Vigor Mortis

VIGOR MORTIS
The End of the Death Taboo

Kate Berridge

P

PROFILE BOOKS

First published in Great Britain in 2001 by
Profile Books Ltd
58A Hatton Garden
London ECIN 8LX
www.profilebooks.co.uk

1 3 5 7 9 10 8 6 4 2

Typeset in Dante by MacGuru
info@macguru.org.uk
Designed by Geoff Green
Printed and bound in Great Britain by
St Edmundsbury Press, Bury St Edmunds

A CIP catalogue record for this book is available from the British Library.

ISBN 1 86197 177 X

For the Loved One
From the Dear Departed
Amoris causa

CONTENTS

ACKNOWLEDGEMENTS

For patience, encouragement and navigation, Andrew Franklin, Penny Daniel, Nicky White, Natasha Fairweather and Bunny Smedley. For perseverance, Joanna Weinberg. For inspiration, and with great admiration, the late Nicholas Albery. For teaching me 'Maintenance of Objective' and for assisting me on my tour of duty as judge of the Cemetery of the Year Competition, my father. For information, and in the hope that they can rest in peace because I haven't done a Jessica Mitford, all the funeral directors, cemetery and crematoria staff, memorial masons and funeral specialists who spoke to me, including Dr Ian Hussain, Derek Gibbs, Roger Gilman, Neil Cocking, Keith Leverton and John Harris. For help tracking down some of the dustier nineteenth-century material, Ros and Sita in the Rare Books Reading Room. For moral support and morbid outings, my dear friends, who showed me not only that if you keep singing you don't hear the storm, but who sang along with me.

NOT IN
FRONT OF
THE CHILDREN

T THE AGE OF EIGHT, WHEN ASKED TO DO A PROJECT ON any aspect of life, I chose death. Although this rather upset my grandmother, I did get a star. We were not the kind of family who sang songs in the back of the car and had fridge-magnets, but we muddled along. There was no obvious reason for my morbidity. I never understood the appeal of crouching in the cramped, gingham world of the Wendy House to play Mummies and Daddies. I disliked dolls, which seemed stiff-limbed, dead babyish and disconcerting. I was far happier grubbing about outside, making dens with dead-leaf walls and running a personal paramedic service for fledglings. No-hope vigils normally preceded shoebox burials and graves marked with pebbles or a cross of twigs.

In the way that parents give children pets to teach them the facts of life; my first exposure to the facts of death was from the same source. These were small, scaly, feathery and furry deaths, each body held and looked at, like Gulliver inspecting a Lilliputian. The first fatality was the Boil-in-the-Bag goldfish, an expensive fish finally won after ten attempts at trying to land a ping-pong ball in a jam-jar at the church fête. Being carried around in a small polythene bag half-full of water on a hot day is not a good way for a goldfish to travel. Once home it swam a curious lop-sided stroke. Next morning it was floating on the surface. To the strains of Armitage Shanks water music my mother flushed it away with the single sweep of a rubber-gloved hand. Similarly ignominious was the mercy-killing of my rabbit. I had released it from its hutch to give it the freedom of the field where we kept chickens, but it got myxomatosis and became Bug-Eyed Bunny. My father finished it off with a spade, but forbade me from witnessing the execution.

Death was filtered through the lens of a childhood in the country. Death was the closed scaly eyes of pheasants dangling from garden string nooses in poignant pairs. These spooky Siamese twins were inanimate, but you felt their presence like walking past mannequins and when they were hanging in the larder I didn't like going in there.

Death was a confusion of crucifixions. Kirk Douglas as Spartacus got muddled with Jesus in *The Greatest Story Ever Told*. Both died to set others free, and the pain and strain of their slow deaths was made even more upsetting by the sympathetic presence of onlookers and heart-rending subplots involving sons. In *Spartacus*, a dewy-eyed Jean Simmons presents Spartacus with his son, pleading; 'Oh my love, my life, please die.' In the *GSET* the terrific storm that coincides with the moment of Jesus's death causes a bystander to observe in an American accent; 'Truly this was the Son of God!' In both films these unhappy endings are accompanied by a heavenly chorus, like a religious version of the *Star Trek* choir but at a slower tempo; and the celestial singing signals THE END.

The End in real life is different. We knew from Easter and Sunday school that death is no fun, especially when compared to the commotion of Christmas, hectic with handicrafts and the Nativity. We once tried to draw the Sunday school teacher on the subject of crucifixion, but she wouldn't co-operate. We would have loved to have put on a Passion play. In the un-Christian system of justice that operates in playgrounds, as punishment for the sins of greed and always coming last we would have 'crucified' the class scapegoat – the fat boy who was bad at games. As it was, Easter was boring: a small congregation singing depressing hymns. In the chilblain-stinging cold of Tansor parish church, I learned that just as the death of Jesus does not receive nearly the same turnout as his birthday, so it is in life. Death-days are unhappy times to get through and get over.

Abstract enquiries of the 'How do you know when you're dead?' school of juvenile philosophy were usually evaded by grown-ups. More direct questions either elicited that 'Trespassers Will be Prosecuted' look, or else we were fobbed off with something unfeasible: notably, in the case of a missing pet, 'He's gone to live on a farm in Wales'. Death did not add up. Just as Valerie Singleton on *Blue Peter* always skipped the difficult bit, and we never witnessed the critical stage in the transformation of the liquid detergent bottle into the Dougal money box, we never really knew what happened between the part where grandmother was just poorly and upstairs with grapes, and the disturbed patch of earth in a churchyard. All we knew was that death made everyone sad. I remember my mother sobbing in front of the black-and-white television set when Andy Williams sang 'Mine Eyes Have Seen the Glory of the Coming of the Lord' at President Kennedy's funeral. Jackie Onassis became a model of death chic: black veil, shift and shades, her feelings as controlled as her lacquered flyaway hair.

Death was not even definite. Jesus rose again from the dead; and so did Tom, after what looked like mortal blows from Jerry. Despite the strongest evidence to the contrary, parents and teachers always insisted dead people were fine and dandy, just not around anymore.

Every year on holiday in Norfolk I used to play with a girl I'd befriended on the beach. One summer, with no warning, I was told that she and I would not be able to play anymore because she had gone to Heaven. I felt short-changed by this explanation for her disappearance. I missed her very much.

To perk me up, my parents presented me with a kitten, which was fairly therapeutic until the milkman ran her over in his electric milk float. The next day they bought me another cat, a ginger tom who emitted guttural growls when I tried to stroke him and kept coming back with bits of ear and fur missing. It is strange, the way adults try to mollify children by replacing dead pets. But it doesn't really work, and it didn't seem to work for the adults either, because even though nobody mentioned my friend anymore, and her mother adopted another little girl soon after, she still looked sad and her fingers shook when she lit cigarettes.

While my friends speculated endlessly about sex, I was always more interested in the other end of the scale. Watching wildlife programmes, I preferred the part where the lion got the gazelle to the bit where he got off with the lioness. Hoping for some real-life experience of 'nature red in tooth and claw', I signed up for a school field trip. After a long journey that seemed even longer because we ate our packed lunches before we had even left the school drive, we eventually reached a nature reserve in north Norfolk. In cold wellington boots we squelched expectantly across the marshes. We watched, waited and kept very still, but nothing mated, nothing was born, nothing died. The greatest excitement was when Mrs Bradley couldn't start the minibus and we had to wait for an AA man. To young girls from a strict Church of England school, men were a rare species, so this was the unforeseen high point of our expedition. On the journey back our behaviour corresponded to the time-honoured rituals of schoolgirls on buses. The goody-goodies in the front singing 'Ging Gang, Goolly Goolly Goolly Goolly Watcha'; the bored and anti-social were in the middle asleep,

and in the back the Lolitas made suggestive faces at truckers, and gave sala-
cious *sotto voce* accounts of things they hadn't really done with boys. Somewhere near Kings Lynn there were complaints about a strong fishy smell.
On the marsh I had found a not-quite-dried-out dead crab and in my damp
pocket on a warm bus, it was becoming quite pungent. Later, I set one of
the perfect secateur claws in plastic with the Plasticraft kit my sister gave
me for Christmas: *memento mori*.

Death is the first big lie parents tell children; a close second to Father
Christmas. The way they act as if death does not exist is just as dogged as
their insistence that Father Christmas does exist. In both cases there is
ample evidence to arouse suspicion but children appease the adults. To preserve the status quo they say nothing. I behaved the same way when I noticed that 'Santa' in the magic grotto at Selfridges did not look a bit like the
Father Christmas who came to our school party, who was a dead ringer for
Sheila's father. Like many children, I cottoned on to the facts of death on
my own. I realised that death disturbed my parents. I realised that my parents were going to die. This reality tremor shook me, and toppled my fantasy that they were omnipotent and infallible. It happened at about the
same time that I rumbled Father Christmas.

Growing up I learned that adults don't like to make a fuss about death.
At boarding school I did a stint of community service at the local old
people's home, an activity which in the argot of school was called 'granny-
bashing'. I was dismayed by the way the old women did death. Consideration for others was their main concern. They kept the communal television
turned down low and they died discreetly, without disturbing others or dis-
rupting the routine. The whole place had the air of people waiting. The living room was even arranged like a waiting room, with chairs against the
walls and very old back copies of *Woman's Weekly* with the teabag tokens
torn out. It was in these surroundings that I learned the power of small
things. It is not the business in the crematorium that makes death real. It is
the dented seat of a favourite chair, skeins of hair on the bristles of a brush,
handwriting. It was not my grandmother's funeral but her dressing gown
that made me cry; it smelt of mothballs and the 4711 cologne that she used
to dab on handkerchiefs and on the pulse points of her wrists.

In the drab old people's home – which with its endless rules, strict meal
times and fire doors was anything but homely – I realised the consequences
of being open about death. Miss Liffin, a resident there, became the second
person after my grandmother whom I managed to offend on the subject of
death. Over the course of a few weeks I noticed that her world-view
seemed to be shrinking: she was squinting over life itself. Someone had

given her a sheepskin foot cosy and she sat for hours with both feet in it. In that beach prank where children immobilise their parents by patting sand tightly around their feet the parents just pretend to be stuck, but Miss Liffin behaved as if she really was. 'I find it so hard to feel enthusiastic about going out,' she quavered. I told her, 'You simply must keep active; as soon as my grandmother slowed down she was dead within a month.' Later my house-master called me in to say that Miss Liffin did not want me to visit her any more because I depressed her. At this point I became aware of the potency of the 'd' word.

My childhood experiences typify the twentieth-century approach to death – death kept at a safe distance by denial and silence. As in the story of the Emperor's New Clothes, we collaborate in the illusion of life without death, we suppress the instinct to expose the myth of invincibility. We collude and deny: *carpe diem*, not *memento mori*. We play our part in the elaborate hoax. We witness all manner of death as entertainment, as sound bites and soap opera, as a shoot-up computer game and a shoot-out in a movie, all conning us that we are getting up close to death, when in reality we have never been further away. Television is the main medium which delivers this paradoxical perception of seeing things close up from a distance – an unreal reality. The 1986 Challenger disaster was an astounding instance of this: an astronautical Daedulus and Icarus. Chernobyl, on the other hand, showed us the perils of over-reaching on the earth, prompting apocalyptic reports of poisoned seas, poisoned skies and poisoned people.

This interplay between private and public experience confers a false sense that we are sharing the drama of death in other people's lives, while in reality we are completely insulated from it. The zoom lens focusing in on relatives visiting the scene of the rail crash, interviews with body recovery teams, close-ups of the teddy bear shrine impart illusory intimacy. Proximity to impersonal experiences of death co-exists with distance from personal experience. For although dramatic death defines the news and pretend death comprises an increasingly significant part of popular culture, the social context for discussion and consideration of death has eroded. Death no longer has a place in everyday life. In real life, we pretend that death does not exist.

I am one of a generation of babyboomers whom peace and medical progress has placed at a greater distance from death than any previous generation. For us – the progeny of a death-denying, death-defying culture – the first experience of mortality is an awesome ambush for which we are completely unprepared. Sudden, slow, young, old, expected, unexpected: death stings. But at the same time, the terrors of death are exacerbated in a climate of repression, denial and secrecy. Just as daylight transforms the monster menacing the child's bedchamber into a dressing gown hung on the back of a door, death is less of a bogeyman when confronted with the lights on.

For my generation, divorce and family breakdown, rather than bereavement, have been the agents of our separation, severing our contact with the living. Ours has been the era of the McDonald's foundling's, the corporate crèche, the latchkey kids. The single mother and the divorcee have become as emblematic of our age as the nineteenth-century widow was of hers. In the twenty-first century, our longing is often for the living, our suffering related to the scale of casualties in our domestic conflict – those missing in acrimony. Where our parents were silent about their losses, we are voluble, as if the melting ice caps are a metaphor for an emotional thaw taking place all around us. Popular culture has exploited our sentimentality. The mourning rituals of romance, not death, dominate the hit parade, with cheesy lyrics conveying what Emily Dickinson expressed more eloquently about the link between romantic and mortal absence:

> Parting is all we know of heaven
> And all we need of hell.

In our child-centred world the adult censorship of death is an anomaly, a glaring omission both in individual homes and in society at large. Death is an integral part of human experience. It resonates through daily life in both factual and fictitious ways. Yet there is a disparity between the level of children's exposure to death as current affairs – *thanatomimesis*, or pretend death – and a cultural conspiracy to conceal real death, the kind most people witness and the kind most people die.

This dichotomy was highlighted for me at a discussion group co-ordinated by the charity Parentlink in which the writers Blake Morrison and Fergal Keane, in their capacity as fathers, were invited to share their insights into bringing up children. Professionally, both men have won critical acclaim for the sensitive way in which they have served up the strong stuff of death and ultra-violence, and yet both conceded that they shirked from discussing death in the domestic context of the family. Morrison, who has written both about the James Bulger killing, and about the death of his own father, said that death was something people didn't like to think about. 'It's quite possible to get to fifty without seeing a corpse.' Keane, who has won awards for his coverage of the genocide in Burundi and Rwanda, admitted that he had lied to his young son when asked a question about death. These exchanges exemplify our squeamishness about death education. They underscore the contradiction between culturally approved representations of death, transmitted via the media, and a blanket ban on addressing, even within the family, a process which is as natural and inevitable as birth. The facts of death, as important as the facts of life, warrant a more enlightened approach.

Increasingly, as the twentieth century progressed, it was against the rules of polite society to speak of death. Dead became the ultimate four-letter word, one letter short of the dread it inspires. Nobody likes to say 'dead', they plug the gap between truth and fear with euphemism. He has 'kicked the bucket', 'passed on', 'passed away'. Death frightens everyone, yet the fear is chiefly performance anxiety about dying. Once it was the last breath that defined death, the absence of mist on a mirror; now, less poetically, it is a flat line on a machine. But death is much more than the moment when a life ends. In the sixteenth century, death was the lens through which people viewed life. Death put life in perspective. In the twentieth century, advances in the control of infectious disease and the pace of medical progress have drowned out, or at least muffled, intimations of mortality.

Scientific and medical progress have contributed greatly to the challenging context of contemporary death. Not least, they have amplified existential anxiety. Death assumes a different dimension of difficulty in a secular age where scientists tell us that the soul is the interaction of nervous impulses in the brain, and love a thought virus. In the past the mental space for the contemplation of mortality was filled with faith. The matrix of death was God, Heaven and Hell. Now, by making what was invisible visible, the camera, the X-ray and the Hubble telescope have contracted the gap between the imaginable and the measurable. Where once there was a leap of faith, there is now data. If the wonder of early space travel was the way it enabled us to look back at earth and see ourselves – a form of cosmic navel-gazing – now space missions such as Pathfinder are about looking out beyond. As the parameters of exploration expand, our stature is continually diminishing; in relation to the rest of the cosmos, we are confronted by our own insignificance.

This reductive view is compounded by the impact of medical technology. Life-support machines, organ transplants, keyhole surgery, genetic engineering – these are just some of the procedures which have transformed the body from the temple of the soul into the object of medical experimentation, preservation, and even replication. Recent work in the field of programmed cell death has paved the way for scientists to flout the laws of evolution by reprogramming the cells that cause ageing. Increasingly, death has become less to do with nature than with man; instead of being a natural event, it is seen as a medical failure. Even the afterlife has shifted into the realm of medical technology. Cryonics specialists offer a 'pay and stay' scheme, which enables participants to have their heads or whole bodies suspended in liquid nitrogen in the hope that, like some futuristic Humpty Dumpties, medical breakthroughs will allow scientists to put them back together again. The twenty-first-century version of resurrection amounts to being defrosted by a man in a white coat.

The body itself has become more significant than shared faith in defining contemporary communality, a shift which has had an important bearing on attitudes to death. A striking metaphor for this was the Body Zone in the Millennium Dome, the scale of which dwarfed the Faith Zone. Fragmentation is the hallmark of contemporary society: of our belief systems, of families and even of our own bodies. In *The Revival of Death* (1994) sociologist Tony Walter observes that 'the human being is no longer shadowed by a single skeleton personifying death but by any number of germs and diseases which attack medically identifiable organs of the body'.

The Human Genome Project which plans to have deciphered all the signals that control what happens in each cell of the human body by 2075, is the ultimate reduction of man to the sum of his parts. Where once the book of Genesis told man who he was, and where he came from, now this happens in a petri dish. The potential power of genetic engineering, the heady sense that by doubling the lifespan of a fruitfly we may be on course to challenge Methuselah: this is awesome knowledge. It is the secular equivalent of the temptation to eat the forbidden fruit, a second Fall with the opposite outcome of immortality. For attempting to defy death is not without its own dangers, scrambling the logic of evolution whereby men die without being forced to compete with their own offspring.

As our world picture expands, our place in it contracts. The unfeasible scale of our position relative to the nearest star – the concomitant confusion of light years, incomprehensible measurements of distance expressed in the dimension of time – these concepts exacerbate the reductive view of our place in the world. This demoralising perspective is not new. Whereas in our age science and medicine, and the increasingly complex offshoots of bio- and nanotechnology, are accelerating the rate of secularisation, for the Victorians it was the natural world as interpreted by Darwin that created a climate of doubt and disorientation. In 1851, Ruskin expressed this well in a letter to his friend Henry Acland: 'If only the geologists would let me alone, I could do very well, but those dreadful hammers! I hear the clink of them at the end of every cadence of the Bible verses.' Instead of galaxies, the dimensions of time expressed by the fossil record diminished man's sense of self. As the geologist's hammer chipped away at old belief systems, the questions the atheists asked became more challenging, and by the end of the nineteenth century there was a climate of change which extended to radically new perceptions of death. A famous article in the *Fortnightly Review* (1899), entitled 'The Dying of Death', announced:

> Death as a motive is moribund. Perhaps the most distinctive note of the modern spirit is the practical disappearance of the thought of death as an influence directly bearing upon practical life ... The fear of death is being replaced by the joy of life. The flames of Hell are sinking low and even Heaven has but poor attractions for modern man. Full life here and now is the demand; what may come after is left to take care of itself.

Hence in the twilight of the Victorian age, the death rituals which formerly had sustained the living were questioned. There was a rejection of extravagant mourning. It took the First World War, however, to turn death into a fully-fledged existential crisis. The annihilation of so many, the government policy of not repatriating the war dead for family burial, and the horrific realisation that in many cases identification of individual bodies was impossible – these caused a seismic shift in the emphasis put on different rituals. After the Great War the emphasis shifted from the body to memory. At the same time, the demotion of the significance of the body in death rituals was accompanied by the promotion of rituals of remembrance.

In the way that it reset the course of death rites for the twentieth century, the First World War is of crucial significance to the modern history of death. Before the war, death had involved a conflation of public and private spheres, and an integration of the physical reality of death with emotions directed at the dead body. The war caused a dramatic schism between the physical and emotional, private and public experiences of death. It separated funerary ritual from commemoration, mourning from remembrance, private grief from public acts of remembering. This emphasis reverberates to the present day in low-key private cremations followed by large, more sociable memorial services.

Importantly, as a result of the war, mourning dress was abandoned. The magnitude of loss meant that the sheer numbers of people wearing mourning would have devastated national morale, discouraging not only the surviving troops, but also those who had yet to take their turn in the trenches. Women were needed for war work and could not afford to be secluded for the old rituals which had segregated them from society. The reduced significance of the body paved the way for the post-war rise in the popularity of cremation. There is a sense after the war of abbreviating death, according it less time and less ceremony. The armband, the poppy and the two-minute silence, compared to the formality and extent of nineteenth-century mourning, in which death was remembered in units of months rather than minutes, indicate this abbreviation. The conscious retreat from mortality was fully under way.

A further change caused by the mass bereavement of the First World War was the exclusion of children from death. Grief-stricken and reeling from the scale of their losses, adults started, in a striking divergence from Victorian conventions, to censor children's experiences of death. The war marked the beginning of shielding, hiding and distancing children from the fact of their own, and others', mortality. This 'not in front of the children' attitude is a distinctive twentieth-century phenomenon which is without precedent. Until the late 1880s full mourning extended to children and was rigidly enforced. Queen Victoria complained in the strongest terms when her eldest daughter failed to put her five-month-old baby in mourning when her husband's grandmother died, and on another occasion was adamant that three-year-old Beatrice wore mourning when her mother's half-sister's husband died. Everything from babies' bonnets to their bed-clothes were adapted. *The Life of Mrs Sherwood* (1854) includes a poignant description of the writer modifying her three-month-old daughter's clothes when her two-year-old son Henry died.

> I remember that day occupying myself in trimming the lace cap with bows of narrow black love ribbon and tying a black love sash round her waist. I was encouraging myself to make a new idol; each idol that I raised becoming more and more precious if possible than the one which had gone before. Still my heart clung to the memory of my Henry.

The importance of the abandonment of mourning should not be underestimated. It signified a literal and irrevocable alteration in the social fabric. When it was a standard part of everyday behaviour for people at all levels of society to don black when someone, either in their immediate circle or of national significance, died, this meant that death was routinely present, domestic, familiar. Mourning almost made death mundane, such was the extent of black ephemera in daily life. The visual impact of mourning is captured in a letter written by a young German prince who was in London in 1827 when the general public was in general mourning for the Duke of York.

> The Duke seems to be much regretted, and the whole country wears deep

mourning for him, crape on the hat, and black gloves, *ce qui fait le désespoir* of all shopkeepers. People put their servants into black liveries, and write on paper with a broad black edge. Meantime the Christmas pantomimes go on as merrily as ever. It has a strange effect to see Harlequin and Columbine skipping about on the stage in all conceivable frivolities and antics, while the coal-black audience, dressed as for a funeral procession, clap and shout with delight. (Butler [ed], *A Regency Visitor: The Letters of Prince Puckler-Muskav*, 1957)

The modification of appearance extended to interiors. The undertaker, as we understand the term, actually stems from 'upholder' or 'upholsterer', and originally the dramatic drapery of rooms and buildings, including overlaying floors with black baize, was a major part of the funeral ritual.

In its most excessive and theatrical guise, black was the basis of the spectacle of a state funeral. The gloomy melodrama achieved by black hangings is evident in a contemporary account of the interior of St George's Chapel, Windsor, 'swathed in its ghastly trappings of black' for the funeral of Prince Albert in 1861.

… black everywhere – black over nave and aisles, and side walls, and deeper and more dense than all seemed the black within the dimly lighted choir, where the empty oaken stalls and vacant canopies of the Knights of the Garter gave a still more desolate aspect to the scene. The steps leading to the Communion table, the Communion table itself, even the walls at the back were hung with solemn black and thus the groined arches and fine white fluted columns of the building had, by contrast, a bleak, shrunk ghastly look; while over all beneath, so absorbing was the dark hue that it was difficult at times to distinguish the forms of the attendants as clad in deep mourning they crowded the floor like shadows flitting noiselessly to and fro. (Blenkinsopp, *Britain's Loss and Britain's Duty*, 1862)

The floor was similarly covered in black; given that the entrance to the royal tomb house was through an opening in the floor, it constituted a potential hazard to mourners. 'The mouth of the gloomy chasm' was 'so little distinguishable amid the general blackness that had not its edge been marked with white bands it might have been dangerously overlooked by those engaged in the choir beneath'.

The phasing out of the use of mourning material, insofar as it represents the physical disappearance of death from everyday life, is a visual corollary to the mental banishment of death from the minds of the living which started to happen at the end of the nineteenth century and which was accelerated by the First World War. Furthermore, the rejection of mourning was but one aspect of a general corrosion of ceremonies and customs to do with death which had involved children. In Cornwall, children would kiss the hand of the corpse in the belief that this would grant them longevity. In close-knit communities in the North children would knock on the door of a bereaved household and ask to see the laid-out body. Children attended deathbeds, funerals and even carried the coffins of their peers with white carrying straps and white coffins for innocence. A visual symbolism which was carried through to the horses, white plumes replacing black and tack similarly modified. Death was a normal part of everyday life.

One of the most extraordinary manifestations of the Victorian child's exposure to death is to be found in the children's literature of the period. Dickens describes attending a funeral as a seven-year-old with other children, where the undertaker was 'handing us gloves on a tea-tray as if they were muffins, and tieing us into cloaks (mine had to be pinned up all round because it was so long for me).' Information about death seems to have been the primary aim of a range of periodicals which were clotted with morbid material. This genre is an intriguing if somewhat disquieting expression of the Victorian volubility on the subject of mortality, and an incomparable benchmark against which to evaluate contemporary reticence. There is an alarmingly high corpse count, most of the fatalities being described in 'Juvenile Obituaries'. Unlike modern obituaries, in which the focus is on the life lived, here the emphasis is on how each child died. Stoicism in suffering is applauded as good behaviour. The macabre equivalent of *Look and Learn*, titles like *Youth's Instructor*, *Aunt Judy's Magazine*, the *Little Gleaner*, and the *Child's Companion* are packed with miscellaneous death-related material including tips on taxidermy, poems about graveyards and human remains, funerary rites in far-flung places and woodcuts of catacombs. These appear between stories where, instead of living happily ever after, the young heroes and heroines die happily, believing in the hereafter.

Intimations of mortality are conveyed with a rich variety of devices ranging from the allegorical to the explicit. An example of the former is a meditation on the phenomenon of autumn, where 'the gradual death of vegetable nature' is likened to the inexorable decay of man, 'like leaves on trees the race of man is found, now green in youth now withering on the ground'. Even a train journey prompts a musing on mortality when two excited children enjoying the new method of travel are interrupted by their father: 'Does not the railroad remind you, my dear children, of the shortness of our lives?' (*Youths Magazine*, February 1843). More forthright is the New Year message of an editor to his readers:

NOT IN FRONT OF THE CHILDREN

You may not live to see the end of the year now just begun. How many little graves you see in the churchyard and whatever your age may be, you
will see graves of children younger than yourselves. Will you not repent
and pray to God? (*Child's Companion*, January 1824)

With a remarkable sleight of prose the same warning is expressed in
'That's a Little Baby's Grave', in which the author describes his encounter
with two small boys playing in a graveyard where they come across a new
grave:

I saw them both look attentively at the spot wondering perhaps how it happened that a little baby should die. And have not some of you my little
readers wondered too? You have walked, I dare say, through many churchyards and have you not been struck as this little boy was at the many little
graves that you saw around you? And who lies in these little graves? Little
children! And if little children die why may not you? Perhaps you may, for
we know not what shall be on the morrow. (*Child's Companion*, December
1826)

The rhythm created by repetition effectively turns the word 'little' into
hammer blows; presumably, the sound of the nails being driven one by one
into a *little* coffin was precisely what the young reader was supposed to
imagine and associate with his own precarious condition.

The *memento mori* theme is not confined to the churchyard, but crops up
in polite society. One of my favourite examples of death discussed in the
drawing room occurs in the *Youth's Instructor* (January 1817). With the delicacy and decorum of Jane Austen heroines, Eliza (aged 19), Mary her sister
(13), Sarah (16) and Charlotte (17) muse on mortality:

CHARLOTTE: Pray Eliza, is it true that your excellent mother was taken suddenly ill a few days ago?
ELIZA: Her indisposition was indeed quite unexpected. One minute she was
playfully caressing little George and the next she appeared in the grasp of
death!
MARY: Oh, it was so dreadful to see my dear mother in convulsions! I nearly
lost my senses while Eliza waited upon her with so much presence of
mind.
SARAH: Alarming indeed! How long did she continue in that state?
ELIZA: Dr L was providentially present, so that proper means were immediately used; and my mother is now so far recovered that she accompanied
my father yesterday to Cheltenham where they intend remaining several
days.

SARAH: I am sorry that the human body is subject to such seizures. If no medical gentleman had been near, probably your mother would have expired. I greatly fear dying suddenly.
CHARLOTTE: Some people have desired to leave the world without previous sickness.
SARAH: But you know, cousin, they were pious people, ready to die at all times; and I am not.
ELIZA: You should be thankful, my dear friend, that you are aware of your unsafe condition; but do you intend to remain in it? It is your privilege to be so happy that the idea of death need not terrify you.
SARAH: Excuse my freedom, but pray, Eliza, could you close your eyes in peace, with the certainty of dying before the next morning?
MARY: I do believe my sister could; for she often says when we are going to bed: O Mary, how delightful it would be to wake no more on earth.

A constant feature is the interpretation of death in a moral context, the interplay between morality and mortality emphasised through a variety of didactic tactics. Often, as in a tabloid headline, a title tells the whole story: for example, 'The Sabbath-Breaker Drowned', 'The Awful Death of a Giddy Young Man'. Even where material does not directly concern death, morality sets the tone of the narrative. Characters are frequently portrayed in symbolic terms with names like 'Emily Mindful' and 'Sally Thoughtless'. The cautionary theme is integral and often explicit. 'A Sunday Scholar Drowned' (for some reason death by water is the preferred punishment for disobedience) describes the fate of an eight-year-old boy who goes for a walk without the permission of his parents. More naughty still, he chooses a waterside walk. He had often been charged by his mother not to play beside water. For this misdemeanour, he drowns slowly in Regent's Park Canal in front of his distraught brother.

> There are three lessons which I hope all Sunday scholars will learn from this painful event. 1. Never disobey your parents. 2. Never play beside deep water. 3. Pray to God to prepare you for early and sudden death. (*Child's Companion*, July 1824)

The innate moral deficiency of children which resonates through nineteenth-century periodicals is a diluted form of concepts expressed in James Janeway's *Token for Children, being an exact account of the conversion, holy and exemplary lives and joyful deaths of several young children*. One of the most influential books in the 'death as self-help' genre, and a bestseller for around 200 years after its publication in 1671, this book's premise is that children are 'brands of hell', 'not too little to die, not too little to go to hell'.

Given that 'a corrupt nature is a rugged knotty piece to hew', the book presents itself as a moral manual designed to knock children into shape in readiness for death. You could almost burn your fingers on the pages, so palpable are the flames of hell fanned by the author's perception of children as intrinsically wicked. Parents are advised to 'take some time daily to speak a little to your child about their miserable condition by nature'. Hell is a fate worse than death, and no effort must be spared to avoid going there.

Yet in spite of Janeway's assurance of authenticity and his claims that 'several passages are taken verbatim from their dying lips', the children he describes sound too good to be true. His exacting standards are revealed in his character study of an eight-year-old girl: 'when she was at school she was eminent for her diligence, teachableness, meekness and modesty, speaking little, when she did speak it was usually spiritual'. Death is presented as the ultimate form of good behaviour. 'Of the Excellent Carriage of a Child Upon His Deathbed When But Seven Years Old' is typical of the tone.

In the nineteenth century the requirement to die a good child was still being powerfully expressed, and the emphasis of juvenile obituaries is on the child's conduct and moral fibre in the face of death. So important is moral virtue that a sanctimonious death is preferable to sinful survival. Hannah Tully, who passed away, aged 12, on 12 May 1824, died a paragon of moral fortitude:

> One of her aunts asked her if she did not wish to get better? She replied, 'No, Aunt, you know I would rather die; for I am sure I shall go to Heaven; but if I were to get better I might fall into sin, and be unprepared for death at last, which would be very awful. (*Youth's Instructor*, June 1825)

One of the best-known fictional figures of the late twentieth century is Bridget Jones, a neurotic thirty-something woman obsessed with her single status, and a boon to readers who identify with her foibles. In light of her present day status as a role model, it was extraordinary to encounter her namesake in a juvenile obituary exemplifying how to die well. In a memoir of Bridget Jones, born Swansea, 26 August 1811, died 26 September, 1826 aged 15 years and one month, Bridget is the epitome of piety. 'Her thirst for the means of grace was great, and she omitted no opportunity of reproving sin.' The nineteenth-century Bridget Jones died of a cold.

> But alas, how frail is man, as a flower of the field he flourisheth! In April she caught a severe cold from which she appeared to recover partially; but

remained weak and languid. This affliction with uncommon growth in a frame rather delicate laid the foundation of the disease that proved fatal.

The focus on other-worldly salvation and moral piety as the key ingredients of the nineteenth-century self-help genre are the antithesis of the self-doubt and neurosis of their present day equivalent. They highlight a society in which women were encouraged to aspire to a good death, rather than a boyfriend.

The most striking aspect of this material is that much of it is designed to prepare children for their own demise. It confronts them with the precarious nature of life, and conveys premature death as a likely, rather than merely a possible, fate. Sometimes the impact of death is conveyed subtly by focusing on the sadness of what is left behind, a sentimental approach familiar from Edwin Landseer paintings of the period such as *The Old Shepherd's Chief Mourner* (1837), or *The Empty Cradle* by W. Archer (1839). In 'The Deserted Nursery' the reader is regaled with a heart-wrenching account of the sad surroundings following the death of 'Augustine who was seized with a fatal disorder that in 24 hours cut short the thread of his life and he was no more'. The reader is shown Augustine's crib, the fireplace, his photograph, the hat and coat he wore 'the last day he spent on earth', the closet and the toys.

> I saw the little boy had been liberally provided with playthings there was a large rocking horse but ah! The once rosy rider was pale and cold in the darkened grave ... Every toy looked as if it had been used but alas they were wanted no more, oh my children learn a lesson from this empty room learn this lesson that none are *too young* to die. (*Child's Companion*, November 1833)

Where 'The Deserted Nursery' implies absence and describes loss by focusing on its physical context, a more terrifying approach to mortality is evident in graphic descriptions of the physical decline of dying children – descriptions which are abhorrent to contemporary sensibility. These are uncomfortable reminders that, as well as worrying about the health of their souls, children were expected to be prepared for the physical ordeal of dying. Articles describe the effects of ruptured lungs, seizures, and the act of spitting up blood. For example, the juvenile obituary in *Youth's Instructor* of Maria Wybourne who died in 1822, aged 13, relates how 'she was seized by a disease accompanied with excruciating pains in her left arm. The pain with which she continually laboured soon reduced her to a mere skeleton and wholly confined her to bed. For five months she bore this pain with exemplary patience, Christian fortitude and holy resignation.' The unflinch-ing realism of these deathbed scenes written to be read by children is in marked contrast to the notoriously sentimental deathbed scenes in nineteenth-century novels, which Gerald Manley Hopkins parodied in a letter to the poet Robert Bridges in 1881: 'Pallid cheek, clammy brow, long, long night watches, surely there is some hope! Oh say not all is over, it can-not be!' The anaesthetic of idealised death was not administered in nineteenth-century writing for children, where instead one finds a striking lack of subtlety and an unfeeling directness. Juvenile obituaries are starkly real accounts of brief lives. Authenticity is what makes Catharine Tait's ac-count of the death of her children so powerful. As memoir rather than novel, descriptions of deathbed vigils kept rather than imagined, it is a soul-destroying narrative by a mother who lost five daughters to scarlet fever be-tween 6 March and 10 April 1856: 'The little body was quite stiff, the arms and legs twitching. It was a sight full of agony; the conflict with death was long.' (W. Benham [ed], *A Memorial*, 1879.)

The corpse was considered a fit subject for children. It is impossible to imagine primary school children today singing the following hymn from *Hymns for Little Children* (1848):

> There are short graves in churchyard, round,
> Where little children buried lie,
> Each underneath his narrow mound,
> With stiff cold hand and close shut eye;
> Bright morning sunbeams kiss the spot,
> Yet day by day, they open not.

Contemporary squeamishness means that we no longer entertain thoughts of entropy, let alone sing about it. Interestingly however, two other hymns by the same author, Mrs Alexander – *Once in Royal David's City* and *All Things Bright and Beautiful* – remain popular.

The prevalence of macabre imagery in material for children is striking. There is something incongruous about the image of respectable children in comfortable parlours poring over accounts of putrefaction, stinking cadav-ers and endless variations on the theme of death. The *History of the Fairchild Family* (1869) describes the initiation of three young children under the age of eight to the facts of death, when their parents take them to view the body of the family gardener.

> 'Should you like to see the corpse my dears?' asked Mr Fairchild, 'you never saw a corpse, I think.'

'No Papa', answered Lucy, 'we should like to see one.'
'I tell you beforehand, my dear children, that death is very terrible. A corpse is an awful sight.'
'I know Papa,' said Lucy, 'but we should still like to go.'

To similarly uninitiated young readers, a full and frank description of the corpse gives a grizzly sneak preview of death.

When they came to the door they perceived a kind of disagreeable smell such as they never had smelt before. This was the smell of the corpse which having been dead now nearly two days had begun to corrupt; and as the children went higher up the stairs they perceived this smell more dis-agreeably … At last Mrs Fairchild said, 'My dear children, you now see what death is; this poor body is going fast to corruption.'

If explicit descriptions of mouldering bodies are disconcerting and guaranteed to make a child think about death, another method of fixing the young reader's thoughts on the subject was by inciting him to ponder his own corporeal fragility. A book entitled *The Peep of Day, or a series of the earliest religious instruction the infant mind is capable of receiving* by F.L.B. Mortimer (1860) was translated into many languages and published in many different versions; it became a set text of the missionary movement. Mortimer interprets biblical themes in a series of descriptive narratives. For example, 'Poor Little Body' is a consummately skilled, if unequivocally sadistic illustration of the biblical theme that all flesh is grass:

How easy it would be to hurt your poor little body. If it were to fall into the fire it would be burned up. If hot water were thrown upon it, it would be scalded. If it were to fall into deep water and not be taken out very soon it would be drowned. If a great knife were run through your body, the blood would come out. If a great box were to fall on your head, your head would be crushed. If you were to fall out of the window your neck would be bro-ken. If you were not to eat some food for a few days your little body would be very sick, your breath would stop and you would grow cold and you would soon be dead. You see that you have a very weak little body.

To the nineteenth-century child, death was a subject to be explored not only for the purpose of self-improvement, but also preparation. Above all, it was personally relevant.

By contrast, the modern child has almost no exposure to depictions of children dying. Child death is one of the most powerful elements of the present-day taboo on discussing death. The representations of death that children encounter tend to be directed towards entertainment rather than education. Death is grand-scale special effects wizardry on the big screen, or realistic but rarely with real dead bodies on the small screen, or an interactive experience on a computer screen. Such encounters make death appear remote and split off from everyday life. Of course, remoteness from death is at one level the privilege of greatly improved healthcare. When they fell ill Victorian children *expected* to die. The scale of child mortality is most poignantly revealed on overcrowded gravestones which, more effectively than any table of statistics, reveal the awesome loss that individual families endured. In Tower Hamlets, London:

> Sacred to the memory of Ellen daughter of Llewellyn and Ellen Llewellyn who died 6 February 1854, aged 14 months. Also Emily sister of the above, who died 29 March 1858, aged 3 years and 9 months; Beatrice Ada who died 26 July 1860, aged 15 months; Horace who died 20 December 1864, aged 3 months and 3 weeks; Cuthbert Llewellyn who died 29 January 1865, aged 5 months.

The constant morbidity and *memento mori* content of nineteenth-century children's literature make perfect sense in the context of relatively low life expectancy. Losing a parent and dying young were legitimate fears, for in the 1830s a quarter of all children lost one or both parents before their sixteenth birthday. In the 1990s this had dropped to 3.3 per cent. Jane Eyre was an archetype in a century of orphans and foundlings, of children despatched to distant relatives or dubious institutions because their immediate family was dead. The highest mortality rates were for babies: 1 in 6 died in the Victorian era, whereas today the infant mortality rate is 2 per cent. The dramatic decline in the death rate for children in the twentieth century is a major factor contributing to the contemporary complacency and disregard of death.

We have had the privilege of being able to put death out of our minds. A comparison of survival rates of children born in 1850, 1900 and 1950 illustrates the point. Of 1,000 children born in 1850, 300 could expect to die before the age of 15; in 1900, 230 would die before the age of 15; whereas in 1950 only 40 would die before the age of 15. In 1999 the mortality rate for children under 15 had declined to the point of being negligible – the precise figure as supplied by the Office for National Statistics is 0.523 deaths per 1,000. This sets the pattern for the modern era. There is a very real sense of being cushioned from death, largely as a result of the conquest of infectious diseases. The history of death is also the history of medicine;

breakthroughs in anaesthetics and antiseptics from the 1850s onwards, followed by mass immunisation at the end of the century, paved the way for progress which has culminated in the current longevity boom.

The increase in the older population, together with the trend towards intentional childlessness and smaller families, mark a milestone in demographic history, for there has never before been a society in which older people outnumbered younger people. This is *terra incognita* and fertile ground for evolving new attitudes towards death. For an ever greater proportion of older people in the population confers a sense of living in the midst of death – for years the Queen Mother has been a state funeral waiting to happen – and in an environment where it is much harder to die, this is going to become a common phenomenon. Within the last 200 years, life expectancy in Britain has more than doubled. Indicative of this is the rising number of British centenarians. Thirty years ago there were under 300; today the figure is nearer 8,000. Ageing focuses the mind on death, and as the baby boomers become octogenarians the contemporary death style is likely to undergo further changes. For as the generation that reshaped attitudes to childbirth and benefited from the freedom of birth control, they are already applying similar principles of autonomy to death.

Shortly after the outbreak of the First World War in the spring of 1915 Sigmund Freud wrote two essays, 'The disillusionment of war' and 'Our attitude towards death', published under the collective title *Thoughts on War and Death*. In the second essay he describes our tendency to live life as if death does not exist. 'We show an unmistakable tendency to put death on one side, to eliminate it from life. We try to hush it up.' For almost seventy years this was an accurate description. For most of the twentieth century we did indeed, in his words, 'exclude death from our calculations'. The denial of death as a distinguishing feature of the twentieth century has been well documented in the work of anthropologist Geoffrey Gorer and in that of social historian Philippe Aries, whose seminal works date from the 1950s and 1970s respectively. Gorer in his famous essay 'The Pornography of Death' (1955) observes that 'in the twentieth century copulation has become more and more mentionable, and death has become more and more unmentionable'. Similarly, Aries, writing in 1974, describes death as 'forbidden', 'invisible' and 'an interdiction to preserve happiness'. He writes: 'A great silence has fallen on the subject of death in the twentieth century'. This idea is reinforced by the bereavement expert and psychotherapist Elizabeth Kublher-Ross writing in the 1980s: 'Death is a dreaded and unspeakable issue to be avoided by every means possible in modern society.'

For most of my lifetime death has been a silence. The fear persists that to talk of death is somehow to invoke it. The general reluctance to address mortality is reflected by the fact that only three in ten adults in the UK have made a will. By comparison the Victorians were voluble: taking pictures of the dead, keeping their hair, marking their passing with mourning dress and jet jewellery. They shared death with the communality of customs, such as Yorkshire funeral teas, or tolling bells: nine strokes for a man, six for a woman, or one for each year of their age. For the Victorians death was both domestic and public. Only in the twentieth century was it driven out and turned into a taboo. For the first time death became private; bereavement became a shameful secret. The funeral parlour, like the massage parlour, became the establishment nobody wanted to be seen entering – plastic flowers and shaded windows, dingy discretion with Kleenex and credit cards – both premises conducting furtive commercial transactions for the relief of socially embarrassing situations.

A curious anomaly of an age that prides itself on information technology is our basic unfamiliarity with the dead. Where once bodies of our loved ones stayed at home, laid out on trestles in open coffins, visible and visited, now they are spirited away to the fake domesticity of the funeral home. The Albinoni tapes, mock Chesterfield sofas and genteel coffee cups are all indicative of the dubious taste of premises contriving to be 'tasteful'. At home the living room is exactly that, and while we do not flinch from death on television – melodramatic or violent, real or pretend – we do not deem our own dead to be suitable family viewing. It is strange that a society that hides from the bodies it has known and loved chooses to spend so much of its fantasy life in morgues. The forensic pathologist is the new breed of popular detective. The emphasis has shifted from whodunnit to what was done. Where formerly the scene of the crime was the focus of enquiry, now the corpse itself is the scene of the crime; where once we watched the cops comb debris and undergrowth for crucial clues, now the trail of clues in organs and cells is our area of interest. The chalk outline of the murder victim has been fleshed out, and the autopsy has become an integral part of the murder mystery, redefining the genre.

Today death is done by rote, not rites, and so in some respects looking back is a depressing reminder of what has been lost. The fast funeral that is cremation suits a society crippled by fear of death, and turns death into waste disposal rather than a rite of passage. Some wonderful bits of funerary flotsam, of the past washed up in the present, are to be found in the parish church of St Mary the Virgin in Abotts Ann, Hampshire. Here, hanging from the roof, are the remnants of intricate crowns made for the funerals of young girls. Known as Maidens' Garlands or Virgins' Crowns, these intriguing concoctions of gilded shells, paper, birds' eggs, ribbon and filigree were carried in front of the coffins. After the funerals they were hung from the rafters of the church; fifteen survive. In a curious custom, four gloves are suspended from some of these. They represent 'lives' or chances, and if after death it was revealed that a girl's reputation was not as spotless as might have been hoped, then a glove was taken down – a post-mortem public humiliation. In stark contrast is the bland uniformity of modern death – MUM written in white chrysanthemum heads, wired wreaths, cellophane.

Compared with the rich visual culture of the past the modern version of death is greatly impoverished. The relentless parade of weeping women and doleful dogs which feature so prominently in Victorian oil paintings on funerary themes has no modern equivalent. Artists no longer paint funerals, graveyards or grief. For most of the twentieth century, apart from official war artists, death disappeared from the sphere of art for public consumption and the market for morbid works of art designed for private consumption also died out. The post-mortem postcards to friends, the marble death-masks, the photographs of graves, which were such a source of solace, these jar with contemporary sensibility. Even though they give the illusion of sleep, the dead babies they depict disturb us. Death is omitted from our photograph albums. John Donne and James Dean, although centuries apart, both posed for morbid photographs in a funeral home with a coffin. Yet whereas Donne was behaving completely in accord with seventeenth-century custom and taste, James Dean's gesture was that of a rebel flouting twentieth-century convention.

Historically, attention was drawn to death not only by commemorative works in public places, such as effigies and elaborate tombs, but also by the vast variety of smaller artefacts displayed in private homes. Anthropologist Geoffrey Gorer famously analysed the social impact of the disappearance of mourning rituals. One facet of this was the disappearance of death from the domestic environment in concrete form: the funeral tea service, the black-edged writing paper, the handkerchiefs embroidered with tears. These details gave death a strong presence in everyday life; they made death mundane, a part of life's clutter. This constant visual presence of death enhanced children's awareness of mortality.

In the twentieth century mourning jewellery vanished from the fingers and chests of the bereaved. Its disappearance was symptomatic of the general mental flight from death which started to gain speed towards the end of the nineteenth century. Prior to that, however, mourning jewellery had been a constant tradition, and in fact constitutes a fascinating visual narrative of changing attitudes to death, encoding different psychological perspectives in a way that is mirrored in memorials. In the sixteenth century great knuckleduster rings of the sort sported by bikers today depicted skeletons, skulls, coffins and crossbones. The overt *memento mori* message shows a society facing death squarely and collectively. In the eighteenth century the macabre motifs provoking general contemplation of mortality disappeared. Instead, elegant neoclassical imagery marked the beginning of euphemism, and the grim reality of death was tempered by gentler expressions of personal loss. Urns epitomised the spirit of elegance and classical restraint and were an extremely popular motif on brooches and rings. In the nineteenth century, however, more overt emotion tipped into sentimentality. Hair, as a relatively durable part of the body, lends itself well to the idea of continued association and mementos made from the hair of the dead became extremely popular. For probably the only time in its history, Tunbridge Wells became famous in fashionable circles. A group of French prisoners-of-war put the town on the map for their dexterity in crafting dead people's hair into beautiful designs for rings and brooches. Antoni Forrer of Hanover Street, who described himself as 'Artist in Hair and Jewellery by appointment to the Queen', fashioned the locks of loved ones into keepsakes for the smart set. The intricacy of Victorian hairwork is extraordinary. Hair was woven into graveyard landscapes complete with trees, monuments and delicate forget-me-nots. Less impressive but equally fashionable was Whitby jet, which worked well against the matt black materials of mourning dress.

Mourning jewellery fell out of fashion in the 1880s as death rituals started to wane; in the twentieth century it disappeared completely. In an era which could not tolerate reminders of death it had no place. Yet it is interesting that the half-folded ribbons which started to appear in the 1980s as symbols of remembrance for AIDS victims are now extending to other causes. The badges worn by the friends and relatives of the murdered schoolgirl Sarah Payne – at once, iconic school portrait, human smiley badge and picture of innocence – are striking examples of the emergence of modern versions of *memento mori*. Victorian hair jewellery also has a modern equivalent in the lockets which contain the cremated remains of a loved one. 'Cremation keepsake pendants' are just one expression of the trend towards confronting death with greater openness, indicating the restoration of mourning conventions and the readmission of death to life after a long absence.

In parallel with the denial of death, a defining characteristic of the twentieth century was its attitude to sexuality, which encompassed self-identification, notions of autonomy and freedom of expression. This upgrading of the significance of sexuality while at the same time downplaying mortality is an inversion of nineteenth-century social mores. Our deaf ear to death mirrors their blind eye to sex. Our ancestors set great store by the relationship between life and death; they better understood the meaning of 'till death do us part'. Queen Victoria was a potent figurehead both as a devoted wife and later as the 'widow of Windsor'. Her mourning for her dead husband defined her, and in turn her character powerfully defined her reign to the extent that her name has become an adjective, loaded with meanings beyond the chronology of her rule. By contrast, personal relationships and fulfilling sex have become the modern standard of happiness and it is increasingly divorce, not death, that parts married couples. Diana, Princess of Wales, the beautiful divorcee and the wronged wife, has assumed a power beyond her actual status. In this regard her influence is an interesting variation on that of Victoria. Diana's little black dresses – notably the one she wore to the Serpentine Gallery on the night her husband gave the most important interview of his life – give an impression of a woman locked in an impossible tug-of-love with a man to whom she was denied access. Victoria's big black dresses fulfilled a similar function. When Victoria said, 'My poor sad face and garb must tell its tale', she could have been speaking for both women, for what clothes they wore and how they wore them were richly expressive of their emotional states. Each was defined by a different d-word – death and divorce – chosen from the same lexicon of loss and longing. The difference between the two women encapsulates the differences between the nineteenth and twentieth centuries, the altered significance of death and sex – one the era of the mourning wedding dress, the other the era of the maternity wedding dress.

If sexuality has eclipsed mortality in defining the social framework, it also lies at the core of our perceptions of child welfare. Whereas the Victorian parent was preoccupied with informing children about death, but ignored sex, the modern parent is preoccupied with sex education and avoids death. The contemporary lack of information available to children about death is in marked contrast to the provision of sex education, the benefits of which are all but undisputed in the face of concern about teenage pregnancy and sexually transmitted diseases. Initiatives like ChildLine, Stranger Danger and powerful NSPCC advertising campaigns emphasise sexual abuse as the ultimate betrayal of the rights of the child, and the paedophile is vilified as the most threatening offender. This is a fascinating inversion of nineteenth-century concepts of child welfare which excluded sexuality from issues of child protection. Indeed, a striking aspect of Victorian attitudes towards children is the socially sanctioned objectification of young girls in the burgeoning child sex trade; until 1885, the age of consent for sexual intercourse was 12. Child brothels flourished in London's East End. When incidents of sexual assault did reach the courtroom there seems to have been no mitigating sense of childhood innocence. During such trials, laughter in the public gallery was apparently a common reaction. In 1889, a famous case of alleged sexual assault against a 10-year-old girl, reported in the *North London Press* (5 October 1889), exemplifies this stance:

> This little girl suffered no injury at the hands of the accused, and she was of such a tender age that it was not likely that she would understand the lewd motive of the way in which she was treated, assuming of course that it was done from a lewd motive.

Erring on the side of adult innocence is completely unlike the highly charged atmosphere of suspicion today; the hyper-vigilance of film processing units concerning bath-time photographs is but one example of this changed climate. Where today there is opprobrium and mistrust, the interest of nineteenth-century adults in young girls was validated as a bona fide cultural phenomenon by the art and literature of the period. The polarity between demonisation and idealisation is striking.

Attitudes to mortality and sexuality are analogous in other ways, for the social response to the problem of sex in the nineteenth century mirrors the twentieth-century response to the problem of death. Modern denial of death mirrors that of the Victorians about sex. Ronald Pearsall, author of *The Worm in the Bud*, a study of Victorian sexuality, observes that: 'Fear, alarm and shame meant that when anything approached sex in the course of conversation, the shutters of the mind came down with a great slam.' This is echoed by Mexican poet and essayist Octavia Paz in his famous book *El Laberinto de la Soledad* (1959). Summarising western society's anxiety about death and contrasting it to Mexican acceptance he writes: 'The word death is not pronounced in New York, in Paris, in London because it burns the lips.' The demystification of sex, which began at the end of the nineteenth century with the development of the formal treatment of the subject in the form of sexology and medical books about the physiology of sex, resembles the evolution of thanatology in the twentieth century. According to American writer Stephen Strack, as recently as forty years ago there was 'no organised scrutiny of everyday matters of death dying and bereavement, no field of thanatology'. The psychosocial aspects of death are a recent field of enquiry, and our tentative exploration in this arena replicates the first pre-Freudian, faltering steps taken by the Victorians towards the subject of sexuality. The way that we have begun to wrestle with the ethics and implications of death control echoes the Victorian sensitivity about birth control. Where euthanasia is fraught with difficulty for us, the Victorians perceived contraception as similarly socially divisive.

Gradually, however, new attitudes to death are emerging. If the popular view of the Victorian period is of a society in which sex was taboo but at the same time sublimated in a burgeoning subculture of prostitution and pornography, contemporary society is informed by the idea of the death taboo, in which denial is sublimated into simulated violence, an appetite for books about serial killers and programmes about real life crime. Yet can we still claim that death is taboo?

In similar rhythms to the changing perceptions of sex over time, the history of death is substantially about death shifting between the private and public realms of experience. Just as the interplay between war, medicine, art and fashion changed sexual attitudes in the swinging 1960s, these factors have also altered the dynamic of death throughout the twentieth century. The death taboo is spoken of as a constant, as if it is an unaltered and unalterable state of being. Yet this is a misconception. In the 1980s the dance of death assumed a different tempo. Without warning, the carefree and confident mood of that decade changed dramatically when AIDS gatecrashed life. After nearly seventy years of taboo and crisis management, we were jolted into a forced awareness of our own mortality. Reminded to remember death, we were reminded of our invincibility. The reverberations are still being felt in many different ways: discount coffins on the World Wide Web, crematoria open days, designer shrouds, DIY funerals, posthumous e-mail services, glossy magazine coverage of celebrity funerals, body part art, fashion shows in funeral homes and death as a theme in advertisements. By moving from the margins of society to the mainstream, and hence becoming social not anti-social, public not private, fashionable not fearful, death is the focus of a new permissiveness. Death is in.

NO MORE
HEROES
ANY MORE

N A HOT CLOUDLESS DAY IN MAY, I WAS HAVING LUNCH with my father in a pub garden when, scanning the landscape and sipping his beer, he said, 'It was like this when we got to Belsen.' It was one of those moments when you are ambushed by the unfamiliarity of your own family, for he had never spoken of this before. Once, when a friend of his came round for supper, he went to his study and came back with a flimsy, sepia-coloured booklet, which looked like an old parish magazine. It was a poorly typed first-hand account of Belsen by a padre. The text was interspersed with black and white photographs of people who did not look like people – pretend people, in piles like kindling. At a self-conscious age I felt most indignant about the dark triangles on all the naked women, their legs akimbo, their rag-doll arms. A shadowy presence that evening, I didn't pick up much of the conversation; certainly I never cottoned on to the fact that my father had been there.

As an officer in the First Battalion of the Herefordshire Regiment he had been among the first to arrive at the scene of crimes against humanity of a magnitude which were without precedent. Shortly afterwards Richard Dimbleby bore witness to these crimes, and broadcast what he saw to the outside world, his words branding into the minds of listeners epoch-changing images of atrocity. Belsen was the first concentration camp to be discovered by the Allies. At the time the military objective of the Eleventh Armoured Division was to reach the River Elbe. Belsen was in their line of advance, a place on the way, with no particular known significance.

Retrospectively, the only ominous sign was a rumour that they were entering a typhus zone; some miles before they got there, they were issued with DDT to put all over their battle dress.

Travelling on top of tanks in flat terrain, about a hundred yards off the road, my father and his men were disoriented to see what they thought were monkeys clinging to the wire fencing of a large compound. As they got closer they realised that these were people. Nothing could have prepared them for what they encountered, and yet my father's tanks were ordered to carry on. It fell to other men to carry out the formal business of liberation and humanitarian relief. Other men bulldozed bodies like human rubble, and endured the horror of witnessing people drop dead from starvation. For finding and freeing Belsen was not a full stop to horror, merely a comma. Death and disease continued. My father speaks little of what he saw, but he says it is the smell that stays with him. It hung in the air for miles.

With his disclosure, I suddenly appreciated that while we were bound by bloodline, we were separated by experience of bloodshed, brutality and death. I have had the privilege of peace and protection from death – witnessing it, causing it, living close to it. By contrast, my father and his father before him had been in gunsights, had been aimed and fired at, and they in turn had killed men. There was a rumour of dubious origin attached to the heavy Zeiss binoculars with which we used to watch birds and point-to-points, but we never asked. As father and son, in different wars, they kept the secrets that only soldiers know – the smell of death, the sound, the sight of men crying and dying. And it is not because time heals that they kept these things to themselves.

They were both part of the tragic cycle that is inscribed on war memorials throughout the country, where the names of those who died in the Second World War follow those whose sacrifice failed to prevent future conflict. Dick, my father's younger brother and an officer in the Second Battalion Scots Guards, was killed in the last week of the Second World War. For years during my childhood when his name was read out on Remembrance Sunday in a disproportionately long inventory of loss for a small village, I would observe my father and grandfather, straight-backed and solemn-faced remembering him. We heard our family name once, but in some cases a surname was repeated three times. In the Sunday best atmosphere of church I used to feel guilty that I could not actually remember Dick at all. I had never known him. He existed for me flimsily, as three disparate things. He was his name being read out once a year by the vicar; he was a portrait in the dining room which shows him with that Rupert

Brooke look, quietly glamorous, better suited to cricket whites than khaki; and he was a wooden cross on a wall in my grandmother's bedroom. The cross was as close as she could get to her son and it comforted her to have it. I later discovered that my father, as a dutiful son (and a guilty survivor), had carried it back from Belgium for her.

These things compel me to consider the comparative lightness of my life. I have been free from the weight of duty, sacrifice and loss that informed my parents' and grandparents' lives. I belong to a generation obsessed with self-knowledge and self-expression – concepts that they regard warily as the prerogative of poets and Americans, and dangerously close to self-indulgence. For my generation, words like 'victim' and 'survivor' are part of the vocabulary of psychotherapy; for them, they literally described the difference between living and dying. Where the self-help culture deliberately sets out to loosen the stiff upper lip, for them it was self-preservation. Self-control was the key to their survival, self-sacrifice a way of life and death, too. In the way that the Chinese used to bind women's feet, in the English tradition my father and grandfather had had their emotions stunted to make them into men. They expressed emotions strategically, not spontaneously.

Every year we went through the ritual of watching the Festival of Remembrance on television – my mother quavering along to 'Oh Valiant Hearts', poppies fluttering from the roof of the Albert Hall, my father and grandmother standing up for the two-minute silence and again for the National Anthem. Over the years, as we graduated to smarter sofas and bigger and better televisions, the number of old soldiers got smaller and granny's hearing got worse. In the last years of her life the festival was on at full volume and when the communal singing reached a certain pitch, glasses in the cupboard would shake in faint reverberation. Then my grandmother died, and the family ritual ceased. I never watch 'cenotaphery' on television now and, like so many who did not live through it, I sometimes forget to buy a poppy. But the poppy is about both forgetting and remembering, ironic flower in its strange marriage of associations between opiates that induce oblivion and a stimulus to remember bloody battlefields.

I have watched the transference of the duty to remember being passed down from one generation to the next. Like 'Pass the Parcel', the next one who gets it has less to deal with. When Vera Lynn handed it to the Spice Girls it was obvious that remembrance had slipped into the realm of consciousness-raising – the poppy a logo, the British Legion a brand. For it is hard to be conscientious about remembering the ever more abstract versions of other people's experience, things that happened not to you but 'for you'.

I have watched my father stand solemn and strong as his father was low-ered into earth beside my grandmother, whose grave bears the cross that once hung on her bedroom wall. Their graves lie beside the lych gate and lichen-covered dry stone walls of a country churchyard. I have watched my father turn into a grandfather and, where once he marched at the back of the parade his father led, now he takes the parade himself as president of a branch of the British Legion. The only bowler hat in a sea of berets, he is one of the few to have seen active service, for the majority of those march-ing alongside him are far too young and lucky to have had their polished jackboots muddied by real war. Although to the fidgety youngsters step-ping out of time my father is an old codger, barking orders with a furled umbrella under his arm, to me he is a brave man, for I know what the small bits of metal on his chest really mean.

In his village, the Little England pomp and circumstance culminates in as dignified a wreath-laying ceremony as it is possible to have when the war memorial is located in front of a chip shop, a video store and a tandoori takeaway. After laying the wreaths and attending church, there is a British Legion time-warp tea in the village hall, complete with tea urns, china cups and brown fruitcake that tastes of burnt currants. The layout of the trestle tables is the epitome of Englishness. In strict pecking order, the vicar and the big cheeses sit at the top table, the Boy Scouts and Brownies at the back; and in the middle is a line of upright citizenship, the social vertebrae: fire-men, policemen, St John's Ambulance men and members of the British Le-gion. For me, living in a city where I have never known neighbours, this manifestation of community feels awkward. Unlike the elderly women wielding the teapots, who have shared the hardship of war and balanced 'make do and mend, privation with 'Down at the Old Bull and Bush' jollity, I don't know what and how to remember.

The fortitude of the women bereaved by war is remote in the contem-porary climate of emotional incontinence where in the 1990s two self-ob-sessed women – the fictional Bridget Jones and the larger-than-life Princess of Wales – became role models for a generation of single women. The sad spinsters who became doughty maiden aunts, the widows, the mothers who lost only sons – it is hard to relate to them. Their daughters – our mothers – are of a different mettle from us, too, enduring endless trau-matic partings – smiling through, in spite of the real possibility that they would never meet again. Plenty didn't. A substantial number became serial widows, caught up in cycles of love and loss, loving and losing fiancés and then risking again, and sometimes losing again, the men they married, often without even having had a honeymoon.

To my generation, bravery is anachronistic and demanded comparatively rarely. 'Brave' is people with cancer, or dumpees, duped by love and dumped after years of keeping the domestic faith. 'Brave' for us is the opposite of cracking up. I had a clearer sense of the wartime meaning of the word recently when my father opened a rusty biscuit tin and showed me a crumpled piece of paper. It read:

> On the afternoon of 1st march 1945, this officer's platoon was attacking enemy positions south of Udem. The forward section became pinned down in open ground by heavy and accurate Spandau fire from their front and right flank, and were suffering heavily, all except one man became casualties. Lieut. Berridge went forward to see the position for himself, and tried without success to signal to his supporting tanks. He then crawled 100 yards under intense fire to the nearest tank, and successfully directed its fire on to the enemy position that was holding up the advance of his platoon. In the meantime enemy shelling had commenced in the immediate neighbourhood of his platoon. Nothing daunted; Lieut. Berridge collected the remainder of his platoon and cleared the area of enemy capturing 20 prisoners and the machine guns, which had held him up. Lieut. Berridge's prompt action and complete disregard for his own safety undoubtedly ensured the complete success of the attack. Throughout the operations on this day this officer's gallantry and leadership were an inspiration to his platoon.

It was a citation for an immediate Military Cross. To a degree, fathers are always their daughters' heroes, but this bit of paper extended the definition.

It is hard to identify with the Pathé newsreel people, yet these are my parents. This is my father with his Ministry of Information voice and endless military-style acronyms: FHB (family hold back); used when people come for supper; MFU (monumental fuck-up); LOC (lines of communication); his habit of ending phone messages with 'Over and Out'; his mantra 'Maintenance of objective'; his wish that my sister walked up the aisle to the theme music from *The Dam Busters*. He carries the war with him still. This is my mother, too: her love of Glenn Miller, her tendency to treat bananas as extravagant rarities. They never talked about the war, but sometimes at breakfast my mother would say, 'Your father was fighting the Germans again last night', meaning that he had had nightmares. Very occasionally she would mention dead people she had lost in the war. And occasionally after supper, warmed up by an audience, my father would tell 'The Jerries were here' stories in which the Eleventh Armoured Division was represented by a napkin ring, a fork and a knife, and the enemy a side plate, in a battle over a stick of celery, which was the River Elbe.

For me the Second World War is a collage of fact and fiction – jumpy newsreels with music and films with actors playing brave men in stories about courage. It is Noel Coward drowning with dignity, Kenneth Moore as Douglas Bader. In real life, my grandfather was a brave man who played life modestly. He returned from the war completely deaf. For him, remembrance was a sixty-year silence, not two minutes once a year. He did not believe in household security. The front door was permanently ajar and most of the windows were open in all weathers; he never locked a car, a case or a door. His vigilance was in a different direction. He had been at Ypres and the Battle of the Somme, and in addition to the loss of so many brothers in arms, he had gone on to lose two of his three sons, a wife, a sister and his parents. This is why, instead of wearing his heart on his sleeve, he had locked it up in a very safe place, and only my grandmother had known where he kept the key.

As a member of one of the Pals corps, a Kitchener battalion raised in the early days of 1914, he had been one of the raw recruits whose military career had got off to an ignominious start. A shortage of khaki and guns had forced them to train in temporary blue uniforms that looked like convict suits and to carry wooden dummy rifles. Yet, from an inauspicious start he went on to become a distinguished soldier. Like my father, he won recognition for bravery. On one occasion, despite suffering from the effects of gas, he went down on record as setting 'a fine example of endurance and devotion to duty' with 'prompt and gallant action which undoubtedly saved the company from being cut off by the enemy'. On two further occasions his behaviour when in mortal danger was singled out for praise, and he was honoured with awards 'for conspicuous gallantry and devotion to duty'. By the end of the war he had six decorations for gallantry, including the Military Cross and two bars. My brother tells me there is a portrait of him in an officers' mess somewhere titled 'The Intrepid Hero of the Regiment'.

In church on Remembrance Sunday my grandfather used to chink when he got up and sat down. After the service the veterans, the vicar and younger British Legion people would come back to our house and have sherry and twiglets. I was given bitter lemon from the cupboard in the corner of the drawing room which still had some port put down for Dick's twenty-first on a shelf that no one ever touched. Some of the old soldiers had child-scarer faces, like Otto Dix paintings. One man looked as if his nose had been carved off like a difficult bit of a joint of meat. Others had disfigured minds, locked in perpetual combat with life.

For the Remembrance Day service, Oundle School provided a bugler who played the Last Post. As a stroppy teenager attending the ceremony on sufferance, this was the only part of the proceedings that held any interest for me. With his scuffed shoes and scruffy uniform, a face that was all acne, he was an ally. Back at the house we were bored and bolshey together, slouching conspiratorially in a corner of the drawing room and keeping our distance from the war veterans. Their watery eyes and baggy suits embarrassed us, and if they tried to speak to us, we fixed our gaze on the floor and mumbled monosyllables.

As a child of the 1960s, that slow-motion mushroom cloud impinged on my consciousness of death more than the death camps and the jerky archive film of packed train carriages and ominous chimney stacks. The nuclear bomb was an abstract but terrifying threat which was compounded by the Cold War tension between East and West. CND, making love not war, stoned hippies, flower power: this was the wallpaper of my early life. My brother had a Mini Moke covered in psychedelic flowers and guitar-playing, barefoot girl friends. He got married in a hippie chapel in Sydney to a barefoot pregnant bride. He wore white, she wore green. In those lazy, hazy days activism tended to be passive; people listened to protest songs, put up posters in their bedrooms and wore 'Ban The Bomb' badges. Sex, not death, was the optic through which we viewed the world. This carefree climate lasted until AIDS brought to a time of peace a new awareness of death. Whereas in 1945 the atom bomb dealt a horrific, invisible, unprecedented death from the outside in, in the 1980s the AIDS epidemic heralded a horrific, invisible, unprecedented death from the inside out. Suddenly, apocalyptic imagery extended beyond nuclear warfare. 'Thunderbolts and lightning, very very frightening': Freddie Mercury was but one of the famous fallen whose passing intruded on teenage cool.

Like a disco when the lights are put on, thoughts of mortality suddenly broke up the promiscuous party that was the 1980s. The sonorous tone of the 'Don't die of ignorance' campaign infused peacetime with a new kind of death threat. Death imagery was everywhere as government campaigns used the bony-fingered Grim Reaper to frighten the population into monogamy. The *Panorama* programme 'A Killer in the Village', about the ravages of AIDS in San Francisco, made me think of Nagasaki. The Castro neighbourhood was at the epicentre of the epidemic in a city devastated by the disease. Red ribbons became the 1980s equivalent of the CND badge as consciousness-raising emblems. The early safe sex messages from the health education authority were as unsophisticated and condescending as the public education 'duck and cover' films produced by governments about nuclear war. In a climate of fear and misinformation, people built mental bunkers in which to shelter their families. Mothers stopped children from using public swimming pools. Bartenders smashed glasses that had been used by gay customers. The crazies called for HIV-positive people to be rounded up and interned on the Isle of Wight.

What AIDS meant for the babyboomers is analogous to what the First World War meant for my grandfather's generation: both are about the tragedy of parents outliving their children. Where they named the glorious dead on pale Portland stone in incised letters, cold to the touch, we named the gay dead on bright panels on the AIDS memorial quilt. They remembered with marching and monuments; we remember with candlelit vigils and needlework. Both are communal sources of consolation, but compared to their walls, our quilt is a metaphor for our softer social fabric. The impact of their trauma of mass death drove death from everyday life and fixed it in the private realm. The impact of the trauma of AIDS put death back into people's minds and reinstated it in the public arena. As one gay male said of life in New York in the 1980s, 'You haven't lived until you've got used to *not* going to your best friends' funerals.' AIDS happened in a climate of medical invincibility when the western world believed it had vanquished infectious disease. The war broke out in a climate of military invincibility. The experience of multiple death in close-knit male communities set apart from mainstream society is common to both generations, and so is the sense of being guardians of the secret of death. In the late 1980s many HIV-positive people kept silent about the status of their condition or even lied about it, like the writer Bruce Chatwin who turned the truth into an elaborate traveller's tale of exotic disease.

> I don't always feel that I mourn fully now because there are so many and they come very close together like we had seven in ten days and you don't know where to start so in the end you don't start at all.

This statement by a gay man in a bereavement research project in 1997 could have come from a soldier at the front. It conveys death ripping through a group with rapidity and power, leaving a trail of numbed survivors. Seventy-six per cent of the casualties of the First World War were under the age of 30, and like them the victims of AIDS are, in Edgar Allen Poe's words, 'doubly dead' because they died so young. The memorials at public schools and universities reveal the extent to which the First World War ravaged the Establishment. (The death toll of Etonians was 20.5 per cent, the Cambridge University toll 26.5 per cent, compared to a general death rate of 11 per cent.) The AIDS memorial quilt testifies to the degree to which AIDS has shattered the world of fashion, entertainment and the media. Where remembrance of the war dead is political in character, remembrance of the gay dead is politically correct in character, with glamorous fundraising benefits and actors wearing red ribbons at awards ceremonies. Where the war was a catalyst for the deritualisation of death, AIDS has generated a different energy. It has created a subculture of creative funerals which have restored to the funeral the ceremony, celebration and ritual that had been stolen from it by the war.

The First World War dramatically accelerated the twentieth-century retreat from death. In the closing years of the nineteenth century the Victorian cult of death was already on the wane. Death was receding as the preoccupation of polite society, partly because improved healthcare had increased life expectancy. The war also repeated the common Victorian tragedy of parents outliving their offspring, although in this case the lost children were young adults, far away. More significantly, the war sabotaged society with the unprecedented phenomenon of manmade mass death, and the collective trauma left a disfiguring scar on the psyche of the British nation from which it never fully recovered. Never before had death undone so many. The scale of loss was such that three million households lost a close relative (husband, father, son, brother and the corresponding in-laws) and many more were affected by the loss of kith as well as kin. The devastation of bereavement was compounded by the savage flu pandemic of 1918 and 1919, which killed 280,000 people in Britain. The virulence of 'The Spanish Lady', as the flu strain was known, coupled with the hideous symptoms – victims coughed blood and their feet turned black – brought ugly death on an epic scale into the domestic environment and reinforced the already crippling impact of military loss. Where the Victorians had integrated private grief into a social context using elaborate funerals and mourning rituals, the decision in 1915 not to repatriate bodies had shattered the coherence of traditional death rites. Without the consoling elements of body, funeral, grave and mourning dress, death slipped into the contemporary realm of crisis management, and practicality took precedence over ceremony in attitudes to the disposal of the dead.

The fact that agents of the state became in effect official body snatchers enforced a demotion of the significance of the body in the death ritual and paved the way for the post-war rise of cremation and the promotion of rites of remembrance.

Victorian concepts of glory sank in the mulch of dead men at the front. The mass mobilisation of the First World War and a revolution in infantry and artillery tactics which gave new force to the concept of 'canon fodder' meant that the broadest possible spectrum of British men experienced for the first time a totally depersonalised rain of death. The impersonality of death made mundane by sheer numbers undermined the ideal of chivalrous martyrdom. In trench warfare, men died like animals rather than gentlemen. This sad way of dying – in circumstances closer to murder than moral mortal combat – made death a hitherto unimaginable horror. Robbed of the romance of heroism and without the comforts of the domestic deathbed, death was visceral and violent, and often a slow agony. This raw war death is powerfully conveyed in the diary of a French soldier:

> Between this war and the last we did not die: we ended. Neatly, in the shelter of a room in the warmth of a bed. Now when we die it is the wet death, the muddy death, death dripping with blood, death by drowning, death by sucking under, death in the slaughterhouse. (Louis Mairet quoted in M. Eksteins' *Rites of Spring*, 1989)

The First World War marks a watershed between the death acceptance of the Victorians and twentieth-century death denial. Nineteenth-century religious doubt was compounded by events at the front. After the war, God receded in the world picture and death became a new form of trauma and taboo. T. S. Eliot's *The Waste Land* resonated in the battle-scarred plains, which Paul Nash, the official war artist, described as 'unspeakable, godless, hopeless'; the Western Front was literally 'a heap of broken images'. Geographically and physically, fragmentation was everywhere – in the broken bodies of dead and maimed survivors, and in the shards of horror that splintered the minds of the mentally wounded. To comprehend the scale of the crisis of meaning that happened in 1914, it is enlightening to look back to the ideological climate immediately before the war, when the meaning of death was much clearer, and faith and social cohesion tempered the trauma of bereavement.

The spirit of nineteenth-century patriotism is encapsulated in a poem entitled 'Wooden Legs' in which a young brother and sister evaluate the risks of a military career:

> 'Then I'll be a soldier,
> With a delightful gun,
> And I'll come home with a wooden leg
> As heroes have often done.'
> She screams at that – and prays and begs
> While tears – half anger start

'Don't talk about your wooden legs,
Unless you'd break my heart!'

He answered her rather proudly,
'If so what can I be?
If I must not have a wooden leg
And must not go to sea?
How could the Queen sleep sound at night,
Safe from the scum and dregs,
If English boys refused to fight
For fear of wooden legs?'

She hung her head repenting,
And trying to be good,
But her little hand stroked tenderly,
The leg of flesh and blood!
And with her rosy mouth she kissed
The knickerbockered knee,
And sighed 'Perhaps if you insist –
You'd better go to sea!'

Then he flung his arms about her,
And laughingly he spoke
'But I've seem many honest tars
With legs of British oak.
Oh darling, when I am a man
With beard of shining black,
I'll be a hero if I can
And you must not hold me back.'

(*Aunt Judy's Magazine*, July 1866)

From the poems of Alfred, Lord Tennyson to the 'blood and morality' tales of George Alfred Henty, risking life and limb for king and country was perceived primarily as duty, but also as an adventurous and noble path to glory. Nowhere was this ethos more enthusiastically inculcated into young Englishmen than in the famous public schools, where attitudes to death in war were akin to kamikaze propaganda:

To die young, clean, ardent; to die swiftly in perfect health; to die saving others from death, or worse disgrace – to die scaling heights; to die and carry with you into the fuller ampler life beyond, untainted hopes and aspirations, unembittered memories, all the freshness and gladness of May – is not that cause for joy rather than sorrow? (H.A. Vachell, *The Hill*, 1905)

The novel from which this extract is taken was a bestseller which was reprinted twenty-one times before the outbreak of the First World War. It is part of a headmaster's speech intended to bolster morale after a favourite pupil has been killed in the Boer War. He continues: 'I would sooner see any of you struck down in the flower of his youth than living on to lose, long before death comes all that makes life worth living.' But in real life people subscribed to this notion of honourable sacrifice. Lord Grey spoke for many when he said; 'None of us who give our sons in this war are so much to be pitied as those who have no sons to give.'

The glorification of death in youth was a forceful ideology. It permeated the intellectual climate, from the popularity of A. E. Housman's 'Lads that will die in their glory and never be old' to classics classes where boys were taught that 'Those whom the Gods love die young'. J.M. Barrie's play *Peter Pan*, which was first performed in 1904, and the subsequent prose version *Peter and Wendy* (1911) provided contemporary reinforcement of the cult of youth.

'They shall not grow old, as we that are left grow old' resonates beyond remembrance rituals. It is the epitaph of a generation of Peter Pans, the 'lost boys' of real life, commemorated on official monuments designed by the artist and architect Sir Edwin Lutyens – the man who, with poetic symmetry, had also designed the stage set for the original production of Barrie's play. Although Barrie claimed to have based the characters of Peter Pan on a composite of the personalities of the Llewellyn Davies boys (he once told them, 'I made Peter by rubbing the five of you together'), the psychological roots of the story stem from the death of Barrie's 13-year-old brother, who died in a skating accident. As the surviving younger brother, Barrie seems to have been profoundly affected by the impact of the bereavement on his mother. She never fully recovered, and admitted that she found some comfort in the idea that her dead son would remain a boy for ever. As Barrie himself put it, 'When I became a man, he was still a boy of 13.'

As lifelong friends, the trajectories of Barrie and Lutyens' creative lives intersect in extraordinary ways: Barrie as the man who created the archetype of the permanent youth, and Lutyens as the man who created the Cenotaph as a permanent memorial to all those who died in their prime. Indeed, the two went to France by boat together in the immediate aftermath of the war. Lutyens, in his capacity as consultant to the War Graves Commission, was advising on appropriate monuments that would help transform makeshift military graveyards into dignified cemeteries. Barrie was making a personal pilgrimage to visit the grave of George Llewellyn

Davies. A further irony was that the war which claimed the life of a role model for Peter Pan was widely referred to as The Big Adventure, which had been Peter Pan's description of death – a line tellingly cut in the 1915 Christmas revival of the play.

The reality of death was obscured beneath a variety of ideological guises. Death was a purifying transcendental experience; for Rupert Brooke, soldiers were 'swimmers into cleanness leaping'. Less esoterically, Peter Pan's 'awfully big adventure' view of death was echoed in thousands of high-circulation boys' magazines. In *Chums*, *The Captain* and the best-known of these, the *Boy's Own Paper*, death is the privilege of a character built of the right stuff. *Men Of Grit*, an anthology from 1916, exemplifies this ethos:

> All the heroes of this little book were men of great daring, and their daring had its foundation, support and stimulus in their faith. They were great doers because they were great believers. They attempted great things for God, because they expected great things from God.

On the pages of *Boy's Own* the war is a real-life action adventure, in which accounts such as 'How "Todger" Jones Won a VC' and 'Allied Aviators' Adventures in the Great War' turn the events on the Western Front into a series of ripping yarns. George Soper's dramatic drawings, such as 'Night Raid on German Trenches at the Front', reinforce the action-packed, fantasy version of war, where the true horror of death and carnage never intrude.

A striking example of the way in which readers' attention was deflected from the human cost of war is an article in *Boy's Own* entitled 'Animals in Gas Attacks', which describes the effects of gas with the detached observation of a natural history feature:

> Poultry of all kinds are useful for giving warning, ducks and fowls becoming agitated ten minutes or so before the oncoming of gas clouds. Many kinds of wild birds are greatly excited, and the usually unruffled owl becomes, as it were, half-demented. Only the sparrow seems to disregard the poisonous vapour and sparrows chirp on where horses are asphyxiated, and bees, butterflies, caterpillars, ants and beetles die off in great numbers. The gas at once kills snakes, and earthworms are found dead in their holes many inches below the ground. (*Boy's Own Paper*, volume 39, 1916)

This is in stark contrast to the searing realism of Wilfred Owen's account of the death of a man from gas poisoning – 'guttering, choking, drowning'. Owen's provocative poem punctures the myth of glorious death, and suggests that if more people witnessed the grim reality of slow, painful death in the primordial conditions at the front they would not

> tell with such high jest
> To children ardent for some desperate glory,
> The old lie: *Dulce et decorum est*
> *Pro patria mori.*
>
> (*Dulce et Decorum Est*, 1921)

The 'old lie' was widely told. Popular culture was saturated with militarism, which masked the facts of death. In all the yarns about heroes and descriptions of every conceivable type of weapon, the emphasis is on the killing, not the killed. Obituaries of war heroes often use the phrase 'was laid low by' for 'killed'. The pages of *Chums* magazine are peppered with advertisements for guns. A banner headline for Gamages toy shop (which also sold guns) in London's Holborn reads: 'Boys of the British Empire, Learn to shoot now and ensure your future usefulness for king and country.' Advertisements for rifles are interspersed with those for cricket bats, but as the war progresses, weapons win, and the military message becomes more overt. Editors start to sound like ventriloquists' dolls as they mouth words supplied by Kitchener:

> We all know, don't we, my chums, that if you want to take care of yourself you must fight. Let us all try to be decent, manly, men with a keen military spirit and a love of our King and Country. (*Chums*, 28 November 1914)

When the magazine becomes the official organ of the sharpshooters' organisation, the editor receives a letter of complaint:

> 'You ought to be ashamed of yourself encouraging boys to learn to kill their fellows.' I can't for the life of me think what sort of fellow could have written that postcard. Thought occurs that he may be a German who is bitterly envious at the splendid response of the boys of Britain to the call to make themselves efficient sharpshooters, so that when they are men they will be perfectly ready to protect their king, their country and their homes from the rapacity of a foreign bully. Yes, the writer must be a German and so we will forgive him. (*Chums*, 31 October 1914)

The juggernaut of patriotism was also powered from another quarter. In the early years of the twentieth century, partly out of concern for Britain's military prowess after the humiliating and unexpected human cost of the Boer War, there was a well-orchestrated campaign to instill military aspirations in the minds of young Englishmen with a view to building up territorial reserves. Where periodicals pedalled myths and filled the imaginations of schoolboys with images of the glory rather than the gore of war, veterans from the Boer War toured schools to drum up enthusiasm for the military life. As war heroes with stories to tell, they too contributed to the misleading idea of war as adventure. The common objective was to take the raw material of a mass of schoolboys and shape it into a new generation of soldiers who would willingly lay down their lives for their country. Special attention was paid to the public schools in recruitment initiatives.

> I look to you public school boys to set an example. – Let it be your ambition to render yourself capable of becoming leaders of those others who have not your advantages, should you ever be called upon to fight for your country. (Field Marshal Lord Roberts, 1906)

The corps became an important part of the curriculum, although the headmaster of one school famously remarked that a school that had a rugger pitch did not need a rifle corps. The association of sportsmanship and fighting was deeply ingrained.

> War as we know is the greatest game there is. But we want other most peaceful games, not only to prepare us for the great game of war but also to prepare us physically and morally – remember that! for the battle of life, which is a struggle in which every one of us is predestined to take part. ('Rugby Football an Asset of Empire' by George H. Harnett in *Boy's Own*)

The same piece continues:

> One great merit of rugby football is that it makes men. In all history there has been no greater test of manliness and manhood than that, without compulsion of any kind, prompted solely by their own patriotism and sense of duty, young fellows of our kith and kin have forsaken ease and comfort and prospects and everything, and have as cheerfully as voluntarily gone forth, to the Great Adventure from which so many never return. No game has sent these heroes forth in proportionately greater numbers than Rugby football ... Rugby football – clean straightforward, free from, any taint – makes men and both in quantity and quality it is *men* that the Empire needs today.

Playing a match was universally regarded as a model for fighting, and whether wielding a bat or a rifle the rules and expectations were similarly perceived:

Situations may arise in a good cricket or football team requiring as quick a decision, perhaps a shade quicker than a company commander with his line of skirmishers in the field. (Colonel O'Callaghan Westropp, 1904)

Public school boys subscribed wholeheartedly to the idea that war, like sport, operated on the principles of fair play, team spirit and competition. They looked forward to fighting with the same sense of pride that was inspired by an important sports fixture with a rival school. The headmaster of Eton wrote in 1915:

> I believe there are still people who believe that the sons of the well-to-do are soft and effeminate. The fact is directly war was declared, they telegraphed from all parts of the country for leave to rush off and fight the Germans. Cricket weeks were dropped, yachting was taboo and the grouse were left to batten among the sunlit burns of Yorkshire.

For many young men, fear of death was sublimated in the fantasy of dying a glorious Greek warrior's death, as much for house and school as for king and country. The *Boy's Own Paper* article entitled 'The Old School' (1916) proclaimed:

> There is no other love on earth exactly like this, except that of motherhood itself, that is so undying, so strong, so rich, and so full.
> It was this love which made the young officer at Elandslaagte rush into the fight waving his sword and shouting as his battle cry '*Floreat Etona!*' It was this love that made Desmond in *The Hill* see Harrow again as a vision ere he died.

One of the most infamous Old Etonians to die with the words '*Floreat Etona*' on his lips was Captain Hook in Peter Pan. But in reality, in the last words of mortally wounded officers, 'Eton' often followed 'Mother'.

The scholar poet Julian Grenfell personifies the idealism of the *jeunesse dore*. When war broke out he was positively excited. In August 1914 he wrote to his mother; 'It reinforces one's failing belief in the Old Flag and the Mother Country and the Heavy Brigade and the Thin Red Line and the Imperial Idea which gets rather shadowy in peace time, don't you think?' The experience of front line fighting at Ypres failed to diminish his fervour. On 24 October 1914 he wrote; 'I adore war. It is like a big picnic without the objectlessness of a picnic. I've never been so well or so happy.' This naivete and cognitive dissonance between perception and reality is similar to that expressed by the fictional 'chaps' in *Chums*. In 'Lion's Teeth and Eagle's Claw, A Story of a Struggle to the Death Between Our Empire and Her

Enemies', the protagonist is overcome with excitement at the news that Britain is at war:

> 'War, war, war – giddy joyful war,' carolled Roy Carrington dancing to and fro snapping his fingers. A moment later he flung himself on his father's broad chest. 'Pater, get me an appointment aboard *The Empire*, she'll be first in the fighting and in the thick of everything'. (*Chums*, 13 December 1913)

Nothing stemmed the misrepresentation. What the virgin soldiers expected and what they experienced were vastly different. Although it describes a scene in the Dardanelles, Ronald Blythe's *Akenfield* (1969), a book of first-hand narratives based on interviews, includes one of the most vivid accounts of the violent ambush of death that was such a widespread experience. Young soldiers who have just landed on the beach glimpse the familiar sight of an English marquee – the kind more commonly seen at village fêtes and agricultural shows, with guy ropes and cream canvas and coconut matting. Making towards it excitedly, they pull back one of the sides and are confronted by a vast number of decomposing Englishmen. The rookie soldiers could be forgiven for their naivete when the sources of their information are subjected to closer scrutiny. One of the more striking publications is a strip cartoon entitled 'Jovial Jottings from the Trenches'. In an alphabet format, 'W is for Wound which the soldier acquires, If not too severe tis what he desires.' This caption is illustrated by a picture of a bedbound soldier, looking a bit like Leslie Phillips with a moustache, one arm in a sling and the other brandishing a cigarette, as two attractive nurses sit at his side, hanging on to his every word. 'Y is for Youth full of keenness and dash, who longs for the head of a German to bash.' This seemingly light-hearted material is likely to have contributed to the false perception the British public had of the war.

A common denominator in the vast volume of material for young men is an emphasis on dying with dignity. This is presented as duty. It is a recurring theme in both factual and fictional formats. For example, an article in *The Boy's Illustrated Book of War* (1914) entitled 'How Officers Die' – 'Splendid in leading, patient in teaching, lofty their ideals and in their code of honour, the British Officer dies as he lives, bravely', resonates in Wendy's words to the Lost Boys as they prepare to walk the plank in the prose version of Barrie's *Peter and Wendy*:

> 'Are they to die?' asked Wendy, with a look of such frightful contempt that he [Hook] nearly fainted. 'They are,' he snarled. 'Silence all,' he called

gloatingly, 'for a mother's last words to her children.' At this moment Wendy was grand. 'These are my last words, dear boys,' she said firmly, 'I feel that I have a message to you from your mothers and it is this "we hope that our sons will die like English gentlemen".'

Another device for distorting the horror of death on active service is to blur the distinction between fact and fiction in increasingly imaginative ways. *Captain Loxley's Little Dog* (1915), which enjoyed great popularity, is an example of this genre. An anthropomorphic version of patriotism, it plays on our dog-loving national characteristic, and fuses it with the duty-ethic in an intriguing narrative, presented as the 'true' story of the sinking of HMS *The Formidable* from the perspective of the dog. The terrier went down with his master when his ship was torpedoed by a German submarine on New Year's Eve with the loss of 5,000 lives. Captain Loxley was on the bridge 'to the last'. As the ship is sinking the faithful terrier gives a dog's-eye view from the bridge where he remained at his master's side:

> 'I'm glad I'm with Big Master on the bridge. He keeps on flashing lights. This is really a very strange muddle – like a fifth of November and a fancy dress party and a rat hunt all rolled into one. I'm not sure I altogether like it. Something's wrong somewhere. I believe it was his danger bark. 'Keep cool, boys. Keep cool. Be British!'

The gap between fact and fiction was a chasm. Where adventure stories always concluded with a happy ending and a victorious hero, at the actual front the Victorian definition of victory was obscured by 908,371 unhappy endings – the British Empire total of First World War military battle deaths. Of these, 702,460 came from the British Isles.

Instead of the clamour and glamour of the cavalry charge, instead of the elegant symmetry of men marching into battle en masse and sweeping over battle plains in great surges, there was deadlock and digging. The initial action of mass mobilisation, with millions of men on the move, ground to a halt. The overwhelming impression is one of immobility and physical constraint, where for much of the time what was not happening was the preoccupation.

The image of men knee-deep in semi-liquid, frigidly cold mud shooting at an enemy who was within earshot but out of sight is as absurd as anything written by Samuel Beckett. The Theatre of the Absurd which emerged from the pens of Beckett and Eugene Ionesco disturbs audiences with plays in which the meaninglessness of life is the theme and what does not happen is the action. Similarly, the theatre of war confronted the Tommys with the meaninglessness of death, and subjected them to a series of dehumanised and absurd situations. The relentless visual assault of surreal images – rats running up the walls of dug-outs, a dead hand sticking out of the side of a trench, a human head used as a football, dead horses in trees – reinforced the mental alienation. The sights men saw compounded their feeling of distance from the domestic world, turning death and carnage into deep secrets to harbour from friends and relatives at home.

'Digging in' epitomises the powerlessness. As one general remarked, the spade was as important as the rifle. To visualise an image of men digging deep with spades, smelling wet earth, seeing worms, bones and rats, is to visualize an image of soldiers as grave diggers, digging their own graves and living in them until death, for the miles of semi-subterranean tunnels afforded limited protection. Ypres, Passchendaele, the Somme – these represent a tragic loss on a scale that is beyond emotional computation. Record rainfall and three months of continuous fighting turned Passchendaele into an awesomely sad swamp in which the dead disappeared and the dying who could not be rescued drowned in mud. After the Big Push on the first day of the Somme, which claimed 20,000 lives, the uncut barbed wire of enemy trenches was draped with death, and for nine months the unburied bodies of thousands of 'Accrington Pals' turned no man's land into a grim Golgotha. In that one day, the British army toll of loss was the same as that for the entire Boer conflict between 1899 and 1902.

The casualty figures are unimaginable. At 'the rottonest place' on the Somme, High Wood, four months of fighting left 82,000 dead. Military historians estimate that by the end of the war, the human cost was equivalent to one dead body for every eighteen inches of the front. Although the twentieth century turned out to be the age of mass death, the famous visual representation of the dead of the Great War, first described when the war ended, has retained its power:

> Imagine the dead moving in one continuous column, four abreast. As the head of that column reaches the Cenotaph in London, the last four men would be in Durham [240 miles away]. It would take those million men 84 hours, or three and a half days, to march past the Cenotaph in London. (Sir Fabian Ware)

The impersonality of 'millions of mouthless dead' remade the imagery of death with an extra dimension of existential horror. It is a telling detail that early on in the war, identity tags had to be redesigned, and the glazed tunic material was replaced with compressed fibre and metal of double-strength durability. Regardless of this provision, the scale of unidentifiable human remains – less than one quarter of all those reported missing after a major battle were identified – and the failure to retrieve anything of some known casualties exacerbated the crisis of death. Loss of identity is the crux of contemporary anxiety about death. The First World War tapped into this fear very literally, for men were annihilated.

The disappearance of the dead was a particular horror. The need for this focus was highlighted when, some years after Kitchener's body was lost at sea, an elaborate hoax was staged in which some enterprising people claimed to have recovered the body, resulting in a short-lived sensational newspaper scoop. This was a desperate attempt to comfort the public by conjuring up the body of their hero. The bodies of the majority of naval casualties were lost at sea, nearly half of the bodies of all those killed on land were never found, and the final resting places of vast numbers are unknown. The scale of anonymous bodies becomes real on monuments covered with the names of the missing. The Menin Gate, Thiepval, Tyne Cot – these places multiply thousands of times the peacetime urban tragedy of those who die the sad bad deaths of anonymity, and are only found when neighbours they never spoke to telephone the authorities because of piled-up newspapers or unexplained smells.

Anonymity in death is heart-hurting; nameless graves are disquieting more than consoling. Rudyard Kipling and his wife spent years trawling the military hospitals of France, desperately seeking news of their only son who had been reported missing after the battle of Loos. Knowing this gives added poignancy to the fact that Kipling composed the official inscriptions for the headstones of unidentifiable human remains: 'A Soldier of the Great War Known Unto God'; and for graves destroyed by continued bombardment: 'Their glory shall not be blotted out'; and where only a rough estimate of the site of burial was possible: 'Buried near this place'.

Obliteration and fragmentation were everywhere. Men were blasted to bits, burned black, buried alive, gassed to death, drowned in dug-outs, disfigured to anonymity, shot to slow-bleeding death. The front was 'rotten with dead', and often chloride of lime and creosote were not enough to mask the stench. The concentration of carnage was such that in places the sandbags used to shore up trenches became contaminated by human remains. In a macabre marriage, the living lived with the dead. Philip Gibbs, the British war correspondent, gives a graphic first-hand account of conditions at Hooge:

> Human flesh, rotting and stinking, mere pulp, was pasted on to the mud
> banks. If they dug to get deeper cover, their shovels went into the softness

of dead bodies who had once been their comrades. Scraps of flesh, booted legs, blackened heads, eyeless heads, came falling over them when the enemy trench mortared their position or blew up a new mine shaft.

It was as if Picasso's deconstruction of the human form in the early years of Cubism anticipated the real fragmentation of the human body that happened in northern France. The people on Picasso's canvasses in 1910 are unrecognisable as people, like the thousands of corpses that were unidentifiable, nameless and in pieces in 1914–1918.

The trauma of the men who had witnessed the carnage was compounded by an overwhelming sense of futility, for what had been gained failed to justify what had been lost. The ratio of cost and acquisition called into question the morality of heroism, and instilled the uncomfortable possibility that 'the glorious dead' were more murder victims than heroes.

The impression of senseless slaughter overturned the conventional meaning of death in war, and the idea of meaningless death signified the advent of death as existential crisis which crystallised in the twentieth century. Many voiced their anger at the end of the war including a young German corporal who asked, 'Was this the meaning of sacrifice? Hatred grew in me, hatred for those responsible for this deed. I decided to go into politics.' He was Adolf Hitler. Anger also informs the French feature film *J'accuse* in which dead soldiers rise from their graves and make their way to villages to ask if their death has been worthwhile. The director, Abel Gance, said that he was pointing his finger at 'universal stupidity'.

The soldiers who had witnessed the brute facts of death with multiple bereavements of comrades rarely spoke of what they had seen; the bereaved rarely spoke of their emotional pain. This replicates contemporary dissonance, where the dynamic of death tends to be repressed emotion and distance from the physical body, which is spirited away by funeral directors as soon as death occurs. Like soldiers harbouring the secrets of death in the war zone, doctors and nurses keep the secrets of the facts of death to themselves in the hospice and the hospital. They are people in uniform with the high-tech machinery of life and death in their hands. The flimsy screen put around the dying in the hospital is a metaphor for the way medical staff hide the truth of death from the living, from relatives and often the patients themselves.

On the home front the news of death was devastating. 'Missing', 'Regret no trace' – these words went straight through the hearts of those who received the telegrams. Barely a line of black print inflicted deep wounds on hundreds of thousands of families. The sheer number of households hit by death made grief ubiquitous. The scale of emotional pain in domesticity was analogous to the scale of carnage witnessed by hundreds of thousands of soldiers at the front. The excess of grief and excess of corpses were collective and comparable traumas, and both situations were complicated by the absence of factors that normally help to alleviate the pain of bereavement. The bereaved received telegrams about their loved ones, but they were not sent their bodies. Conversely, those on active service and dealing with the bereavement of brothers-in-arms were surrounded by bodies but deprived of the chance to grieve.

The physical and emotional splitting around death that happens in war is analogous to the dynamic of sex without emotion, and the difference between pornography and romance. In a sense, the carnival of dead flesh at the front was a macabre form of pornography, for it objectified the body. The orgy of killing was like a sexual orgy, entailing abandonment of inhibitions and loss of individuality. Similarly, the unbridled grief at home became a form of emotional fantasy, in so far as the emotions were not fixed to the physical dimension of death, since the body was not seen or touched but pictured in the mind. This splitting is a significant aspect of death becoming taboo and anti-social. It marks the evolution of a climate of repression and denial that replicates the Victorian model of sexuality which has similar anomalies.

In the nineteenth century, the more repressive the official cultural stance on sexuality became, the greater the subculture of pornography and the tension between the personal and social sexual arenas. In *The Other Victorians* (1966) Steven Marcus writes of Victorian sexuality:

> By a variety of social means which correspond to the psychological processes of isolation, distancing denial and even repression, a separate and inculcated sphere in which sexuality was to be confined was brought into existence.

The tension between the personal and social aspects of death in the twentieth century has a similar dynamic. A repressive climate of taboo around mortality has spawned a subculture of death. The First World War heralded the advent of the contemporary climate of concealment, distance and secrecy. The post-war popularity of spiritualism was symptomatic of this segregation. Instead of being integrated into society, after the war bereavement became an isolated experience which was to be coped with in private and kept distinct from the public rites of official remembrance.

The war enforced a revision of Victorian funerary ritual. It created a context where elaborate family funerals for individuals were anathema.

The Easter sermon delivered at St Paul's Cathedral in 1918 included an entreaty to stop 'parading bereavement', and as early as 1914 there were calls in society magazines for mourning dress to be abandoned in bereavement of men who had been killed in action. Less orthodox voices also championed funeral reform. The spirits of dead soldiers, speaking via mediums, also apparently called for restraint in mourning rituals. In *Talking with the Dead* by J.F. Rutherford (1920), a dead Tommy asks his bereaved relatives to stop crying and to cease wearing black clothes, a fascinating ideological use of the dead as conduits for an important social change.

If, as the saying goes, religion is for people who are afraid that Hell exists and spirituality is for those who have been there, then after the war society moved in a more secular and spiritual direction because from 1914 to 1918 Hell *happened*. The two-minute silence, a rite with a spiritual dimension that was not mediated by priests and happened outside places of worship, signified this secular shift. For many, belief in God's grace was untenable after the war. On hearing of the death of her fiancé, Vera Brittain wrote in her memoir *Testament of Youth* (1933): 'I knew now that death was the end, no hereafter, no Easter morning, no meeting again.'

For many of the bereaved, conventional Christianity and the notion of Heaven became insufficient sources of solace, and there was an instinctive migration to spiritualism. Whereas the nineteenth-century concern with spiritualism had been motivated more by a sense of intellectual crisis in a general climate of religious uncertainty, the post-war upsurge of interest was borne out of extreme emotional disturbance. The war dramatically tested the tenets of theology, and found them unable to confer meaning on the epic scale of loss. Many of those who turned in droves to mediums after the war were buckling under the weight of bereavement exacerbated by feelings of futility and waste. British society was thrown into theological turmoil. In 1915 the headmaster of Eton wrote of the war that

> It has brought us to a new idea of death. I may be wrong but I think that since the casualty list began its record there has been less talk of death being the end. It is not possible for some of us to think of these personalities as annihilated, and yet in the paganism of our times of peace how common is it for people to talk of death as if they never heard of the Resurrection!

In 1914 the Spiritualists' National Union could claim 145 affiliated branches; in 1919 this had risen to 309, and by 1938 it had increased to 539. But interest went beyond consultations with mediums. After the war, 'I died' books 'written' by soldiers from the other side proved very popular.

They include *A Subaltern in Spirit Land* (1920), *A Plain Record of the After Life Experiences of a Soldier Killed in Battle* (1917) and the bestseller *Raymond or Life After Death* (1916), which was reprinted twelve times between 1916 and 1919. Written by Sir Oliver Lodge, an eminent scientist who served as President of the Society for Psychical Research in 1901 and 1903, *Raymond* was persuasive both on account of the credentials of the author and because it was rooted in personal tragedy which he takes pains to justify making public. In the book's preface the author explains why he has chosen to reveal family matters to a wider audience:

> The amount of premature and unnatural bereavement at the present time is so appalling that the pain caused by exposing one's own sorrow and its alleviation to possible scoffers, becomes almost negligible, in view of the service which it is legitimate to hope may thus be rendered to mourners, if they can derive comfort by learning that communication across the gulf is possible.

One impassioned 'scoffer' was Walter Cock who vented his scepticism in *Reflections on Raymond* (1917). His powerful critique was a deliberate attempt to deter people from 'the present notorious revival of a dangerous and deceptive anachronism'. He hoped to dissuade the bereaved from looking for hope where 'no real or healthy consolation can be found', and yet his arguments are damaged by his insensitivity. 'Not grief but pride is the adequate emotion we feel in face of these countless sacrifices so cheerfully and nobly made and still to be made by it almost seems the whole youth of England.' Pride, however, was not the emotion that was inducing the bereaved to rush to the nearest medium with their guineas at the ready.

The psychological role that post-war spiritualist literature fulfilled for the bereaved is revealed by the nature of the 'communications' from the dead soldiers, which continually stress how comfortable things are on the other side. In *Raymond* the comforts of the afterlife include whiskies and soda and cigars. One of the most interesting passages, highlighting the consolations of spiritualism, is that in which Sir Oliver's dead son reveals via a medium that bodies are whole on the other side:

> ... Oh, there's one thing, he says, I have never seen anybody bleed.
> OJL [Oliver Lodge]: Wouldn't he bleed if he pricked himself?
> He never tried it. But as yet he has seen no blood at all.
> OJL: Has he got ears and eyes?
> Yes, yes, and eyelashes and eyebrows exactly the same and a tongue and teeth. He has got a new tooth now in place of another one he had – one that wasn't quite right then. He has got it right and a good tooth has come in place of the one that had gone.

He knew a man that had lost his arm but he has got another one. Yes, he has got two arms now. He seemed as if without a limb when first he entered the astral, seemed incomplete, but after a while it got more and more complete until he got a new one.

The concept of the afterlife as a supernatural cosmetic surgery clinic in which shattered bodies are reconstructed fulfilled a crucial role for the bereaved. It tapped into the same fundamental need for positive imagery which is behind the twentieth-century embalming trade and the transformation of the common corpse into the 'Beautiful Memory Picture' that Jessica Mitford mocked. Deprived of any view of the body, the bereaved sought solace in imagined versions of it. Although an unorthodox form of bereavement therapy, conjuring up tragi-comic scenarios of moving tables and sad strangers trying to get connected via the psychic switchboard, spiritualism was a valued form of solace. It superimposed a comforting fantasy on the unbearable reality that lost relatives had died maimed, mutilated or blown to bits. In this way it met a mental requirement still powerful today, namely a sense of the sanctity of the body. The insistence that the body remains intact in death is as emotive an issue today, as demonstrated by public outrage about the removal of organs from children who died during surgery at hospitals in Bristol, Liverpool and elsewhere, as it was then.

It is understandable that so many of the bereaved rejected conventional Christianity. To consider any representation of the Crucifixion is to understand the appeal of the bloodless afterlife described by the spiritualists after the war. In particular, the *Isenheim Altarpiece* (1513) by the German painter Matthias Grünewald highlights the brutality of crucifixion, which is such an integral part of Christian iconography. Dying is conveyed with graphic realism. The body of Christ is punctured with thorns. A jet of blood gushes from a deep chest wound. Christ's thorns and wounds and blood were too close to the truth of barbed wire and wounds and blood. People did not want a mutilated dead man to remind them of their own dead men. They wanted no more of Rupert Brooke's symbolic blood of martyrdom, 'the sweet red wine of youth'. The absence of blood, *'no blood at all'*, was a way in which the spiritualists could palliate almost unbearable pain. It helped the bereaved to deny the horror, which in turn was a way to deny death – and denial is a recognised stage of grief.

Interest in the concept of the continued existence of the dead spiralled beyond the seance and post-mortem autobiography and into the visual arts, where artistic interpretations of the ghosts of the departed were extremely popular. An oil painting entitled *The Menin Gate at Midnight* (1927) by the Australian war artist Will Longstaff depicts the ghostly figures of dead soldiers in a supernatural crowd, clustering around the vast monument to the missing at Ypres. Churchill said of Ypres 'a more sacred place for the British race does not exist in the world', which may in part account for the reverential demeanour of the crowds who filed past this painting wherever it was exhibited on tour, with solemn music playing in the background. Similarly popular were Mrs Deane's spirit photographs, including a famous image of the ghosts of dead soldiers mingling with the crowds at an Armistice Day ceremony at the Cenotaph in 1922.

Interring the dead and marking where their bodies lie is a deep-seated human need. Even before the Bible when the angel explained to Adam and Eve that something had to be done with the dead Abel, man has had an instinct to do something about his fellow humans who have ceased being. The earliest record of ritualistic inhumation in Britain is in Gower, where a young man was buried with grave goods and seashells circa 24,830 BC. The Ancient Greek heroine Antigone went so far as to sacrifice her own life so that her dead brother could be buried. At the front it was impossible to honour the dead, and the blocking of this instinct compounded the crisis of death. Decent burial, let alone ceremony, was often not viable, and continued fighting made violation of bodies and graves a routine horror. In an ambitious attempt to reassert humanity in the midst of barbarity and to bestow a vestige of dignity to ignominious death, the Graves Registration Commission (which later became the War Graves Commission) was established to inter and record the resting places of the fallen. Graves were marked with temporary crosses; in some cases these were wrapped in canvas and shipped home to relatives who ritually buried them, but in most cases all the relatives received was a photograph of a grave taken by one of the Commission's photographers. Such attempts to impose order on chaos were largely symbolic. It was as if the physical acts of systematic registration and subsequent arrangement of the military cemeteries after the war were paradigms for the mental processes. They represent an attempt to confer meaning on apparently meaningless tragedy. Early in the war, Fabian Ware, the founder of the Commission, who became known as 'Lord Wargraves', wrote that

> Many graves are frequently under fire and inaccessible. I regret to say that not only have a large number of bodies been destroyed beyond all recognition, by the enemy's artillery fire, before burial, but that all traces of graves themselves have in a large number of cases been obliterated.

In a letter to his wife, Sir Edwin Lutyens gives a first-hand account of the desultory landscape of death before the temporary burial sites were re-arranged into immaculate military cemeteries in the 1920s. His description echoes John McCrae's poppy poem and highlights the visual impact of the flower on the crater-scarred barren plains of Flanders:

> The cemeteries – the dotted graves are pathetic, especially when one thinks of how things are run and problems treated at home. What human-ity can endure, suffer is beyond belief. The battlefields – the obliteration of all human endeavour, achievement and the human achievement of de-struction – is bettered by the poppies and wild flowers that are as friendly to an unexploded shell as they are to the leg of a garden seat in Surrey.

The state control of the disposal of the war dead was controversial. In the early days the War Graves Commission received, on average, ninety re-quests a week from relatives seeking permission to repatriate the bodies of their loved ones. In the House of Lords, Viscount Wolmer described the Commission's policy as 'a terrible confusion of thought' and objected in the strongest terms to the idea that the government felt entitled 'to take the bodies of heroes from the care of relatives and build them into a national state memorial'. The state also overruled the wishes of relatives by impos-ing a ban on personal memorials and imposing instead a strict policy of uni-formity. This very un-English insistence on equality and a democratic approach to death represented a major break with tradition. For the first time, banning the use of monuments to express differences in social status meant that death was truly the great leveller.

The serried ranks of headstones – 2 feet 6 inches high and 3 inches broad, made of stone the colour of bleached bones, charnel house grey – were designed at the suggestion of Frederic Kenyon, director of the British Museum, to 'carry on the military idea, giving the appearance as of a bat-talion on parade'. This uniformity has persisted in peacetime, where the symmetry of the military cemetery is echoed in the manicured municipal cemetery, where the rows of rose bushes and headstones all look the same. An early report clarified the policy of standardisation: 'Those who have given their lives are one family; and children of one mother who owes to all an equal tribute of gratitude and affection.' This view of communality transcending distinctions of rank led to the decision that comrades-in-arms in life should be treated equally in death. An official statement in 1918 from the War Graves Commission clarified the policy of standardisation: 'In death all, from general to private, of whatever race or creed, should receive equal honour under a memorial which should be the common symbol of their comradeship and of the cause for which they died.'

Unable to bury their dead, the British people were determined to honour them in other ways. The two-minute silence, which was introduced on 11 November 1919, has significance both as a new rite of remembrance and as a signpost in the secularisation of death. The *Daily Express* applauded the distinctive quality of communality, so different from a church congregation:

> There was no mechanism of ritual or service. Those who went to church missed the stupendous thrill and mystery of the greater service in which men and women confronting their God held communion without the hindrance of formula.

This conveys the spirit of modernity and demonstrates a simple human response, an informal action made powerful and ritualistic by the participation of an entire nation. As in a freeze frame, normal life was temporarily stilled, paused for two minutes of public unity and private thought. More than eighty years on the corporate silence has permeated society at large as a more general mark of respect in the event of tragedies and the high-profile deaths of public figures.

In the aftermath of the war, secularism seeped into society, steadily spreading as both a style of monumental commemoration and a way of thinking. Apart from the cross of sacrifice, the official commemorative iconography was non-denominational and neutral, with military cemeteries controversially choosing rectangular headstones over crosses. The centrality of the Whitehall Cenotaph – a classical, not a Christian symbol – to remembrance rituals gave added weight to secularism. No prayers were said there in 1919. Although some memorials took the form of village crosses, a vast number were secular in character and placed in public schools, working men's clubs, sports clubs and village halls, rather than consecrated places.

A powerful totem of grief, the Cenotaph was originally intended as a temporary structure, designed to provide a focus for a grand procession as part of the celebrations for Victory Day in 1919. A temporary altar shrine designed by Lutyens for Hyde Park in 1918 had proved extremely popular with the general public, with people queuing from dawn to dusk to pay tribute to the dead. This predisposed the Prime Minister, Lloyd George, to commission Lutyens to provide a large-scale structure as a ceremonial focus. The Prime Minister's original design request was for a catafalque, a temporary stage or platform normally erected by way of honour in a church to receive a coffin. Lutyens proposed instead a cenotaph, an empty tomb which commemorates a body buried elsewhere. This distinction is important in the history of the semiotics of death, for the former design is associated with the presence of a body in a Christian environment, while the latter has classical connotations and is associated with the absence of the body. Such was the impact on the public that by popular demand it was agreed to make the Cenotaph a permanent memorial. The wood and plaster of the original was replaced with Portland stone, and the ceremony for the unveiling of the new monument was staged on the same day as the funeral of the unknown soldier in Westminster Abbey on 11 November 1920.

Just as the Cenotaph is an empty tomb, in a sense the Tomb of the Unknown Warrior was empty because the body interred there was symbolic. The idea of a public funeral for an unidentified body from the Western Front was intended to assuage the private grief of individual households. It was an attempt to provide one body as a surrogate for all the bodies that had not come home, one funeral for all the funerals that had been prevented. This symbolic action was carried out with a series of elaborate rituals. Six bodies were exhumed from different areas of the front, Aisne, Marne, Cambrai, Somme, Arras and Ypres. The criteria were that they should be from graves marked 'Unknown British Soldier', and from early in the war to ensure they were only bones. They were put into sacks and transported to a military hospital at St Pol, where they were laid on stretchers and covered. A British officer selected one. The chosen body was then placed in a coffin made from oak from a tree at Hampton Court, and started its journey home. From the outset there was great ceremony. A grand cortège accompanied the coffin to the quay, from whence it was transported to England on a British destroyer, flanked by six further destroyers. Its arrival at Dover was signalled with a ten-gun salute from Dover Castle. Then, in a specially adapted passenger luggage van, the roof of which was painted white so the crowds en route could identify it, the South Eastern and Chatham Railway Company carried it to London. Although hidden from public view as a mark of honour, the interior of the luggage van was draped in purple and hung with a trellis of fresh bay, rosemary and chrysanthemums. On the morning of 11 November the coffin was placed on a gun carriage of the Royal Artillery and escorted by Coldstream Guards via the Mall to Whitehall for the ceremony of the unveiling of the permanent Cenotaph. From there, the funeral cortège moved next to Westminster Abbey. The King and the Prince of Wales walked behind the coffin, which was carried by distinguished pallbearers including the Commander-in-Chief of the British Army Field Marshal Douglas Haig and flanked by a guard of honour made up of one hundred soldiers who had won the Victoria Cross. A predominantly female congregation of specially invited bereaved women – including those who had lost both husbands and sons, and those who had lost their only sons – contributed to a service at which emotions were more palpable than politics. The Royal Family were more visible than the Prime Minister and the Cabinet, while the politicians who were present were notable chiefly as fathers who had lost sons. In the closing moments of the ceremony, the coffin was sprinkled with French soil from a silver shell; further bags of Flanders earth were used to fill in the grave.

The congruence of the unveiling of the Cenotaph with the funeral of the Unknown Warrior was like an official cultural hand-over, marking the transition from corporeality to remembrance as a key component of mourning. Henceforth, society's relationship to the dead was more abstract. The distancing from the dead body that had been imposed by the war created a context in which society was more receptive to the concept of cremation. The conjunction of the two ceremonies in 1920 signified the psychological transfer from the body as the focus of the death ritual and the grave as a site of mourning, to the memorials, monuments and rituals of remembrance. The two-minute silence was particularly powerful and universally respected. A good example of this appears in the *Manchester Evening News* on 11 November 1920 under the heading 'Silent Cells'. It reports that 'prisoners in their cells, some awaiting removal to Strangeways gaol to serve sentences, rigidly observed the silence'. After the war, the grave became less important than remembrance of the dead in a wider context. Stones supplanted bones in significance. Names increasingly stood in for bodies and graves, on rolls of honour, inscriptions on memorials, and in books of remembrance. The lists and lines, ink and inscriptions were an effort to return to each individual his identity, and to tease out of the trauma of mass death something personal, human and emotive. They were an attempt to stave off the nihilism inherent in all the anonymity of the Great War. The names were proof of the existence of the missing. They were a token presence in the midst of the anguish of absence keenly and universally felt.

In the 1920s some 4,000 headstones were shipped weekly from England to France for the military cemeteries. Throughout that decade, all over England – from town halls and squares to villages, schools and colleges, sports clubs and railway stations – the British people built memorials to the war dead. The rich diversity of civilian memorials is a counterpoint to the restraint and uniformity of the official memorials, and a powerful visual testament to the degree to which death, like a precarious emotional fault-line ran through every strata of society. As a nation of animal lovers, even the four-legged fallen were remembered. At Lake in the Isle of Wight a drinking trough commemorates the 'the horses and dogs who also bore the burden and the heat'. At Meriden in the West Midlands there is an obelisk dedicated to 'the lasting memory of those cyclists who died in the Great War', while in Victoria Embankment Gardens in London there is a splendid camel monument to the Imperial Camel Corps. From a simple oak wall memorial in a working men's club in Durham to the elegance of Asquith's memorial to his son at Mells, Somerset with lettering by Eric Gill and a wreath by Lutyens, the poor and the privileged, socialists and capitalists, rural and urban dwellers were united in their drive to commemorate the dead, and united in loss.

If the First World War had a cataclysmic impact on British attitudes to death, the Second World War also influenced the course of the modern way of death, but it did so in a different way. Notably, as the People's War, it brought violent death to the domestic arena with a national, catastrophic catalogue of carnage and loss, which claimed 60,000 British civilian lives. Unlike the consciously risked death of those on active service, the large-scale, unexpected and unprotected random death of ordinary people was unprecedented in modern history. The plight of people often dressed in their pyjamas, dying ugly deaths as their bedchambers became their burial chambers, required the British people to mine new reserves of fortitude. By the end of the first year civilian losses outnumbered the military losses of the British Army, and by the end of the war civilian loss represented one-fifth of the military death toll, which in turn was about half that of the First World War.

The Battle of Britain in 1940 tested the mettle of English men and women. They responded to Churchill's entreaty and 'braced themselves for their duties'. With barbed wire on the beaches and the Home Guard going through gun drills with broomsticks, there was an all-pervasive sense of an under-protected country fighting for its survival. For five years the British public lived in a state of perpetual insecurity and were subjected to relentless aerial bombardment from which inadequate civil defence afforded scant protection. Throughout the country families huddled in back-garden Anderson shelters during the onslaughts from the skies. Every large city became a target – notably London, Coventry, Clydebank, Hull, Plymouth, Birmingham and Manchester. As the war progressed, the sites of Luftwaffe bombing became ever more scattered as less populous places with no tactical significance were chosen – most vengefully in the Baedeker bombing raids where, as a reprisal for Bomber Harris's attack on Lübeck, Radio Berlin announced: 'We shall go all out to bomb every building in Britain with three stars in the *Baedeker Guide*.' Exeter and Bath were early targets, increasing the toll of death and devastation among the unsuspecting participants of war.

As firebombs ripped apart suburbia, it fell to elderly volunteers to quell the devastation with sandbags, stirrup pumps and buckets of water, and ordinary people were called upon to join together and quite literally pick up the pieces. In Coventry, an eyewitness describes the grizzly process of body recovery, with people 'picking up bits of arms and legs and putting them in potato sacks as if they were working in a harvest field'. An interesting aspect of the civilian effort is the polarity of the age groups witnessing and dealing with this devastation, since it was the very old and the very young who were involved in the ghastly aftermath of bomb damage. A friend of mine corroborated this recently. When she was about fifteen and staying with her parents in a B&B in Canterbury, the proprietor told her that he had been younger than she was when, during the war, he had been sent to collect human body parts into a wicker basket for some sort of general burial. They had apparently looked like butcher's cuts. She never forgot this.

At least 20,000 Londoners were killed during the Blitz. The suffering was great. Given the status of the capital as a major target for relentless attack, civil defence was woefully inadequate and people sought refuge in the Underground. On one tragic occasion in Bethnal Green, a place of safety became a death trap. On the congested staircase the people going down panicked and, misinterpreting the sounds of discomfort, those already at the bottom thought a bomb had fallen on the station itself. They sought to escape and, in the confusion of attempts to get in and get out there was a devastating human crush in which 178 people suffocated. On 29 December 1940, the City of London was decimated by air raids; incendiary bombs claimed 1,500 lives and the flames could be seen for fifty miles. Another shocking toll in a single night was the raid of 10 May 1941, which left 1,436 dead. When Chelsea was bombed, Frances Faviell who had studied anatomy was called upon to help sift through the site of carnage in Cheyne Walk. Her macabre assignment was to piece bodies together so that relatives could view them:

> It became a grim and ghastly satisfaction when a body was fairly constructed but if one was too lavish in making one body almost whole, then another one would have sad gaps. There were always odd members who did not seem to fit and there were too many legs. Unless we kept a very firm grip on ourselves nausea was inevitable. (D. Flowers, *The Taste of Courage*, 1968)

In contrast to the First World War, better communications and the more immediate involvement of civilians in the action meant that death was shared and public. Communality was one of the ways people coped. The radio played an important role in keeping up morale and imparting a sense of sharing the hardships and losses. In the face of tremendous privations, the enforced separation of evacuation and the horror of bombs, the radio was an important medium for preserving morale, and the perfect forum for Churchill's powers of oratory. There were 9 million licensed wirelesses at the height of the war, and Churchill's grand statesman's voice crackling over the airwaves was a boon to the British people: calming, authoritative and inspiring. Jaunty songs such as 'Wish Me Luck When You Wave Me Goodbye', Tommy Handley comedy, and Churchill-style British bulldog stoicism provided padding from the reality of mortal danger, and protective mental armour when death was perilously close. When death did happen, life went on. Business as usual was the spirit of wartime death and this stance left a mental residue after the war.

Air raids caused a sharp increase in cremation rates. Practical and economical, cremation encapsulated the chief requirements of coping in wartime and it complemented a mentality that was all pervasive in the domestic war effort. It exemplified the 'get on with it and get over it' attitude, turning death into simply another hardship to be borne with fortitude and a stiff upper lip. This sense that even the trauma of bereavement should be endured with equanimity set a new standard which lasted for years. In the 1960s and 1970s the cultural requirement for a show of strength at funerals resulted in a trend for doctors to prescribe tranquillisers to the principal mourners to help them get through the public ordeal. Another modification to funerary ritual enforced by the war was that, owing to the difficulty of procuring the black Belgian horses used for horse-drawn hearses, more people began to use motorised hearses. This reinforced the demise of ceremony and the rise of the fast funeral. Practicality and restraint carried through to commemoration of the war dead, with their names simply being added to existing war memorials. Under the guidance of the British Legion and the Church of England, Armistice Day became Remembrance Sunday. But the privations and suffering of civilian life in the UK were dwarfed by the suffering of the victims of Nazi persecution in Europe.

More than any other atrocities in wartime before or since, the Holocaust defined the imagery of death in the twentieth century. As an event in the past, it retains great power to put us in touch with our own mortality and humanity in the present. The systematic extermination of the Jews in Europe, carried out through a complex industrial infrastructure of mass killing, brought to death an unparalleled barbarity. This institutionalised atrocity sets the Holocaust apart from previous and subsequent genocides. The technical capability was all too readily available; the history of cremation shows that Germany was developing expertise and interest in cremation at a considerably faster pace than other European countries. Germany was one of the first European countries to advocate cremation as early as 1855, and in 1876 the Germans constructed a crematorium at Goth some nine years before crematoria reached the rest of Europe. In 1914, when England had thirteen operational crematoria, Germany had forty-four. In 1930, there were ninety German crematoria compared to twenty-two in England. The German equivalent of the Federation of Cremation Authorities had an industrial division. The negative application of knowledge to manufacture gas chambers and ovens for the express purpose of mass murder is one of the most chilling aspects of the Holocaust, and extends the circumference of collaboration and culpability in man destroying man.

In much the same way that the police describe crime so that it sounds as if they have strip-searched language and confiscated the feelings, historians tend to speak of the past in statistics and dates and numbers which dull, rather than sharpen, the emotional impact. But feelings, not figures, are my preferred way to register the past and ponder the dead. It is the difference between humanity and human interest. Feelings are more effective than big figures in appreciating the meaning of mass death, and smaller units create an emotive context in which the bigger reality is better grasped. An empty bedroom, an unlaid place at a family table is a way to extrapolate from the mass death of the First World War a vivid sense of what the vast numbers mean. Similarly, concerning the Holocaust, the statistics and pictures of body pits are fraught with the difficulty of impersonality. Repetition calms a shock wave down to a flat line of familiarity.

Recently I heard something I had not heard about the Holocaust, which moved me greatly. Three vans. Vans that look like old-fashioned bakers' vans. These were mobile gas vans (*Spezialwagen*), which were experimental prototypes in the mechanics of mass murder. Each had the capacity to hold twenty people a time; in the first five months of 1942 on the Eastern Front, 97,000 people were killed – 'processed' – in these vans. Three vans.

Mass murder with the paradoxical purpose of hastening peace was the justification for dropping the bombs on Hiroshima and Nagasaki in the summer of 1945. The use of nuclear weapons introduced into the collective consciousness the awesome prospect of total annihilation, setting a new standard for the dangers of the negative application of man's scientific capability. Man made into a shadow on scorched earth by the application of science, man as self-destroyer on a hitherto unimaginable scale – these were shocking truths to bear. Winston Churchill expressed his apprehension to the American war secretary Henry Stimson: 'What was gunpowder trivial? What was electricity? Meaningless. This atomic bomb is the Second Coming in wrath.'

From the moment the tests in Los Alamos were deemed a success, the atom bomb was described in apocalyptic terms. 'I am become death the destroyer of worlds': J. Robert Oppenheimer's choice of quotation from a Buddhist text resonated with portents of doom. When the bomb was dropped on Hiroshima, the language Oppenheimer used to talk about it invoked concepts of evil, and he opined that for the first time in history, physicists had known sin. A year after the bombing he wrote that

> It did not take atomic weapons to make war terrible ... it did not take weapons to make man want a peace that would last. But the bomb has made the prospect of future war unendurable. It had led us up to the mountain pass and beyond there to a different country.

The fallout from this invention reached well beyond Japan. Now the end of the world would be foretold by a four-minute warning.

From 1945 onwards the safety of the whole world has felt precarious, dependent upon a little red button not being pressed. The knowledge of mutually assured destruction placed the superpowers in a terrifying deadlock, and yet this did not curb the arms race. If Armageddon was the result, the means by which it would be achieved became ever more competitive. The technology of the atom bomb was quickly trumped by the development in the 1950s and 60s of the hydrogen bomb, in which the power of fusion dwarfed the atom bomb's fission reaction. If Little Boy was the equivalent of 20,000 tons of TNT, the new generation of hydrogen bomb – delivering 1,000 times that power – was extremely grown up. Nuclear proliferation was the strange competitive psychological warfare that characterised the Cold War, in which knowledge of the consequences of action became a frightening form of peace keeping. For a second generation there was fear of being blown to oblivion. Yet unlike the experience of our parents who had lived through the Blitz, this was an abstract fear, a threat, something that was possible but not likely. It was a psychological terror. The end of the world hung in our minds as a billowing cloud, and like a talisman the CND emblem became a way to ward off anxiety and powerlessness.

Over time, if the threat of nuclear Armageddon has receded in our consciousness, mass death has recurred. The shame of the twentieth century is that mass death did not end with the Holocaust. Death camp survivor Primo Levi's view that man is amoral, unpredictable and massively violent has been borne out. Instead of being the unrepeatable extreme of man's capacity for brutality, the Holocaust has become a benchmark against which more recent atrocities are compared. Events in other parts of the world in subsequent decades have extended the definition of man's inhumanity to man, which should have closed in 1940s Europe with Auschwitz, Buchenwald, Belsen, Dachau, Majdanek and Treblinka. Yet Cambodia in the 1960s and Rwanda and Kosovo in the 1990s have continued the narrative of genocide, atrocity and murderous death.

The twentieth century was the age of both mass death and the mass media, and attitudes to death have been greatly influenced by the changing relationship between reality and media representation. Like fish not seeing water, we have become oblivious to the moving images that make up the sea of information in which we swim. The late twentieth century has spawned a culture of immediacy. And yet the evolution of this phenomenon is recent history. A distinguishing feature of the First World War was the remoteness of the action from the British public. The printed word and newsreel misrepresented the reality. Such was the impact of a film about the first day of the Somme that one woman viewer apparently jumped up in amazement, exclaiming, 'My God, they are dead!' The film played to packed cinemas. Debate raged in the pages of newspapers about the merits of showing dead Englishmen to the general public, and the government was compelled to acknowledge the power of the moving image. In the twenty-first century there are still formal limits to what can be shown. This accounts for the fact that on television everyone dies with their eyes closed and viscera more or less intact, and that dead black people feature more than dead white people, because even when decomposing they look better on camera. If the twentieth century was about mass death repeated, it was and is not always reported. It is interesting to conjecture what would have happened if the Ministry of Information had broadcast images of Belsen sooner. Similarly, Fergal Keane's reports from Rwanda were filmed days and weeks *after* the event. By the time he brought to our living rooms piles of Hutu skulls it was too late for intervention, and the programme was more retrospective documentary than current affairs. Belsen and Rwanda were both tidied up for public viewing, but by different means and for different reasons.

We have become viewers and listeners of war. The modern theatre of war is a form of armchair entertainment and, as with the drama of the theatre, the conflict we witness at a distance in other countries is a moral playground for our conscience. The lines between representation and reality are ever more blurred, with the weapons named after science fiction films, as in the case of the 'Son of Star Wars' missile defence programme. To compound the confusion, the actor Michael Douglas recently performed a one-man show at the Houses of Parliament in the role of ambassador against nuclear proliferation. Modern war is played out in the media and presented to us via army press officers on podiums at press conferences using euphemisms like 'collateral damage' and 'friendly fire' to cover the human cost. Military action is treated as a showcase for 'smart weapons', which beguile us into a false impression of what we see on the news, and into moral amnesia about the mortality part of combat. The First World War version of patriotism by sheer manpower has been superceded by the impersonality of the Patriot missile and a theory of maximum military gain for minimal human loss, which in practice does not run as smoothly as the spokespeople would have us believe. The First World armies may expound media-friendly concepts of 'precision bombing' and 'smart weapons', but in reality – as in Kosovo / Serbia – this translates into minimal loss of life for allied forces and no 'body bags' to be sent home; the necessity of achieving enemy casualties for a variety of tactical reasons is downplayed.

The dichotomies of reality and representation surrounding death and war have changed since the First World War, when newsprint was the primary medium and headlines such as 'Great day on the Somme' hid the facts of mass death. Newspaper sales soared during the war, with daily sales rising from 850,000 in 1914 to 1,580,000 in 1916. Such was the gulf between the front and Fleet Street that soldiers joked about it. In the *Wipers Times*, a satirical newspaper circulated by British forces in the trenches, they parodied the letters pages of *The Times*:

> Sir, Whilst on my nocturnal rambles along the Menin road last night I am prepared to swear that I hear the cuckoo. Surely I am the first to hear it this season. Can any of your readers claim the first distinction?

This was a war where the American ambassador observed, 'When there is nothing to report from France that means the regular 5,000 casualties that happen every day.' In the Second World War the wireless was the main news medium. A memorable BBC broadcast gives a first-hand account of a dogfight over Dover in a style which anticipates the modern coverage of war where the reality of death is obscured, and killing becomes a spectator sport: 'We just hit a Messerschmitt. That was beautiful! I've never seen anything as good as this, the RAF have really got these boys!' In the late twentieth century the visual image became the primary medium. The Gulf War was like a giant Nintendo game, where people had a bomber pilot's-eye view of an attack, with targets and sights looking like an arcade game, and the Scuds and Patriots as unreal as icons on a Playstation war game.

Distorting in a different way was the tint of political expediency which characterised the cosmetic coverage of the Falklands War. This last-ditch whimper of old school imperialism was memorable not only for the battles at Tumbledown and Goose Green, but for the battle of the headlines – 'Kill an Argie Win a Metro' jingoism. And in the background of all these conflicts has been the wallpaper war of 'The Troubles' in Northern Ireland, in which the coverage of carnage and outrage is formulaic except when bombs go off in mainland Britain. Because they are closer to home, Brighton, Birmingham, Manchester and London get more sound bites and come first in the headlines.

Television has brought to a global audience the horrors of genocide and the almost medieval rape and pillage that characterised the Bosnian conflict. Yet in much the same way that gung-ho periodicals championing patriotism at the start of the century gave a distorted view of war, supplying the public with a sanitised version of conflict, arguably the contemporary representation of war is similarly skewed. The official concern with preventing the reality of death from intruding into our lives should not be underestimated. In light of anticipated casualties in the Gulf War and the risk of British boys returning home in body bags, it is rumoured that pressure was brought to bear on the organisers of a major exhibition of Victorian funerary art at the Victoria and Albert Museum, asking them to postpone it. The combination of a constant diet of fictional violence and mass death in movies with edited television news reports of real conflicts means we are similarly distant from, and have a comparably distorted view of, the reality of death. War has become bulletins with airbrushed visual content designed to protect viewers' sensitivities. The war reporter's catchphrase, 'scenes too disturbing to show', is a metaphorical 'Censored' stamp. Martin Bell vociferously objected to this when, while reporting for the BBC in Bosnia, he was only allowed to show a sanitised shorthand version of an atrocity, while the same event was graphically represented in the BBC drama *Warriors* where bodies were shown burned alive in a house. Media policy of war reporting is to show war but not death, to focus on the weapons not the casualties, the news networks send clean-shaven well-turned-out journalists to bear witness to war, but they deny the viewer the evidence. Thus there is a split between representation and reality at the crux of how death is perceived more generally in society. The attitude to reporting the reality of war reinforces the paradox of contemporary life, where exposure to simulated death is at variance with distance from real life death. This echoes well-documented debates about sex, where representation and simulation are acceptable, but real copulation is still deemed pornographic and subject to restrictions.

If representation and reality have distorted our perception of death in terms of the coverage of twentieth-century wars and genocides, they also have a bearing on how we remember these things. As the actual events fade into the annals of history and those who lived through the wars die, there has been an enormous rise in the commitment to remembrance – the Royal British Legion Poppy Appeal has gone from raising £106,000 in 1921 to £18 million in 1999 – and an effort to reconstruct the past in order to instill remembrance in new generations. Remembering has assumed a pedagogic function; increasingly, memory has become both a deterrent and a form of emotional correctness. Remembrance of the dead has metamorphosed into an important form of morality, extending the eighteenth-century idea of the grave as the cradle of civilised society. It has become an important way to link us with our common humanity and our own mortality. Like people gripped with the need to trace their family tree, we have become obsessed with the wartime death and suffering endured by our parents and grandparents. In part, this could be due to changing perceptions of identity. Where our grandparents and parents were defined by stoicism, we live in an era where suffering is a valued part of identity.

In 1978 The Commonwealth War Graves Commission received around 2,000 enquiries from the general public. Today it receives about 50,000 and its internet archive registers over 250,000 'hits' a week. Likewise, the Public Records Office at Kew receives an average 130 enquiries a week. Interest in the war takes a more involved form at the Great War Society. Founded in the 1980s, its members are enthusiasts who want to emulate what Tommy went through. To this end they don the uniforms, eat the food, sit in the trenches, sing the songs and recreate the First World War as authentically as they can – minus the killing, death, wounds, rats and lice. But this drive to simulate privation takes on a different dimension in the latest BBC reality show due to be filmed in autumn 2001. Volunteers will live in a specially dug trench, although unlike their forebears they will receive psychological counselling before and after the experience. Even more crass, the stench of rotting bodies will be chemically replicated, and the experiece of bereavement of a comrade in arms simulated by randomly removing one of the particiapants. Similarly, battlefield tourism is booming. Where once the majority of visitors were veterans and relatives making personal pilgrimages, there is now a thriving market for the casual visitor. Tours like the 'All's Quiet on the Western Front Tour' to Ypres, Picardy and the Somme – costing £229 per person, complete with bed and breakfast – enjoy a high take-up rate. Superimposed on the reality of the past is a new layer of representation. Like seams of old trees preserved in peat, the past is being petrified under increasingly thick layers of reconstructed versions of it. Kristallnacht as a broken window display in a Holocaust memorial museum, personal effects of soldiers in lighted cases, a multi-million pound museum 'In Flanders Fields' located in the old cloth hall at Ypres are but a few examples of the new direction of remembrance – the educational experience, the postcard shop. Where one of the distinguishing traits of the Victorian way of death was the commercialisation of funerary ritual, a distinguishing feature of the twentieth century is the commercialisation of remembrance, which is fast falling into the territory of daytrips, 'teas and toilets'. Le Tommy bar in Pozières, in the heart of the Somme, is the equivalent of a First World War theme bar: 'It's a long way to Tipperary' and others of the Great War's greatest hits play in the background; instead of a beer garden there is a trench outside with dug-outs and mannequins shouldering Lewis guns. In Krakow the concentration camps have generated a cottage industry: the big tour-operators hover outside hotels and, with desperate irony, divide the innocent tourists with their offers of 'Salt mines to the left' and 'Auschwitz to the right'.

How to remember is the challenge of the twenty-first century. It is not a new problem. The debate about memorials for Diana echoes the dissent in the post-war period about the appropriate behaviour for Armistice Day. There was a conflict between the survivors who wanted to celebrate and forget, and the bereaved who wanted to be solemn and remember. In 1925 the 'Talk of the Town' section of the *Daily Express* remarked: 'The really astonishing feature of Armistice Day this year is its pronounced seriousness. As time passes the sense of jubilation on this day of memory decreases.' Immediately after the war it was impossible to get a dinner reservation at top restaurants in London on that day and the victory balls were packed. In the 1930s there were signs that commercialism was on its way when the poppy was used for product placement. In a notable advertisement for Ovaltine, an attractive woman with the ironic combination of come-to-bed looks and a go-to-sleep drink was captioned 'May the Ovaltine girl suggest that you please give generously for your poppy today.'

The conflict between those who lived through the First World War wanting to forget and those who did not experience it wanting to remember is particularly evident in a recent trend for arranging elaborate and formal interments for bodies uncovered in old battlefields. As a new century begins, the battlefields of the past century continue to disgorge the dead. The fields around the Flemish town of Ypres, for example, where some 250,000 British and Commonwealth troops died in the First World War, still yield a body or two a year, ploughed up by local farmers. In a single field, near Boezinge on the outskirts of Ypres, which lay untouched until the late 1990s when plans were made to build a factory there, local 'diggers' have uncovered more than a hundred bodies of French, German and British troops. Continental Europe is dotted with similar fields.

Under the articles of the Geneva Convention, supported by national legislation, the bodies of the war dead are supposed to be identified, if possible, and then buried in an appropriate military cemetery. Not so long ago, however, reburials took place with minimum ceremony, if any at all. The quiet, informal disposal of stray human remains under, say, a particular tree or in the corner of a village churchyard was not unknown. Increasingly, though, these long lost body parts and whole bodies are seen both as worthy of respect in their own right, and as a particularly powerful conduit for reconnecting with the past, both on a personal and national level.

In April 1998, three Royal Fusiliers were buried in the British War Cemetery at Monchy-le-Preux, eighty-one years after they fell in the battle of Arras – eight days of otherwise inconsequential fighting which produced approximately 159,000 Allied casualties. Frank Harold King, George Hamilton Anderson and an unidentified British soldier were buried with full military honours, while twenty-four other anonymous men were also commemorated. HRH The Duke of Kent, the British Ambassador to France, and relatives of the identified men all took part; the Royal Regiment of Fusiliers supplied pallbearers and fired off three twelve-gun salutes.

Private King's story is at once tragic and typical. Aged 23 when he died, he was one of three brothers killed in the war. Two of his nieces, who had not known him personally and whose father had never mentioned him after receiving news of his death, attended this ceremony. Through King's private papers they tried to draw closer to his memory – to make him seem like a real person – while at the same time they acknowledged him as emblematic of a generation:

> My father never talked about Frank. We knew nothing, only that his brothers had been killed in the War. And then … this. I feel honoured to be here.

I only wish there were more of his generation here as well. So many were killed so young. It was a terrible waste. (*Electronic Telegraph*, issue 1056)

Private Anderson's nephew, Robin Anderson, aged 54, echoed their sense of disbelief, the difficulty in bridging the gap between personal and historical remembrance: 'I am [Anderson's] sole remaining relative. And yet I didn't know the man or anything of him. Things like this take time to sink in. Our generation will never, can never, fully understand.'

So anonymous death by mud or shellburst, hasty and inadequate burial under fire, and terse telegrams are transformed into reverence for human remains, solicitude for the feelings of 'loved ones'(who may never have known the deceased), and poignant attempts to recapture the reality of a kind of suffering few of us will ever experience. In peace, we have the luxury of being able to accord this sort of respect to the remains of victims of long-ago wars. But we also have the inclination – the compulsion – to do so, and this is something distinctive about present day attitudes towards death. War memorials are about the legendary dead, people we have never known, but the physicality of human bones brings home the individuality of the deceased, and individuality and physicality are familiar concepts for which we feel immediate sympathy. Others, who have had years in which to reconcile themselves to a different understanding of death and identity, do not agree. According to Dennis Goodwin, chairman of the First World War Veterans' Association, the 300 or so members of his organisation do not share this preoccupation with physical remains. 'We had a discussion with our old soldiers about the number of bodies never recovered, and they are as one in saying 'Why disturb them?'

It is interesting to reflect that the reorientation of death rituals in the direction of remembrance, which hinges to a large degree on the symbolism and timing of the funeral of the Unknown Warrior, nearly did not happen. It was a close call. It was not until October 1920 that the Dean of Westminster mooted to the King's private secretary the idea of selecting one soldier from the multitude who had no known grave to 'represent all those who fell'. The initial response was negative:

His Majesty is inclined to think that nearly two years after the last shot was fired on the battlefields of France and Flanders is so long ago that a funeral now, might be regarded as belated.

Thankfully, the Prime Minister persuaded him otherwise, and it was all within the space of a month that the extraordinary plans were laid and executed. The King's reticence is intriguing, for it strikes a chord with the sentiments of those who actually fought. Certainly my grandfather was of the opinion that forgetting was preferable to remembering. In a recent book about his regiment, *The Mobbs Own* by David Woodall (1994), one paragraph states his case, and, like the women who used private papers as a lens to bring their dead relative into sharper focus, these few lines allow me to see my grandfather more clearly. 'To most [the war] was a terrible experience they wished to forget. Even Captain Berridge, undoubted hero in the true sense, has said that all he wanted to do when he got home was to forget.'

The issue of how to remember the Holocaust is particularly challenging. It is being subjected to the pressures of reconstruction. Two piles of shoes exemplify the disparity between representation and reality. At Auschwitz, as you walk around a display of shoes belonging to internees, you become aware that they have been arranged in such a way so as to magnify the sense of scale. In a storehouse at Majdanek, unarranged similar shoes are poignant for being a pile of shoes, authentic rather than a display. Films play a major role in the reconstruction of history, and it is a sign of the times that visitors to Poland are less interested in going round Majdanek than in seeing the sets for the film *Schindler's List*. In the recent past the Holocaust has been an NBC mini-series, many Hollywood films, twelve hours of real survivors' testimony as *Shoah*, a course in the National Curriculum and a self-contained canon of non-fiction and fiction.

The death rituals of post-war society have, to a degree, inverted the Victorian emphasis. The cult of the funeral has given way to a cult of remembrance. Low-key, fast funerals epitomised by the production line cremation characterise the modern way of death, and memorial services have become positively fashionable. In the wider social context – pink ribbons for breast cancer awareness, black ribbons for Diana, AIDS awareness ribbons, the AIDS memorial quilt, the reinstated silence for Remembrance Day, a newly designated Holocaust remembrance day, the National Memorial Arboretum and the Beth Shalom Holocaust Memorial Centre – all these testify to the changed emphasis. As recently as May 1999, a memorial to the Londoners killed during air raids was erected in the churchyard of St Paul's Cathedral. Another poignant example of contemporary memorialisation is *Lost Lives*, a memorial book to the 3,636 ordinary people who died in The Troubles in Northern Ireland between 1966 and 1999. It consists of a brief summary of each life lost, including name, date of death, religion, age and marital status.

At the start of the twentieth century, the image of Christ on the cross was a potent symbol of meaningful sacrifice. In 1995 a contemporary version of the Stations of the Cross, by Professor Norman Adams, Keeper of the Royal Academy, depicts Christ as a war victim, His face a mask of suffering, simultaneously evoking Holocaust horror and the flash of fear in the faces of those fleeing bombs full of Agent Orange. The first major publicly commissioned work of religious art since the Second World War, it moved many of those who saw it to tears. It tapped into contemporary values whereby suffering has become its own meaning, and soldiers and policemen get compensation for trauma. The cult of the victim is so widespread as to have spawned a hybrid of celebrity victims, people who have become famous for dying in the public eye.

The Princess of Wales was the ultimate celebrity victim. Her life was a short-running drama in which, with the exception of fashion icon and benefactress, every role she played was on a theme of suffering: victim, martyr, scapegoat, sacrificial virgin, outcaste, bulimic, abandoned wife. When not starring in her own suffering, she co-starred in the suffering of others, touching people with AIDS, hugging the bereaved and the terminally ill. In the eighty years between the funeral of the Unknown Warrior and the funeral of the Princess of Wales, Britain has evolved from a society centered on the archetype of the hero to a society centered on the archetype of the celebrity. It changed from a society in which death was interpreted in the context of beliefs to one in which death was interpreted in the context of feelings. The response to Diana's death in 1997 shows the degree to which attitudes to death have changed since the First World War. Her death was caught in the full beam of the searchlight first held up by Sigmund Freud at the beginning of the century. It revealed a society underpinned by psychology rather than theology – a society enduring the crisis of not believing in something bigger than the self – a society where, in T. S. Eliot's words, 'hell is oneself'. In 1915 Freud wrote that 'We can no longer maintain our former attitude to death and have not yet found a new one.' By 1997 there was evidence that we had started to find a new attitude. For eighty years after the First World War we tried to live as if death did not exist, but when Diana died there was no place to hide.

DIANA AND THE 'OUTING' OF DEATH

IX-THIRTY A.M. ON 31 AUGUST 1997, IN A COLD BEDROOM IN an old house in the village of Lullington, Somerset, England, a woman is a restless muddle of eiderdown and pyjamas and is only dimly aware of a phone ringing. Her head hurts with tiredness. She has become such a townie that without police sirens and the night calls of *Homo inebrietus* she can't sleep. The peace and dark of the country keep her awake. She needs noise and neon. She had tried sleeping with the lights on, and the radio, low volume. Now, near her ear she registers what sounds like martial music. She twiddles dials to re-tune, but can't find anything familiar. Where Radio One should be, there is lift music. It suddenly dawns on her that the Queen Mother must have died. Just as she is pondering this, her brother comes in with a cup of tea: 'The Princess of Wales is dead.' In a telling sign of the speed and span of the global news network, his Australian in-laws had just telephoned him with the news which, because of different time zones, broke there before Britain woke up. This is where I was when …

Like millions of people in households all over Britain, for me hearing the news marked the start of a surreal week: cellophane meadows, condolence books in supermarkets, shop shrines. For a week normality took leave of its senses. A tourist stealing a teddy bear nearly got lynched by the mob; a flower-thief was sentenced to twenty-eight days in prison; the Queen was commanded by order of tabloid headlines to come to London. Hit by the biggest shock in its recent history, Britain suffered a temporary loss of normal transmission and then experienced the further strangeness of having this broadcast back to itself in an epic tape-loop of grief and disorientation. Diana's death made real life unbelievable. It was like the clichéd, cop-out ending of a made-for-television mini-series – a high-speed car crash in which, miraculously, the beautiful heroine is unmarked by the accident in which she dies. As Bridget Jones wrote in her fictional journal: 'Is unbelievable. Like dream or sick newspaper April Fool. Is unbelievable. Diana dies is just not the kind of thing she would do.'

Facts failed to make it real: chauffeur Henri Paul's reckless speed of 121 mph; the 290,000 people signing forty-three books of condolence at Kensington Palace; the 35 million visits to the royal website; the 15,000 tons of flowers and tributes; the million people who flocked to London for the funeral; the 31 million British people who watched it on television; the 1,217,978 copies of the special memorial issue of *Hello!* magazine. Similarly impressive in the ensuing months were the 8 million tickets for visits to her island burial site at Althorp sold on the first day the hotline opened, and the 33 million sales of 'Candle in the Wind', certified eight times platinum by the Recording Industry Association of America. The statistics made it, if anything, even more unbelievable, harder to grasp.

From the moment when, newly engaged to the Prince of Wales, a photocall revealed the outline of her thighs in a skirt made see-through by sunlight, there was a sense that from now on Diana's body was going to be dissected by lenses. Shortly after the thigh shots, stooping to get out of a car, one of her breasts spilled from a strapless taffeta gown and the photographs, shot from an unforgiving angle, filled the front pages. This fragmentation continued for years: close-ups of dimpled thighs, haircuts as headline news, upper arms analysed for pre- and post work-out changes, double-page spreads of paparazzi bikini shots, a navel gazed at by the whole world.

Marlene Dietrich famously complained, 'I've been photographed to death.' Diana *was*. Like a rare animal with a price on its head, she was permanently stalked – the zoom lens was a long-range weapon, the viewfinder a gunsight. Like an automatic rifle, a modern camera shoots repeatedly and in rapid succession. The metaphor extends to the terminology, with the paparazzi hunters talking about 'banging', 'blitzing' and 'ripping' their prey. Her brother, Earl Spencer, expressed it well in his funeral eulogy: 'A girl given the name of the ancient goddess of hunting was in the end the most hunted person of the modern age.' Even when she was a car-crash victim, the cameras continued to click. It is widely known that pictures of the dying Diana staring straight into the camera were circulated internationally by way of a Paris picture agency, although to date only a German tabloid,

Das Bild, has been bold enough to print crash scene pictures in which two bodies are visible.

In merely a month Diana was transformed from mourner to mourned, from comforting Elton John at Gianni Versace's memorial service in Milan to being the object of grief herself. But her whole life had been a constantly shifting narrative between subject and object, alleviating suffering and suffering herself, talking to victims and being a victim. With almost pornographic objectification, the medical details about the state of her dying and then dead body were relayed to a global audience with varying degrees of sensationalism. Headlines in the *Sun* proclaimed: 'Heroic Doctors Massaged Diana's Heart by Hand.' The graphic details echoed the way her body had been cut up by cameras in life. In *Newsweek* :

> Diana showed signs of cranial trauma, a broken arm and leg and severe wounds to one thigh. Most important, hospital doctors found a severe lesion to her pulmonary vein. In lay terms, 'her heart had been ripped out of its place in her chest', says Mailliez (an English-speaking emergency doctor).

Similarly explicit were the details released at an official press conference by Bruno Riou, head of the intensive care unit at Salpetriére Hospital:

> Her chest cavity was urgently opened up, revealing a significant wound to her left pulmonary vein. Despite a closure of the wound and an external and internal cardiac massage lasting two hours, no effective circulation could be re-established and death was noted at 4 a.m.

For the British people this was *Casualty, ER, Emergency Ward 10* – every hospital drama they had ever watched – with the top spin of authenticity and a surprise performance from the biggest star in the box office of real life.

In life and in death, Diana was at the apex of the eternal triangle of celebrity, press and public. Like her marriage, there were three parties in her relationship with the world. The dynamic was one of symbiosis between emotions and economics, her image being the commodity on which these forces were fixed. The market was constant, lucrative and mutually beneficial until Diana's sudden death abruptly halted the supply, thereby greatly increasing the demand. In the immediate aftermath of her death there was a seemingly insatiable appetite for images. Pictorial biographies, supplements and pull-outs, special issues and souvenir commemorative editions rolled off the presses in their millions and flew off the shelves of news stands all over the world. Overnight her image acquired new status as the currency of commemoration. Tied to trees, attached to bouquets, posted on internet home pages, displayed in windows – pictorial representation quickly spiralled into a fully fledged merchandising industry with adverts and price tags – mugs, matches, stamps, spoons, coins, candles, T-shirts, ties, Diana dolls, plates, thimbles, endless poor-resemblance figurines, and even memorial margarine.

As the most photographed woman in the world, Diana appeared on an unrivalled forty-three covers in the 23-year history of the American magazine *People*, and was a perpetual presence in the national and international press. It was claimed by the editors of women's magazines that the perfect cover for a sell-out issue included the words 'Diana' and 'Diet' either related or separately. The familiarity of her image made her more present in households than many real life relations, which in part accounts for the reaction to her death. For many people it felt like a personal bereavement, although the feelings of devastation lasted for less time. Her looks created the market, and it is because of her looks that her death acquired a further dimension of grand tragedy, for beautiful women confer romance on death. The freeze frame of a woman in her prime, radiant and glossy, spares her the fate that is almost worse than death – the fate of growing old in pictures, *à la* Brigitte Bardot. 'She shall not grow old as we that are left grow old' resonated in the coverage of Diana's death, where even *The Times* felt the need to reassure the public that 'the Princess's face was reported to be have been unmarked by the accident.' Concluding his funeral oration, her brother also extended the idea that in some way the fact of her youthful beautiful death was a consolation in the tragedy:

> I would like to end by thanking God for the small mercies He has shown us at this dreadful time, for taking Diana at her most beautiful and radiant and when she had joy in her private life.

The fact that this is the conclusion of one of the most widely heard speeches ever adds to the impact of the emphasis on physical attributes.

The dramatic death – the Marilyn Monroe, Jayne Mansfield, bang not a whimper death that spares the beautiful being damned by age and slow decline and turns them into icons, the death that fixes an image of eternal beauty in a million minds by 'mixing memory with desire' – this was Diana's death. It calls to mind an observation by Thomas de Quincy in his essay 'Joan of Arc', (*Last Days of Immanuel Kant and Other Writings*, 1963) from an age without flash-bulbs, in the days before men with cameras played catch-chase with celebrities:

Yet, sister woman, though I cannot consent to find a Mozart or a Michelangelo in your sex, cheerfully, and with the love that burns in depths of admiration, I acknowledge that you can do one thing as well as the best of men – a greater thing than even Milton is known to have done or Michelangelo: you can die grandly, and as goddesses would die, were goddesses mortal. (1897)

Diana's death was made epic by the response to it. It was grand because it was global, grand because it held the world in thrall.

Because the death happened on a Sunday, the national press was caught out. Initially television took the place of the daily newspaper as the principal medium of coverage. For a whole day people watched and listened. The news chain started less that two hours after Diana was pronounced dead at 3 a.m. – 4 a.m. French time. At 4.21 the Press Association put out a news flash. It fell to BBC World TV presenter Nick Gowing to break the news to up to half a billion people around the world:

> At 1.10 I received a phone call from a BBC editor saying Dodi was dead and Diana seriously ill. I thought it was a wind-up. At 2.30 I was on air. Soon after, there was one very dangerous moment when someone called in with passable French saying they had seen Diana walk away from the crash. We decided it wasn't true. Then at 5.17 I made the announcement. Twice that Diana was dead.

Suddenly, Diana's image on postcards and keyrings was *memento mori* as poignant as the pictures of the dead that appear with their obituaries in newspapers. Her smiling face, oblivious of her fate, underscored the fragility of the present, and cheap souvenirs made tourists cry.

From that moment the mass media became the vehicle for a single story. Radio, television and the press provided continuous coverage. Each programme or edition was a morbid medley: part obituary, part postmortem, part crime investigation, with a measure of bereavement counselling. Ironically, blanket coverage of her death in special memorial issues ran in tandem with calls for a shake-up of press practice specifically relating to privacy issues. The internet assumed an important role as a public forum and a medium of mass mourning. Merely two hours after the news broke the first home page for condolence was posted on the World Wide Web by a couple in Santa Clara, California, and in two weeks 600,000 condolences were logged on the Royal website. The speed and style of information encapsulated the smallness of the modern world in which, metaphorically, outside every sickroom, deathbed and intensive care ward where there is a celebrity there is also a camera crew on standby and a reporter with a hot line to a newsroom. The changing headlines of the early editions of the newspapers testify to the impressive speed of contemporary communication networks. The progression in three editions of the *Sunday Mirror* ran: 'Dodi Dead, Diana Hurt in Smash', 'Dodi Dead, Diana Critical', 'Diana Dead'.

In death, as someone once remarked of Eva Perón, Diana ceased to be what she said and what she did and became what people say she said and what people say she did. The myth-making took on a frenzied momentum: fictive last words, talk of an engagement ring in the mangled metal of the Mercedes, whispers of cocaine, and – most gripping – the rumours of murder, conspiracy and cover-up. It was as if the whole world was playing Chinese whispers with megaphones. Then the myths started to manifest a religious dimension, notably with claims of a vision of Diana's face, cast by light, appearing on a portrait in the room of condolence books at St James's Palace. Almost within hours of the announcement of her death, Diana's face appeared not supernaturally, but photographically, superimposed on religious icons in cut-and-paste tributes amidst the flowers outside Kensington Palace. One card which read 'born a lady, became a princess, died a saint' was seized upon by the media and referred to so frequently it became a slogan of hagiography. The extraordinary synchronicity of Mother Teresa's death occurring on the day before Diana's funeral proliferated the concept of saint by association which the media coverage did little to assuage. Rather, at every turn the flames of beatification were fanned. Reporting on the crowds camping out near Westminster Abbey to secure a good view of the funeral, a *Guardian* article (6 September 1997) frequently used the metaphor of pilgrimage:

> 'Yes, it is a pilgrimage,' says Jason from Newcastle. He and his family set off early and have driven all night [...] 'Here are the AIDS victims, the Falklands and Gulf War veterans, the homeless, the divorced, the mentally ill, the unemployed, those who have also mourned the loss of a loved one. Almost to a person they say that they feel that Diana spoke to them personally, and gave them hope when they were at the bottom. Ex-prisoners, single mothers, the deaf, the lame, the crippled lie down together. She cared, they say; others who should have known better did not.

In the reverential atmosphere of queues and crowds, with the air heavy with the scent of flowers and the flickering of hundreds of votive candles around a multitude of individual shrines, Kensington Palace started to feel like Lourdes. Were it not for the absence of candle stalls and nuns in Nike trainers wheeling mobile sick beds it could have been Lourdes. The fervour and homage were the same, and in an atmosphere charged with people power one felt it was only a matter of time before the first crutch appeared on the railings.

Smaller scale tributes in secular settings were replicated throughout the country as the British people, instead of turning a deaf ear to death, marked it everywhere. The inmates of Brixton prison made and wore black ribbons; a single black kite was flown before the start of an annual kite festival. The grounds of Kensington Palace were studded with the colour and confusion of hundreds of improvised shrines, like Mexican home altars: a jumble of ballet slippers, balloons, teddy bears and bottles of champagne. From the formality of lilies and dignified condolence cards in smart shop windows to tabloid portraits taped to the windows of mini cab companies, ordinary people reacted to the most extraordinary event in their recent history with visual gestures. There was no post on the day of the funeral. Sporting fixtures and some weddings were postponed. Even the traffic of commerce stopped. Many tills were silent when shops closed on the day of the funeral – the ultimate mark of respect from a nation of shopkeepers who normally don't allow even Good Friday to interrupt the kerching and swipe of sales.

Looking in the mirror held up by the media, the country did not recognise itself. The mood was febrile, fearful and tearful. A whole nation was acting out of character; a country known to quail at emotional expression was suddenly incontinent. Perceptions of protocol changed from the desirability of concealing feelings to revealing them. Even the Queen was held to account for not only failing to show feelings but for failing to show up. In the new climate, those who did not seem to be moved were universally derided. Even the normally instant reaction of the City to tragedy – the spawning of a mass of crass jokes in minutes – took longer. It was not until Wednesday that the Square Mile started to diffuse the shock of Diana's shattering death by means of the joke cycle, a phenomenon peculiar to the late twentieth century, which interestingly had no equivalent in the days before television. But such responses felt more subversive than usual, and people were more measured about risking anything that might cause an explosion of hostility in the combustible climate of shock, sadness and supersensitivity.

At one level, a particular sadness of the twentieth century is the disappearance of the idea that there is something bigger than the self to be a part of, to count on – to make life and, by extension, death meaningful. If the First World War highlighted the limitations of conventional religion, the death of Diana – a divorcee and an outcast from the Royal Family – tapped into a feeling that even the family has ceased to be a cohesive social unit. In death as in life, Diana was poignantly alone, dying in a French hospital with the British Ambassador in a room nearby, and then lying dead in a stateroom, away from home. Images of aloneness abound in her biography: estranged at the Taj Mahal, or home alone on Christmas Day after a visit to her therapist. A striking vignette of Diana provided by her friends and staff recalls her watching *EastEnders* by herself: tuning in to a mediated fiction of family and close community because her status, fame and personal misfortune had deprived her of the real thing. She seemed to distil the sadness of every dysfunctional family, the loneliness of the broken home, and in this there was something symbolically modern about the nature of her demise.

In a bizarre exchange, ordinary people vicariously lived through her public life – as a strange, luminous constant household presence in newspapers, magazines and on television – and she, in turn, lived through them, sustained by the feedback of fame. The tears that people shed for her dissolved private and public barriers, and blurred the line between the simulacrum of kinship intrinsic to celebrity and the real pain of personal bereavement. There were those who felt they knew her, and were crying for her, and there were others for whom her death provoked a grief by proxy response. Whether consciously or not, they wept for other personal losses, for distant death resurrects others closer to home. Other people's deaths are filtered through a prism of personal experience; it is not right to say the tears are not 'real'.

Whereas the First World War forced people to ponder mass death, and to remember the deaths of others with official rites of remembrance, the mundane nature of Diana's sudden death in a drunk driving accident impelled people to ponder their own mortality: there but by Fate, fluke or the grace of God go I. As with the First World War, her death caused a collective crisis characterised by an excess of feelings in relation to structures in place to deal with them. It highlighted the absence of a modern protocol for mourning. It revealed a society that no longer knew how to 'do' death socially, because it had turned it into a personal matter and relegated it to the private realm. The contemporary apartheid of bereavement forces people to talk to strangers on help lines or buy a self-help book from a burgeoning bottom-shelf selection. Diana's death highlighted the need not only to modernise aspects of the monarchy, but also to modernise attitudes to death.

Diana's death elicited a style of mourning that was essentially feminine in character, and distinctive in its emotional expressiveness. With her vulnerability, beauty and motherhood, she represented a potent feminine equivalent to the masculine ideal that permeated the era of the Great War. As was appropriate for the manly business of military death, the mass mourning in 1918 was essentially masculine in character. It is interesting that bereaved fathers were not invited to attend the funeral of the Unknown Warrior at Westminster Abbey; and with the exception of bereaved politicians, the congregation was mainly bereaved women. The mourning was restrained and rational with political overtones, while from the outset politicians played a more prominent part at the Cenotaph ceremony than priests. It was suffused with the masculine ideal of heroism embodied by the Unknown Warrior.

Diana's funeral cortège fulfilled for the masses a comparable function to that of the Unknown Warrior, for it provided a focus on to which the general public could project their grief and feelings. A card written by the King and displayed on the Unknown Warrior's coffin included the lines 'In proud memory of those who died in the Great War. *Unknown and yet well known.*' With this particular phrase a sweeping cultural arc connects both funerals, for the Princess of Wales was also *unknown and yet well known.* The difference is that whereas the mourners in 1920 projected the identity of people they had known – family and friends – on to a nameless corpse, the mourners in 1997 projected the identity of a person they had never really known on to a named corpse: 'Goodbye England's Rose, we never knew you at all …' The Princess of Wales had only existed for the general public as a celebrity, a personality and a media construct, and yet her funeral became a conduit through which people could channel sadness for personal losses, not unlike that of the Unknown Warrior.

There are further parallels. Just as the body of the Unknown Warrior – in effect 'The People's Soldier' – was repatriated from France, the body of 'The People's Princess' was repatriated from France and transported on a gun carriage past the Cenotaph to Westminster Abbey. Reinforcing the democratic thinking behind both ceremonies, on 11 November 1920 the *Manchester Evening News* referred to the Cenotaph as 'the people's lasting monument, a monument for all'. Just as the Cenotaph is an empty structure, the focal points of the mourning for Diana were buildings without people: Kensington Palace, Buckingham Palace. Both services generated popular commercial recordings. The gramophone record of the funeral of the Unknown Warrior – the first commercial recording made at Westminster Abbey – was priced at 7s.6d. Other echoes are the record sales of newspapers, the flowers and the crowds. In the first week after the ceremonies in 1920, more than half a million people poured into London to visit the tomb of the Unknown Warrior and the Cenotaph. Extra trains had to be arranged to cope with the influx of people. Seven-mile queues developed as people waited to place flowers at the Cenotaph, turning it, in the words of one newspaper, into 'a mighty bed of blossom'.

Diana epitomised the secular style of the late twentieth century. She lived a high-profile life as a key member of the super-rich G&T (Gym and Therapy) set. She did not manifest any obvious Christian faith, but believed in faith healers and astrology. She was more famous for her failings and self-disclosure than as a model of rectitude and religious virtue. Rarely heard, when she did speak her views were expressed in the vocabulary of personal problems and the self-help shelf. There was something touchingly naive about her belief in psychobabble and greetings-card truths of the sort conveyed by a poem she once recited: 'Life is mostly froth and bubble, two things stand like stone, kindness in another's trouble, courage in your own.' She was the perfect figurehead for a society over which psychology had come to exert a greater influence than religion. In her lifetime, as the pace of secularisation quickened, the church pews emptied and the consulting room couches filled up. Talking about feelings was seen both as a cure for the ills of the chattering classes – as a one-to-one private session, Susie Orbach style – and as a confessional television chat show format, Oprah style, for everyone else. The reaction to her death showed a society where it was for the first time permissible, if not preferable, to show feelings. Her death released bottled-up British emotion. Even television anchormen, who were presumably inured to reciting a daily litany of carnage and calamity in the name of news faltered, and the lights caught their eyes glistening as their voices stuck in their throats. The sound of keening in Kensington was the sound of a nation doing death differently. Similarly, the sound of thousands of camera shutters clicking showed something had changed, for people do not normally take cameras to funerals.

It was the first grand public funeral where feminine traits were not obscured by pomp and ceremony. The card inscribed 'Mummy' on the coffin was poignant amidst all the pomp. The Royal Family's view that children should be born and not seen, let alone heard, was anathema to Diana. Motherhood and delight in her own children were some of her most revered attributes. Her love of children generally was an important part of her popularity and one of the most striking features of the mourning after her death was the centrality of children to it. Importantly, the response to her death heralded the readmission of children to death rituals. As early as Tuesday week after the crash, Ladybird had published *A Tribute to Our Princess* for grieving toddlers. But it was not just children who were mourning the loss of the myth of the fairy-tale princess who got married but failed to live happily ever after. Adults were compelled to acknowledge the myth of their own invincibility. Suddenly all the wrinkle creams and workouts, diets and dreams were exposed as but flimsy protection against the troubling trinity of human frailty, mutability and mortality.

In a self-perpetuating cycle the mourning became the subject of analysis. The behaviour of the British public jostled with details of the death and funeral for position in the news. Reactions ricocheted off the media as the epithets which had originated from television were recycled in millions of memorial issues of newspapers and magazines 'The People's Princess', a caption of condolence, the Queen of Hearts playing card, a name tag on votive offerings. The recycling was also evident in the use of newspaper pictures as the basis of tributes and the backdrop for poems and expressions of condolence. In a week suffused with irony and paradox it was no surprise that the behaviour of newspaper readers started to constitute their content. Throughout what became known as 'Weird Week', the people started to eclipse the Princess as news. Journalists, flanked by camera crews, stalked the sad crowds, while the clumsy trappings of television – ugly metal scaffolding, satellite dishes and television vans – turned central London temporarily into a giant film set with cables, catering and a cast of thousands. But it was not just professionals who surveyed the crowds. Tourists took pictures of the pilgrims placing flowers; Kensington Palace became the most impressive interactive display in the capital, a must-see sight on every visitor's itinerary. There was a strong sense of theatricality, camcorders and cameras, spectators and performers. The giant screens in Hyde Park and the loudspeakers outside Westminster Abbey, supplied for live coverage of the funeral, exacerbated this. Those scavenging for sound bites extended their search beyond London, where not having anything new to add or anything interesting to say was no bar to being sought out to address an international audience. Typical of the media madness was the way in which television crews from six different countries queued to interview Betty Andrews, 76 – once a housekeeper at Althorpe, now a guest on a global chat show.

The might of the media was such that the lines between reporting events and directing them became ever more blurred. On one occasion outside St James's Palace the crowd took a reporter to task for fabricating the time of day. In the midst of so much that did not seem real, reality mattered more than usual. The reporter was trying to film his reports starting with the words 'It is the middle of the night'; every time he said it there was loud heckling and shouting – 'No it's not, it's the morning!'

A recurring theme in the miles of words written about Diana's death is the unprecedented nature of the public response. Yet the outpouring of sadness, mass mourning and the surge of commercial commemoration are not without precedent. They echo with remarkable resonance elements of the reaction when, on 6 November 1817, Princess Charlotte of Wales, aged 21, died after giving birth to a still-born son, and the country was plunged into national despair. Charlotte was second in the line of succession. She was the daughter of the Prince Regent (later George IV) and Queen Caroline, granddaughter of mad King George and married to Prince Leopold. The scale of grief is vividly conveyed in a special supplement of *Bell's Court and Fashionable Magazine*:

> At Bristol, in expectation of the arrival of the London mail, a great crowd had been collected, and when enquiry was made to the guard, the fatal sentence of 'both are dead' reverberated like lightning, dejection was painted on every countenance, nor is it a false assertion to say that almost every eye was wet with tears; and every public sign of woe that could be made was done.

The Times leader of 7 November 1817 observed: 'It is but little to say that we never recollect so strong and general an expression and indication of sorrow.'

Here, I would like to pay tribute to Stephen Behrendt whose brilliant book, *Royal Mourning and Regency Culture* (1997) introduced me to Charlotte and inspired my comparative analysis between the two Princesses of Wales. Comparing responses to the deaths, nearly two hundred years apart, provides a fascinating perspective from which to gauge three distinguishing features of the twentieth-century context of death that were brought together in such a spectacular configuration when Diana died. These are the cult of celebrity, secularism and the media. They are important crosscurrents with a major bearing on the direction of death from the late twentieth century onwards, determining its changing profile in the public arena. Looking back to the public reaction to Charlotte's death is a way to extrapolate from the mass of analysis what was and what was not unprecedented about the response to Diana's death. Unlike Diana, Charlotte died a member of the Royal Family. Consequently, her death was managed within the tight protocol of court formality, whereas Diana had been stripped of her royal title and was therefore technically outside the jurisdiction of royal protocol. Diana was not given a state funeral, although interestingly, in accordance with the tradition of royal coffins being made ahead of time, her zinc-lined coffin was a vestige of her former royal status, having been made for her some years earlier when she first became Princess of Wales. Notwithstanding the technical differences of official status, there are compelling parallels between the two deaths.

Like Diana, Charlotte was very much 'the people's princess'; she was a firm favourite with the British public on account of her looks, charm and charity. Captain Gronow described his impression on seeing her at a ball at Carlton House in 1813 in his memoirs entitled *Reminiscences being anecdotes of the camp, the court and the clubs at the close of the last war with France, related by himself* (1861):

> She was a young lady of more than ordinary personal attractions; her features were regular and her complexion fair, with the rich bloom of youthful beauty; her eyes were blue and very expressive.

In conjunction with her physical charms was an appealing personality. The account continued:

> Her manners were remarkable for a simplicity and good nature which would have won admiration and invited affection in the most humble walks of life. She created universal admiration and, I may say, a feeling of national pride, amongst all who attended the ball.

This natural manner drew crowds of cheering admirers at her public appearances. She seems to have anticipated the title of Queen of Hearts: it was said that 'her sweetness void of art made her the ideal of each British heart'. Accounts of her charitable works and sympathetic nature were a staple of magazines and newspapers, such as the time when, in the event of a bad harvest she gave doles of 'bread, meat and flannel petticoats' to poor households in her local village. As one of the eulogies at her death noted:

> She felt the woes and wretchedness of the distressed: and whenever a well-authenticated case of human suffering was submitted to her the ear was as open to hear as the heart was ready to receive it.

One vicar hammered the point home to his parishioners in an impassioned sermon: 'Lament ye laborious and afflicted for your best benefactress is no more!'

In 1815–1817 when her public profile was at its peak, fashion magazines like *La Belle Assemblee*, *Lady's Magazine* and *Ackerman's Repository* monitored every detail of her style – her jewels, hairstyle and outfits were all keenly followed. Her support of the British textile industry was encouraged at a time when trade with France was fiercely competitive. Like her glamorous twentieth-century counterpart, Charlotte became an ambassador of British fashion, although the Albermarle Street shop of her dressmaker, Mrs Bean, had a French name, Magasin des Modes. Charlotte mania spawned a burgeoning industry which was capitalised upon by artists, engravers and publishers. In a letter to a female friend, Charlotte makes an observation about the voracious public appetite for information about her in words which resonate with relevance to contemporary preoccupations: 'What odd mortals we are, and how little likely to be understood or faithfully represented by those who don't know us.' Her popularity sowed the seeds of the cult of celebrity, which germinated so dramatically in the twentieth century when Diana became the prize bloom of a culture nourished by the media, as with rich manure.

Charlotte's relationship to the public also anticipates the emergence of royal soap opera. In her lifetime the monarchy started to be perceived for the first time primarily as a royal family with domestic dramas like all families, rather than as a remote constitutional totem or powerful hands-on rulers – a concept of monarchy her grandfather Mad King George had undermined. In this context the public were hungry for domestic detail. They wanted to know about, and felt entitled to know about, the private lives of the Royal Family. In the time before photographs and television, the closest most people came to seeing royalty in the flesh was in the form of a tableau of wax portraits in Marie Tussaud's travelling exhibition. It was hugely popular on account of its authenticity; made from lifecasts, in every detail it was an accurate representation of their appearance.

Like Diana, Charlotte came from an unhappy family background, which has led one commentator to observe of the House of Hanover: 'One wonders if ever there could have been maritally so tragic a family?' (H. Corbett, *A Royal Catastrophe*, 1984.) Her parents were at loggerheads and early in her childhood she was separated from her mother. The Prince Regent was a dissolute debauchee who loathed his wife and attempted to divorce her in 1820. Domestic instability was compounded by the illness of King George III, putting the spotlight on the young princess in the hope she would be able to restore a sense of hearth, home and marital harmony as an example to the British people. The high hopes concentrated on her marriage to Leopold and the eagerly awaited birth of their first child are conveyed in the subsequent tone of the commemorative material, such as a popular print entitled 'Britannia's Hope Her Love and Now Her Grief.'

One commentator went so far as to say:

Such is now the fate of Britain; her tutelary Angel is gone! She shone like a
bright meteor in the splendid track of her course, and in a sudden vanished
from our eyes, no more to bless us with her radiance. The shock was felt
the more, as coming unexpected, it came like the charged shell, exploding
amongst us with a horrible crash, destroying at one fell swoop, the hopes,
the happiness of a nation. (Robert Huish, *Memoirs of Princess Charlotte of
Saxe-Coburg*)

Like Diana, she was no sop. Charlotte and her father had big fallings out –
most notably when she refused to marry the man of his choice – and her
strong will was a source of disapproval in some circles. One feels that
Nicholas Soames, Prince Charles's crony and chief proponent of the theory of Diana as loose cannon, would have got on famously with Lord Holland, who deplored Charlotte's lack of judgement, manifested by 'love of
exaggeration, if not a disregard for truth and a passion for talebearers and
favourites'.

Charlotte's death stunned the British nation and the shock waves rip-
pled abroad. Lord Byron wrote from Venice: 'The death of the Princess
Charlotte has been a shock even here and must have been an earthquake at
home.' Shock was exacerbated by the expectation of celebration, for the
whole country was poised for the celebration of a royal birth, and celebra-
tory bonfires had been laid the length of Britain. At 2.30 on 6 November
1817 at Claremont, after a disastrous 50-hour labour, Charlotte gave birth to
a stillborn son. Early official announcements gave no cause for concern re-
garding the health of the princess. At 9.15 the announcement of the still-
born child was accompanied by assurance that 'Her Royal Highness is
doing well'. The British public was therefore stunned when they eventually
learned of her death. Her sudden and fatal decline provoked speculation
and suspicions of medical incompetence. The hatred vented towards the
doctors who had attended her reached such a pitch that three months later,
one of them shot himself. People were deeply aggrieved that there had not
been better medical supervision of a birth that had such an immediate
bearing on the succession. 'Of what did the Princess die?' was the refrain in
a pamphlet entitled *Authentic Particulars of the Death of the Princess Charlotte
and Her Infant 1817*. As the search for blame escalated, a Frenchman was
prompted to question, 'What has happened to the English that they have
not stoned her *accoucheurs*?'

Not only were the medical establishment harangued – there was even
talk of foul play and intimations of a cover-up. Our appetite for sensation-

alism is clearly not new, as evidenced by the following letter, which appeared in the *Sun* newspaper on 13 November 1817:

> I shall not only shew contradiction (in the information available beyond the 'authenticated dispatches' released by the authorities); but I shall also shew apparently designed omissions of very great importance, and such omissions as clearly prove, to my mind, that they ought not to have been kept back from the public knowledge.

One feels the historical distance evaporate between the quill pen of Jesse Foot, the author of this letter, and the slick spokesmen who expressed similar speculation on behalf of Mohamed Al Fayed, which was then taken up by the press. Conspiracy theories about Diana spawned thousands of websites and the search for someone to blame veered wildly out of control. Accusatory fingers were pointed at the French medical authorities, the paparazzi, and the hapless Prozac-popping Henri Paul. As Radio One disc jockey Simon Mayo recalled: 'On air that week – with the dictatorship of grief in full effect – I read countless faxes and e-mails from listeners who found a different villain every day.'

The vocabulary of emotional expression is distinctive in the coverage of Charlotte's death. One of the most popular commemorative poems was entitled 'A Sincere Burst of Feeling', and from every quarter sentiments of sorrow poured forth. The preface to a commemorative anthology described 'a sudden and unprepared explosion of grief and esteem'. Like Diana, Charlotte exemplified the feminine ideal of charity; aesthetic charms and her pregnancy completed the picture of womanly perfection with the promise of motherhood. These qualities informed the reaction to her death, which was processed in a context that was more emotive than political. The tragedy was:

> as affecting to private feelings as the event itself may be esteemed publicly calamitous; for if there is an occasion on which the infliction of universal doom excites peculiar sorrow, it is that wherein the more tender sex is alone exposed to pain and hazard. (William Hone, *Authentic Particulars of the Death of Princess Charlotte and Her Infant*, 1817)

Three days after her death another commentator observed that

> The first and greatest feeling of the country on this occasion is certainly not a political one: it is real sorrow and sympathy. If any dreary sceptic in sentiment should ask why the sorrow is so great for this young woman any more than another, then we answer, because this young woman is the representative of all the others because she stood on high, in the eyes of us all,

as embodying, as it were, the ideal as well as the actual images of youth and promise, and blooming woman hood.

Personal memoirs of the period give vivid impressions of the profound sadness that subdued England. The wife of the Russian ambassador noted that

> It is impossible to find in the history of nations or families an event which has evoked such heartfelt mourning. One met in the streets people of every class in tears, the churches full at all hours, the shops shut for a fortnight and everyone from the highest to the lowest in a state of despair which it is impossible to describe.

The lawyer Henry Brougham remarked that 'it really was as if every household throughout Great Britain had lost a favourite child'. He describe how tramps and beggars tied black rags around their sleeves. The overriding impression is of a country immobilised by mourning and united in a sense of sorrow. Public functions were cancelled; public buildings were draped in black; theatres, law courts, docks, shops and the Royal Exchange were all closed. Bands were forbidden to play, while muffled bells tolled solemnly in cathedrals and parish churches. On 6 November 1817 in London's Cornhill, the following announcement was made: 'Drawing of the state lottery postponed in consequence of the lamented death of HRH the Princess Charlotte of Wales.' The *Sun* newspaper put it more succinctly in 1997 for Diana with the headline 'No Shops, No Footie, No Lotto'.

As tears poured from the general public in the wake of Charlotte's death, torrents of words poured from the printing presses. A market was established in which emotionally fuelled demand for information was met with an economically based supply. The vicar of Lewes remarked: 'Every publisher feels a melancholy satisfaction in collecting and detailing every fact that serves to keep alive the honourable sympathies of the nation.' There was a veritable deluge of details about Charlotte's death, the funeral arrangements and the funeral itself. Hottest off the press was a pamphlet entitled *The Virtuous Life and Lamented Death of Her Royal Highness Princess Charlotte, including every interesting particular relative to her accouchement and death; second edition with account of the embalment and funeral preparation.* This was reprinted six times before 1818. Replicating the pathological interest in Diana, pamphlets spared no details, including an account of how Charlotte's viscera were removed and packed 'in coarse sweets' in accordance with royal death rites and her heart placed in an urn of Honduras mahogany, covered with Genoa velvet and lined with white satin.

A plethora of pamphlets, songs and poems published separately and in anthologies appeared in the weeks and months after her death. Many of them bear an uncanny resemblance to the sentimental outpourings for Diana. A popular anthology was *A Cypress Wreath for the Tomb of Her Late Royal Highness Princess Charlotte of Wales*. Given the events of 1997, some extracts merit being quoted at length, both because they work as apt descriptions of that time and because they are relevant to our interpretation of it.

> The fate of a young and beautiful princess, connected with circumstances of uncommon peculiarity, have doubtless contributed to her elevation in the public esteem. Hence the tributes paid to her memory have exceeded all precedent, perhaps in this or any other country!
>
> It is besides unnatural to associate youth and blooming health with the idea of death ... An event therefore of this kind always inspires terror as well as grief. It places before our chilled imagination the frailty of life, and the uncertainty of our dearest connexions. The Princess was one of the last persons whose demise any one could have contemplated. She always presented herself as abounding with health and gaiety, and as one whose path was strewed with the flowers of public affection. In her glance, her smile and in all her movements there was a gracefulness of animated sensibility, which always left the most pleasing impressions.
>
> There was no display of haughty condescension; but the effusion of a tender heart unstudied spontaneous and warm. Hence the expression of the public feeling on her loss was the impulse of genuine sorrow. Hence the tear, the sigh, the mournful look, the thought dejected and the doubt presaging fear: and a general depression of the public spirit, a commiseration and sadness met with at every step such as has been without any example or similarity in circumstance.

Where the iconography of Diana was almost entirely dependent on the veracity of the camera lens and the moving image, in an age before photography the visual image played a lesser role in the construction of the Charlotte myth, being confined to prints and engravings. It is interesting, however, that although expressed in different media, the commemorative iconography is the same. Both women are elevated to the status of secular saints. In an etching entitled *Britannia's Hope Her Love and Now Her Grief*, Charlotte is depicted as a Madonna, and this idea is reiterated in the language used to describe her, where she is variously referred to as Our Lady and a saint. Another popular engraving entitled *The Royal Rose* shows the face of the princess at the centre of an open blossom. The sheer volume of references to Charlotte as a rose suggests that she is the first rightful claimant to the title of 'England's Rose'. Particularly popular was a poem printed on memorial cards called 'The Coburg Rose', but commemorative anthologies are strewn with roses:

> Sweet rose of England! Fare thee well,
> Bright blossom of a royal line,
> Ah! Who without a tear shall tell?
> A tale so sorrowful as thine.

And, in 'The Royal Rosebud'

> On Brunswick's stem a rosebud grew,
> So fair to ev'ry eye;
> But while it budded, bloomed and smiled
> This rose was doomed to die.

Where the British public in the twentieth century had access to a glut of instant television biopics about Diana, those mourning Charlotte relied on the written and spoken word. Sermons were the most immediate medium through which people heard her life discussed, while in the published form sermons comprised an important part of the canon of commemorative literature. 'Her sun went down ere noon' was a common theme, and the basis of reflections on impermanence and *vanitas*. One popular anthology comprising 120 sermons delivered all over the country on the day of the funeral provides an interesting glimpse into how the tragedy was interpreted within a religious context. The editor of the anthology comments:

> The clergy with the most commendable zeal, seized and endeavoured to convert the melancholy occasion into the means of good to their fellow creatures by their exhortations, by the inculcation of religious truths and by displaying for the benefit of the rising generation in the character of our lamented Princess, an epitome of all the virtues that could adorn the woman, or the Christian.

Before the advent of broadcasting, poems and eulogies comprised an interesting variant of the commemorative surge. They were often performed at theatres, as in the case of *A Monody on the Lamented Death of HRH the Princess Charlotte of Wales Spoken by Mr Huntley at the Olympic Theatre Thursday 20 November 1817*. Songs were also popular tributes and large-circulation fashion magazines reprinted the lyrics of requiems for Charlotte. Anticipating modern marketing methods, various ploys were used to harness public interest in the dead princess in order to sell products outside the normal commemorative parameters. Typical of this exploitation of association was the way in which an upmarket firm of piano manufacturers diversified by publishing sheet music, including a special commemorative song 'Sweet Rose from Kindred Branches Torn' – a ruse, no doubt, to persuade more people to gather around their very expensive pianoforte!

In the aftermath of Charlotte's death there was a proliferation of commemorative merchandise, although the means for mass production were woefully primitive compared to the quick transformation of Diana into a panoply of goods which appeared as far afield as street markets in Bangkok and chi-chi shops in New York. Tea services, pitchers, jugs and printed handkerchiefs bearing Charlotte's image were all extremely popular; their manufacture depended on transfer-printing, an inexpensive and simple method by which engraved impressions were stamped directly on to fabric or vessels to created an easily legible image. Similarly popular were medals which, struck in a variety of metals, afforded the consumer products at the broadest range of prices. When death has curbed the source of new images, those with a commercial interest need to be ever more enterprising in the way in which they keep the pilot-light of public interest high. In 1818 an enterprising publisher reproduced 'an EXACT copy' of Princess Charlotte's hymn book which, it was claimed, had been 'found after her lamented decease under the front cushion of her pew' in her local parish church in Esher. The top spin of authenticity in any shape adds value to commemorative material. This was similarly proved when Andrew Morton's biography of Diana took on a new lease of life after her death following the revelation that the original story was, strictly speaking, autobiography, compiled from taped transcripts: it was reissued as *Diana: Her True Story in Her Own Words*.

Reviewing Charlotte's death throws into relief the paucity of twentieth-century social conventions for coping with death. By the time Diana died, society lacked the struts of religion and a common social code of mourning which historically had helped people to deal with death. Unlike the crowds who gathered for the funeral of King George VI, a solemn block of black, those who turned out to pay tribute to Diana were colourful and informal in their dress – a testament to the fact we no longer have a uniform for mourning. But perhaps the greatest difference between the mourning rituals for Diana and Charlotte is the contrast between the religious response to the earlier death and the predominantly secular response to the latter. All denominations marked Diana's death. Responses included special prayers in mosques and the Hindu and Sikh temples at Bradford, a full requiem mass at Carlisle cathedral, an evangelical open-air service in Nottingham, and a service of tribute at Western Marble Arch Synagogue. Yet for the majority of people it was a secular experience, and for many a passive one: listening to the radio, watching TV, reading a newspaper. Where people felt the urge to act, they did not go to church. Most of the mourning rituals for Diana happened outside churches. A striking vignette of the modern way of death is the image of people lining up to sign a book of condolence near the busy checkout of a crowded supermarket.

When people heard that Charlotte had died, there was an instinctive and collective migration to Dissenting meeting-houses, synagogues, Roman Catholic and Anglican churches. Indeed, where services had not been scheduled, people demanded them. Sermons about the princess were the primary medium of analysis of the shattering events, whereas for Diana it was television. The distinction between listening as part of a congregation and watching as part of a television audience seems important, for while both involve passivity, the religious context confers a weight of meaning on the way in which the message is heard. Sermons acted as ciphers to decode the death of Charlotte, whereas television programmes merely relayed Diana's death as a bewildering barrage of information. This transition from active participation to a more passive role goes in tandem with the rise of broadcasting. A transitional point was the death of the current Queen's grandfather, George V, in 1936, when, for the first time, the public heard a broadcast of a royal funeral and listened to muffled drums and the tramp of feet. Olivia Bland makes the point that this was the first major royal death

> upon which there had not been the usual spate of eulogies and funeral sermons in all great churches … The whole world heard the Archbishop of Canterbury preach at the funeral service and the day after Baldwin broadcast to the nation. The BBC held its own memorial service broadcast to the nation from a concert hall at Broadcasting House. Eulogies were fewer, but more widely heard. (*The Royal Way of Death*, 1986)

The role of the media in the evolution of a secular society is significant. The emergence of the illusion of attendance, as well as the transformation of people from active participants in mourning rituals to passive listeners and later viewers, is as relevant to how the nation mourned Diana as to how it mourned the war dead. The rise of the radio correlated with the decline of individual participation in local ceremonies on Armistice Day. The radio displaced local community activities by enabling people to become passive members of a much larger community focused on London, where the Cenotaph ceremony – broadcast live from 1937 – became the natural centre of Armistice Day. In 1927 there were 2,178,259 radio licences in the UK, while in 1939 there were 9,082,666. In each era a different medium has dominated and as these have developed, our experience of death has altered. In the 1930s it was the wireless, in the 1960s television, in the 1990s global colour television, and in the first decade of the twenty-first century it is the internet. The net was to Diana's death what television was to President Kennedy's. It marked an historic point in the evolution of the way in which private households participate in public tragedies. Specifically, as an interactive medium, the web signifies a host of new possibilities for the rituals of mass mourning. The pace of change is evident when comparing coverage of Diana's death with that of the last high-profile royal death, that of King George VI in 1952, when there were still only 350,000 television sets in the UK and one television channel, the BBC. Television was still regarded as something of a technological miracle in 1965 when there was widespread admiration for the coverage of Sir Winston Churchill's funeral, which involved 35 cameras and inspired newspaper columnists to pay tribute to the power of 'the Great Pagan God Telly!'.

In the nineteenth century the illusory function filled by television – something that we take so much for granted – was exercised differently. In a fascinating way, in 1817 going to church played a role in creating for individual congregations the illusion of attending the actual funeral of the princess which took place at night at St George's Chapel, Windsor, on Wednesday 19 November. The historian Stephen Behrendt describes how the impression of simultaneity was created when sermons at services which took place before Charlotte's funeral or the Sunday following were peppered with references to 'now' in such a way that the congregation had the 'illusion of attendance at the obsequies'. If church services were one way to hear about the funeral, pamphlets also supplied detailed descriptions, complete with diagrams showing where mourners stood and the location of the catafalque that lowered Charlotte's coffin into the mausoleum. For Diana's funeral the illusion was altogether more sophisticated, with twentieth-century technology enabling millions of people all over the world to watch a live broadcast. Her funeral was the biggest broadcasting operation in history, with a worldwide audience estimated at 2.5 billion. The BBC had 100 cameras in central London, 300 technicians and 22 outside broadcast units, and they also had crews operating around the country.

The development of the media and its relevance to the British way of death should not be underestimated. As well as being part of the process of secularisation, it has promoted detachment from death and turned us into voyeurs. It has heightened the gulf between proximity to the deaths of others and distance from personal experience of deaths. In the words of poet-undertaker Thomas Lynch,

Being there for perfect strangers has never been easier. When they've had enough they can grab a Dove bar, flick to the movie channel or the home shopping network and wait until the helicopters locate another outrage to zoom in on. (*Bodies in Motion, Bodies at Rest,* 1999)

As the technology has improved, so has the quality and quantity of false intimacy in our daily lives.

Yet one of the more interesting responses to Diana's death was the backlash against passivity. The response was not entirely voyeuristic. For many people it was not enough merely to watch the blanket coverage on television or read all about it. The need to act was demonstrated by the sheer number of people who ran off to London to join the media circus. Certainly in 1817, there was a similar thirst for immediacy; the crowds that lined the route from London to Windsor to get a glimpse of the cortège showed that for many, it was not enough to hear all about it at church or in a newspaper. In response to public interest in the funeral procession, inns along the route upped their rates and families hired out window views. Yet in 1817 the wish to see for oneself seems more understandable, given that staying at home did not assure one of a bird's-eye view of the proceedings.

When Diana died, the thirst for communality was impressive. The acts of assembling a makeshift shrine, laying flowers or camping out to secure a good view of the funeral were part of a contemporary coming-together – a way to express solidarity – informal modern versions of formal, traditional rituals, and a secular alternative to the congregation of church and the kinship of prayer. Joining a queue to sign a book of condolence, sharing thermoses, participating in candlelit vigils were entrées into a new society bonded by ritualistic behaviour, sympathy and the comfort of strangers. The instinct to lay flowers for the dead predates Diana, and has become a standard part of modern death rites, not least at the sites of car accidents. Just as the tributes to Diana were not exclusively floral, in the late twentieth century the instinct to dedicate a token of remembrance for the dead has been expressed in different ways, for instance by teddy bears at Dunblane and scarves at Anfield after the Hillsborough disaster. The modern way of laying tokens of remembrance, whether soft toys or cellophane bouquets, extends the scope of tradition by its refusal to focus exclusively on the burial site. Tokens appear at the sites of sudden violent death – they appeared, for example, around the tunnel in Paris – as well as at sites which have no direct connection with the death but become the locus of remembrance – for example, Kensington Palace and the Shankly Gates at Anfield.

The scale of the floral tributes to Diana and the sheer diversity of tokens tend to distract our memories from other public responses to national tragedy. Yet there are similarities between the mourning for Diana and the public reaction to the Hillsborough tragedy in April 1989. Both disasters 'happened on TV'. At Hillsborough this was literally so, while in the case of Diana's death the security camera footage of her leaving the Ritz, the smashed car and the sense of witnessing events as they unfolded imparted a directness to the experience of tragedy. The facility to witness death unfolding in this way – through moving, not static, images – exemplifies the contemporary culture of immediacy. Sociologist Tony Walter argues that the degree to which the mourning after Hillsborough was publicised may have helped to influence the way in which the public behaved when Diana died. It was not a case of Hillsborough starting this behaviour, but rather of it disseminating it more widely, so that by the time the King's Cross fire and the Dunblane massacre happened such behaviour had been assimilated as convention. According to Walter, an important way in which Hillsborough set a precedent was by prompting the first two-minute silence other than at the conventional Remembrance Sunday observance, after a disaster.

Certainly things happened on a small scale at Hillsborough, which were then greatly magnified when Diana died. Within hours of the Hillsborough tragedy, the public started to lay flowers and other tokens at a place that was not the site of death. There was a powerful sense of a pall of sadness enveloping a major city, Liverpool. Whereas Diana's death affected all strata of society, there is a sense that Hillsborough happened within a more clearly identifiable community who had already learned something about the shared rituals of football-related grief through the Heysel Stadium disaster. Beyond this cohesion, there was a sense of pre-existing conventions being adapted, for example, in the way that scarves were put on the altar at Liverpool's Roman Catholic cathedral, a vast football banner hung up, and a massive service attended by overspilling crowds who participated from outside the building. The comparisons to the service for Diana are obvious. In both cases there was much media comment, both at the time and later, about how the tragedies had been commemorated and how the media had covered these commemorations. From the position of hindsight, it does seem possible that the public may have been 'educated' in how to mourn later disasters, including Diana's death, by what they remembered about Hillsborough.

It felt in 1997 as if, for the first time in years, death was once again a social experience, with people congregating to pay tribute and pulling together to 'do' death. The diversity of the crowd – where, on a couple of occasions, the Crown joined the commoners to look at the flowers –

strengthened the impression of death as a social, public and corporate experience. Sadly, however, the united front was not maintained when it came to agreeing on a permanent memorial. The wrangling and indecision about how to remember Diana notwithstanding, the vast resources of the memorial fund stand in contrast to the admirably democratic way in which the people rallied to commemorate Charlotte. Through a public subscription campaign co-ordinated by the Duchess of York whereby contributions were capped at a guinea and no contribution was deemed too small, £12,340 19s 6½d was raised. This was used to commission a memorial by the sculptor Matthew Cotes Wyatt which was, in effect, truly a people's memorial for a people's princess, although there was some controversy about putting it in St George's Chapel, Windsor.

Both tragedies elicited such an overtly emotional response from the British people that it is easy to forget that in reality, the women the people mourned had been remote public figures, familiar but unknown. They were women who were looked at more than listened to, seen not heard, women whom people felt they knew because they regularly read so much about them, women who had influenced fashion more than politics – women made extraordinary by they way in which ordinary people perceived them. With extraordinary synchronicity, both their deaths coincided with and eclipsed other significant high-profile deaths. In the case of Diana, her death was followed by that of Mother Teresa; with Charlotte, it was the public execution by hanging, drawing and quartering of three workers for an anti-government protest which took the form of a march in Nottingham. In each case, these other deaths failed to divert public sympathy away from the dead princesses; as significant events they were completely overshadowed, and received scant attention.

One of the most pertinent cultural commentaries about this discrepancy, and one which has great relevance to the reaction to Diana's death, is a pamphlet by Percy Bysshe Shelley published under the pseudonym 'The Hermit of Marlow'. With audacious timing, it appeared shortly after Charlotte's death. From a contemporary viewpoint, it reads as a searing critique of the cult of celebrity, which it debunks by questioning the justification for grand-scale public sorrow over a death that has neither personal nor political significance. Appropriateness is the central theme. 'We cannot truly grieve for everyone who dies beyond the circle of those especially dear to us.' This links up with observations made by Thomas Lynch on the death of Diana, in which he suggests that some people were more solicitous and responsive to a beautiful stranger than they had been to dead family and friends, with 'global hyperbole' compensating for 'local understatement'.

Shelley distinguishes throughout between events that warrant private versus public mourning:

> There should be public mourning when those events take place which make all good men mourn in their hearts – the rule of foreign or domestic tyrants, the abuse of public faith.

He develops this idea:

> This solemnity should be used only to express a wide and intelligible calamity and one which is felt to be such by those who feel for their country and for mankind; its character ought to be universal, not particular.

A recurrent theme is the rationale for directing extreme emotions at a remote public figure, and he implies that Charlotte's death does not fall within the category that warrants national protestations of grief. Daringly, given the charged climate, he presumes to challenge Charlotte's contribution to the public life of the nation, 'For the public she had done nothing either good or evil; her education had rendered her incapable of either in a large and comprehensive sense.' And

> She was not like Lady Jane Grey or Queen Elizabeth a woman of profound and various learning, she had accomplished nothing, and aspired to nothing and could understand nothing respecting those great political questions which involve the happiness of those over whom she was destined to rule.

Reverberating through the piece is the fallacy of the fame game, which then was nascent but which subsequently, powered by the mass media, became almost the main motor of twentieth-century society.

> If beauty youth, innocence, amiable manners and the exercise of domestic virtue could alone justify public sorrow when they are exiting for ever, this interesting lady would well deserve that exhibition.

Shelley's pamphlet starts brutally and bravely:

> The Princess Charlotte is dead. She no longer moves, nor thinks nor feels. She is perhaps as inanimate as the clay with which she is about to mingle. It is a dreadful thing to know that she is a putrid corpse, who but a few days since was full of life and hope, a woman young innocent and beautiful snatched from the bosom of domestic peace, and leaving that single vacancy which none can die and leave not.

By demoting the significance of the death of the princess at the very time when people were distraught with grief, this polemic is extraordinarily bold.

> There were thousands of others equally distinguished as she, for private excellencies, who have been cut off in youth and hope. The accident of her birth neither made her life more virtuous nor her death more worthy of grief.

He punctures the status of the death as a uniquely tragic event by considering it in relation to the deaths of thousands of 'the poorest poor' whose passing we barely register. Our reaction to Charlotte jars with our antipathy to the deaths of the underprivileged, and our emotional response to the former is at odds with the way that the deaths of a multitude of poor women fail to prick our social conscience. 'None turn aside and moralise upon the sadness they have left behind.'

Evaluation of the public sympathy for Charlotte is juxtaposed in Shelley's pamphlet with the comparative indifference to the fates of the three young men – Brandreth, Ludlum and Turner – victims of a most bloody public execution, an intended deterrent to others contemplating insurrection against the state. He leaves the reader in no doubt as to the event he feels more deserving of public mourning:

> The execution of Brandreth, Ludlum and Turner is an event of quite a different character from the death of Princess Charlotte – men shut up in a dungeon with fear of hideous death ... Nothing is more horrible than that man should for any cause shed the life of a man. For all other calamities there is a remedy or consolation.

State-sanctioned murder is to his mind 'a calamity such as the English nation ought to mourn with an unassuageable grief.' The fact that a politically charged event of the utmost gravity and significance to the country had been eclipsed by an emotionally charged tragedy with no major ramifications to the British people, for Shelley represents a serious misjudgement.

For Shelley, public mourning should not be made 'lightly or in any manner that tends to waste on inadequate objects those fertilising streams of sympathy which public mourning should be the occasion of pouring forth'. His belief in the 'fertilising streams of sympathy' as the basis of social cohesion is a potent idea. It is at the heart of the relationship between the living and the dead. The end of the pamphlet is steeped in sentiment and drama. To read the final lines is to feel a psychological closeness between

the responses of the British public to the deaths of these two young women
– a closeness which transcends the temporal distance of 180 years.

> Mourn then people of England, clothe yourselves in solemn black. Let the
> bells be tolled. Think of mortality and change. Shroud yourselves in soli-
> tude and gloom of sacred sorrow. Spare no symbol of universal grief.
> Weep, mourn, lament. Fill the great city – fill the boundless fields with the
> lamentation and the echo of groans. A beautiful princess is dead; she who
> should have been the Queen of her beloved nation, and whose posterity
> should have ruled it for ever. She loved the domestic affection and cher-
> ished arts which adorn and valour which defends. She was amiable and
> would have become wise, but she was young and in the flower of youth the
> despoiler came. Liberty is dead.

The final three words are brilliantly placed because they leave the reader in
no doubt as to where Shelley's sympathies lie. It is clear that he regards the
implications of the execution of the three men as of far greater national
importance than the demise of Charlotte.

The most compelling aspect of the close comparison between the public responses to the tragic death of the Princess of Wales in 1817 and the
tragic death of the Princess of Wales in 1997 is the continuum of sentiment.
For, looking back to the dramatic response to Charlotte's death in a world
without television and cameras, it is not enough to say that, the response to
Diana's death was *entirely* media-made. It shows that while the way in
which people mourn changes, why they mourn stays the same. It is reassuring to be reminded that, irrespective of the medical and industrial
changes which are the flux of history, there is stability in the sentiments of
sympathy we feel for the dead. Binding people across time is the drive to
mark, mourn and remember the deaths of others, although the expression
of these impulses varies as religious and social codes wax and wane, and as
technological advances alter our commemorative capability. George Clay-
ton said in a sermon preached at Walworth, on the day of Charlotte's funeral:

> Britain has offered to surrounding countries, a sight rarely beheld. A great
> nation dissolved in the sorrows of an unfeigned condolence, voluntarily
> paying a tribute of loyalty and affection to their departed Princess, and
> bound to each other, by the ties, not of political concord and of civil inter-
> est, so much as by the bonds of a generous and all-pervading sympathy.

Consideration for the dead is at the root of our humanity. The grave is, in
this regard, the cradle of civilisation. Freud went so far as to say; 'Consid-

eration for the dead, who after all, no longer need it, is more important to us than the truth, and certainly for most of us, than consideration for the living.' (*Thoughts on War and Death*, 1915.) The levels of disgust and disturbance we feel towards the Holocaust deniers or our indignation about the omission from war memorials of the names of those shot for cowardice in the First World War all show the importance to us of honouring the dead. It is also evident in the outrage of the Belgian people at the cover-up over the deaths of the children murdered by a paedophile ring. In 1996 this provoked what came to be called the White March. This moving expression of solidarity by ordinary people in numbers estimated at between 250,000 to 325,000 was one of the biggest peacetime protests. Demonstrators converged on the capital, carrying white flowers, white balloons and wearing white clothing – gestures laden with the symbolism of innocence and mourning traditions for children which focus on white, not black. Many of the demonstrators also carried pictures of the victims in keeping with an emerging trend for the use of photographs in modern mourning rituals. The White March was also distinctive for its symbolic silence. This, more than anything else, conferred on it the aura of mourning and solemn remembrance.

Bound up in our drive to mourn the dead with expressions of sympathy and condolence is a more complex dynamic concerning the realisation of our own death. This is brilliantly conveyed in Adam Smith's *Theory of the Moral Sentiments* (1759), in which he explores and explains the relationship between the living and the dead. He develops the idea that a significant component of our morality is determined by the fact that the dead function as a mirror of our own mortality. Empathy for the dead is at the root of our compulsion to honour them.

> It is miserable, we think, to be deprived of the light of the sun; to be shut out from life and conversation, to be laid in a cold grave, a prey to corruption and the reptiles of the earth; to be no more thought of in this world, but to be obliterated in a little time from the affections and almost from the memory of their dearest friends and relations. Surely we imagine we can never feel too much for those who have suffered so dreadful a calamity. The tribute of our fellow feelings seems doubly due to them now, when they are in danger of being forgot by everybody.

Mentally, we change places with the dead, and this transference influences the way in which we grieve. We lodge

> our own living souls in their inanimate bodies and thence conceiving what

would be our emotions in this case. It is from this very illusion of the imagination that the foresight of our own dissolution is so terrible to us, and that the idea of those circumstances, which undoubtedly can give us no pain when we are dead, makes us miserable while we are alive. And from thence arises one of the most important principles in human nature, the dread of death, the great poison to the happiness, but the great restraint upon the injustice of mankind, which while it afflicts and mortifies the individual guards and protects the society.

Our sympathy and condolence for Diana occurred in part because we imagined ourselves in her place. Her death was a reminder to remember death. It showed us the degree to which we have put death out of our minds. It pulled us to our senses, and fixed in our minds the fact that to live without awareness of death is to live with a false sense of security. It reminded us that we couldn't take for granted the concept of a natural order. The death of the Queen Mother – whose funeral is rehearsed each year as Operation Sea Lion – we could have borne with greater equanimity, but the violent, premature death of our favourite celebrity in her prime caught us out. Death rates have lulled us into complacency. In 1880, out of 1 million people, 300,000 could expect to live to age 65; today, 840,000 can expect to live to 65 and 300,000 to 85. In an era which digests death in a palatable formula of short-lived crescendos of calamity in headline news – Hillsborough, Lockerbie, Dunblane – an era which serves up daily sound bite tributes to the famous dead, all of which fade away to silence and forgetting except for those directly affected – Diana's death was louder and bigger and longer. It compelled us to ponder what our ancestors never forgot: *Mors Certa, Hora Incerta* – death is certain, its hour is not.

How we mourned and why we mourned are but two elements of the extraordinary response to Diana's death. Another interesting aspect is what it all meant for the British way of death. Firstly, Diana's death was made even more significant for happening in a year of iconic celebrity deaths. Gianni Versace in July, Diana in August, Michael Hutchence in November – these interconnected celebrity deaths resulted in a spate of celebrity congregations, as people more commonly seen on the catwalk and film premiere circuit gathered at the funerals of their famous friends. Invitations to these occasions became hot social tickets, and for a while *Hello!* magazine threatened to turn into *Goodbye!* magazine, such were the number of photospreads of the death styles of the rich and famous. Autograph hunters and paparazzi had a new stamping ground as a heady combination of fame, fashion and fatality started to turn death itself into the biggest star of 1997.

The devastation to the celebrity circuit was compounded by the fact that it had lost three key stars whose trajectories overlapped. As a leader of the fashion pack, Versace made clothes for royalty and rock stars. Diana and Michael Hutchence were dedicated followers – Diana followed the fashions, Hutchence the models. When three links in the fame chain die within months of each other, the impact is bound to be dramatic. Three modern tragedies – a murder, a car crash, a suicide / misadventure – all were violent, unhappy and unexpected endings. Like the Emperor's New Clothes, they revealed as so many illusions all the layers of meaning with which we dress our lives.

The fashion world is notoriously fickle – a world of instant forgetting, where the preoccupation of the present is the future. The events of 1997 forced the fashion mavens to stop and look at the real world. For nearly six months, teary eyes kept intact with waterproof mascara shone dewy as reminiscence of the famous dead made small talk bigger at parties. The little black dress went retro in meaning, back to mourning black. The fashion world – in which age, let alone death, is the enemy, and 14-year-old models are used to keep intimations of mortality at bay – could not keep death out. The echelon of society that hires bodyguards to keep safe was forced to acknowledge that death is an unstoppable stalker.

Versace's violent death at the hands of a gay serial killer was the first of that fateful year to focus the media gaze on mortality, and it set the tone for what followed. There were so many striking vignettes: the golden box containing his cremated remains, displayed not with a prayer book but his own book, ironically entitled *Do Not Disturb*; the Princess of Wales consoling Elton John before he got up to sing Psalm 23 with Sting; Naomi in a black lace mantilla flanked by Donatella, a long black veil over long bleach-blond hair; models with mournful Modigliani faces that have graced a million magazines. The spectacle of so many of the rich, the famous, the fashionable all paying their respects to a man who built a billion-dollar business on the high-class hooker look was death as it had not been done before. It was death remade as a media event, death presented with the patina of glamour, death exposed with the brightness of Klieg lights. As one journalist wrote,

> For the hordes of invitees who flocked to the Duomo in the centre of Milan for yesterday's memorial service, not to mention the crowds of bystanders who pressed against the security fences, it looked like just another fashion show, a great excuse for celebrity spotting under a blazing Italian sun. (Andrew Gumbel in the *Independent*, 23 July 1997)

Then Diana died, and like a supernova her stardom dramatically increased in the catastrophe of the crash. Her funeral was a triumph of media technology, recorded and filmed, in stills and moving images. It was a magnificent global production, a talking picture with a silent star. Again, it signified modernity, as Westminster Abbey was infused with the gloss and glitz of Hollywood: Tom and Nicole, Steven Spielberg, Donatella (this time in a cameo role, not as co-star), a live performance by Elton John, a passionate address by Diana's brother. There was clapping. The sound of clapping blurred the line between congregation and audience, service and performance.

This line was similarly blurred at the funeral of Michael Hutchence: Kylie in silver stilettos, supermodel Helena Christiansen in shades and Paula Yates, bare-armed and buxom in a low-cut dress, cradling Heavenly Hiraani in her arms. Again, screens relayed the funeral to fans, and the theatricality was enhanced by Michael's own voice filling the cathedral with 'By My Side'. The pop-star pallbearers, the celebrity mourners, the television cameras all shunted death into the public eye. These three funerals meant that death could no longer be kept out of sight in order that the living could keep it out of their minds. Where once the funeral had been a dry eye and black tie occasion, dignified and private, for family and friends, suddenly it involved fans and followers. Instead of a ceremony co-ordinated by priests, it was a media event run by PR executives.

Of the trinity of celebrity deaths that year, Diana's had the greatest impact on the British way of death. Yet it is not right to say that her funeral was innovative in terms of style. It signified a modern response that was already much in evidence among the funerals of ordinary people. A pop song, a warts-and-all address by a family member, being buried in one's own clothes (in Diana's case, a Catherine Walker dress) a woodland burial site – these elements characterise the modern preference for personal relevance, a trend which has been gathering momentum since the 1980s. As Keith Leverton, seventh-generation funeral director with Leverton & Sons Ltd, the firm that conducted the Princess's funeral, commented: 'In my forty-two years in the profession the biggest change is in people's awareness of their rights to have a service tailored to suit them. Ten years ago you were unaware of an alternative to a rota clergyman at the crematorium who would not mention the name of the deceased for fear of getting it wrong, but would say "brother" or "sister".'

Diana's funeral crystallised in the minds of the British public the importance of personally relevant ritual. Apart from the gun carriage, Diana died in character, from the congregation with its blend of celebrity and charity to the choice of music and the vast numbers of children who lined the funeral route.

Of the modern elements, with connotations of Rousseau and Ermenoville, her burial in a romantic woodland setting on a private island gave social acceptability to a movement more commonly associated with ageing hippies and the 'green' fringe. The week after her death, sales of burial plots in Oakfield Woodland Burial Ground in Essex doubled, and enquiries soared. Peter Kincaid, the director, explains: 'We got about six enquiries a day. Of course we couldn't say "Excuse me, did you come here because of Princess Di?" but we felt that was the reason for the sudden increase in volume.'

For some people the funeral was a more immediate source of inspiration. For Anita Hildretch, the whole event was inextricably and poignantly bound up with the death of her husband, John. He became critically ill on the day Diana died and died himself on the day of Diana's funeral. She watched the funeral in a hospice with the volume turned down. 'I felt emotionally inspired by her funeral. My husband was buried at Greenhaven in a beautiful hand-made willow coffin which was borne on green boughs on the back of a farm cart pulled by two shire horses with purple plumes. Apart from that it was very simple with just white lilies. A local Anglican vicar read the 23rd Psalm and a Buddhist priest did a death chant. Everyone there agreed it was a vast improvement on the traditional funeral.'

Greenhaven Woodland Burial Ground is located just a few miles away from Althorpe in Northamptonshire amidst rolling hills. The elasticity of Diana's funeral seems to have struck a chord with the population at large. By infusing into the formality of a quasi-state event a personal and poignant relevance, it demonstrated to millions that it is possible to amend traditional forms. As for Anita and John, traditions can be reinterpreted and melded to create a ritual which is meaningful, modern and individual.

The power of publicity should not be underestimated. In 1987, a single picture of Diana shaking the hand of a gay man with HIV is credited by campaigners with doing more to change attitudes to AIDS and homosexuality than any single event in the past decade. As a gay-friendly figure, Diana did much to promote a greater understanding of homosexuality and AIDS. At the time, AIDS was a source of prejudice, fear and public misinformation, and the popular perception of gay life saw it as a promiscuous sub-culture of bathhouses and discos. Just as she helped to promote a more enlightened view of gay life, indirectly in death she has helped with the 'outing' of death, too. Her untimely end catapulted death from the margins to the mainstream. It jolted us out of death denial. As someone whose belief system was founded in psychology more than theology, it seems appropriate that she un-stoppered death. There is a sense in which the British way of death will never again be dry-eyed and downplayed, with funerals an ordeal of stoicism triumphing over sentiment, in which children are banned from taking part and where men are expected to muzzle their emotions. In her dying, she has conferred on people cultural permission to express their feelings. This is an important legacy. Like sex, death is a social minefield – a minefield which, in death, Diana, Princess of Wales, has helped to clear for us all.

DEATH
AND THE
SALESMEN

I CAN ARRANGE YOUR FUNERAL NOW. IT WILL ONLY TAKE A minute.' It is Saturday morning at the Scottish Exhibition Centre in Glasgow. The Cliff Richard's Hits tour is sharing space with Funeralcare, a public exhibition of funeral crafts and services staged by Co-operative Funeral Services. At the pre-paid funeral stand, a dapper funeral director ushers me to a deep sofa, opens his executive briefcase and talks me through a selection of glossy brochures. I feel as if I am choosing a package holiday, rather than negotiating the price of a one-way ticket for the ultimate getaway. You could fly to the Caribbean for the same price as the top-of-the-range Sussex casket. You would definitely be travelling first class. Economy would be £310 – still plenty of legroom, but without a glass partition and hinge for viewing. Pens and peppermints, business cards and brochures – the marketing arsenal is impressive. I also get a voucher that entitles me to a 10 per cent reduction if I pay for my funeral before June. The basic all-inclusive trip is a £645 funeral package and, as with the travel agent, it is the package that the funeral director prefers you to buy. The person who wants a coffin only, or just an overnight stay in the mortuary, is as irksome to the funeral trade as the person who stockpiles his camper van with food to the tour operator. In both cases, independent travellers are more trouble than they are worth.

At another stand, women potter in pairs around a carousel of coffins, eyeing up the frills and ruffles, pillows and padding which are such an important part of the myth of corpse comfort. 'Och, Glenys! Feel the quality of that!' a woman urges her friend as they run their fingers admiringly along the white satin interior of Jura, from the Scottish Islands Collection. 'Looks awful comfy', her friend agrees, as if sizing up a suite at the Ideal Home Exhibition. Teresa accompanies her elderly mother, Margaret, who walks with a frame. A woman with a clipboard accosts them with a consumer survey. While Margaret enthuses about the coffins, her daughter prefers the embalming display, but overall both feel the atmosphere is more conducive to browsing than to buying: 'Like buying curtains, you want to stand back and have a look and a private word. We'd have talked seriously if they'd had a wee partition.'

It seems that old habits die hard, for part of the objective of the exhibition arranged by Co-operative Funeral Services, the first of its kind in Britain, was to present death in a more familiar context. The organisers hoped that the event would not only stimulate discussion, but might even clinch some 'pre-need' sales of funeral plans, unofficially referred to as 'pay now, die later'. The operations manager explained that 'there is a definite barrier for a person to go into a funeral director when they are not arranging a funeral. Our aim was to take death into a non-threatening, off-site environment with an informal friendly atmosphere.'

Most popular with the browsers is Stand 17, where the Dodge Company is displaying its wares. Since 1893, they have been the largest supplier of embalming products to the United Kingdom funeral trade. The modern mastery of the macabre makeover means that we can all look our best when we face the final curtain, for just as the living are not allowed to look old, we do not like the dead to look dead. It is no surprise that the land obsessed with eternal youth should have monopolised the market in products designed to help the dead to keep up appearances. One enterprising funeral home in Boston, Massachusetts even devised an intriguing scale of charges according to the achieved 'look': for 'quiet resignation $2', for 'giving the features the appearance of Christian hope and contentment $5'. The young Scotsmen on Stand 17 demonstrate a more sensitive approach to their trade as they discuss it with the public. At their premises in Glasgow, they embalm about a hundred bodies a week. In run-of-the-mill cases it takes an hour and a half, ranging up to nine hours for more extensive restoration and reconstruction in the event of violent death.

In glistening cabinets are old-fashioned tins of wound filler, feature builder and lip wax, available in either 'youthful' or 'adult'. 'We won't do you up so you look as if you're going out dancing,' they reassure me, as I eye up a pot of French Rose intended 'for delicate cosmetic tinting' and the most frequently used product for skin tone. If you pinch the skin on the top of your hand for a moment, you will get a sneak preview of your complexion as a corpse, a thin-skinned translucence. Men are finished off with a glossy look achieved by the application of a patina of hair spray to the facial features, and women a matte look with 'Perma-powder'. All this is applied with subtlety, for less is more, even in death; it is vital that the embalmed can pass the 'kiss test'. Similarly, the embalmers strive not to make the loved one look as if he or she has spent too long under a sun lamp. 'We refrain from using the phrase "life-like", and I wouldn't call it healthily pink, but we try to achieve a natural effect.'

Formaldehyde, pink plastic mouth-formers, surgical instruments: I'm temporarily distracted by the observation that, hung in a Hoxton gallery, this morbid cabinet of curiosities would be considered cool and collectible – such is the contemporary art market's love affair with death. As art it would command many times a mortician's annual salary. The entrepreneurial lobe of my brain then reformulates this as many times *my* annual salary, and for a nanosecond I toy with the idea of doing a Damien and pitching up at packing-up time to talk.

I'm brought back to reality by a baby in a pushchair grizzling to attract the attention of her young mother, who is listening intently to the young mortician telling us some of the tricks of his trade. 'They used to put Bibles under the chin to keep the mouth closed, but these days we tend to use clinical adhesive.' This struck me as a singularly vivid sign of our secular times. It also conveys the impoverishment of the modern imagery of death. Where once the woman who did the laying-out placed coins to close the eyes, the less esoteric modern way is plastic eye caps, which apparently require a certain knack in order not to make the dear departed look as if they are squinting. Gone, too, are nature's herbal helpers – the nosegays of rosemary, the oil of lavender – replaced by industrial-strength disinfectants. Instead of homely lengths of muslin and calico, arranged by women, boards cut by a local carpenter-cum-artisan undertaker, the personal has become professional. The body has moved to a sterile environment of trocars and tubes, rubber gloves and masks, stainless steel gurneys with ominous gullies. With the resonances of efficient disposal, those whom we have only moments earlier covered with kisses and tears, held and watched, we witness being removed in zip-up sacks, as if in death they have become as undesirable, untouchable, as inappropriate to keep in our homes as toxic waste.

The Funeralcare exhibition crystallised my resolve to write this book. It was one of many examples I have witnessed in recent years of the demystification of death. It exemplified on a small scale what is happening on a large scale throughout the funeral trade. For, like a mummified cadaver exposed to daylight after centuries in dust and darkness, the taboo-driven model of death that dominated and distinguished the twentieth century is crumbling before our eyes. After years of downplaying death and going to the funeral director for the death style equivalent of a short-back-and-sides, new consumer demands are transforming the funeral trade.

As I flipped through the coffin catalogue and sampled corpse cosmetics, as I queued with children for hearse rides to the nearby crematorium for 'a funeral education experience' and browsed memorial pendants, it was as if I were experiencing a real-life version of *The Loved One*, Evelyn Waugh's wicked, witty parody of the American cemetery Forest Lawn. Scottish brogue aside, the pre-need advice that I got was not so different from the sales spiel directed at Waugh's protagonist concerning 'Before Need Provision Arrangements':

> Choose now at leisure and in health the form of final preparation you require, pay for it while you are best able to do so, shed all anxiety. Pass the buck, Mr Barlow; Whispering Glades can take it.

In the fifty-odd years since the book's publication, Waugh's smooth-talking mortuary hostess with her range of choices, from casket suits to how the Loved One should be embalmed – 'Rural, Athletic and Scholarly, that is to say red, brown or white' – has proved oddly predictive. For as death is ceasing to be taboo, it is becoming a market, and the funeral has become a plethora of consumer options.

Until fairly recently, the paraphernalia of death was a safe outpost from the consumer boom. Now, inexorably, it has become caught up in the proliferation of choice that afflicts western society in general and which is threatening to turn the American dream into a trans-Atlantic nightmare. From supermarkets to satellite channels, the concept of multiple choice that is intended to be a boon to the consumer is in danger of becoming the bane of modern life. Whereas twenty years ago a supermarket stocked on average about 5,000 lines, today it offers in the region of 40,000 different products, including a hundred different kinds of water. Compared to this, the changes in the funeral trade seem relatively restrained although, having said this, just as choosing a cup of coffee has become a complex decision-making process – size, bean, milk, sugar, topping – so it is with coffins. I've seen the coffin as a backpack, flat pack and even shoe-rack. The coffin is at the centre of a massive merchandising boom. Within a few years the range of models has more than doubled. Many funeral directors now have showrooms. But the fundamental problem with the coffin is encapsulated in the undertaker's riddle: 'The man that makes it doesn't want it, the man that buys it has no use for it, the man that's in it doesn't see it.' Even the use of the word 'coffin' is not what it was; the gravedigger may still call a spade a spade, but increasingly the funeral trade talks of 'caskets'. It's the difference between a limousine and a vehicle that simply gets you from A to B. Caskets look and sound impressive – the Baronet, the Chesterfield, even the Last Supper – a magnificent handmade Italian model with a choice of seven religious scenes for the side panels. Another model displays artwork on the inside of the lid, affording the ultimate in private views. The range of colours is impressive. Jesus even comes in black or white versions. A smart Chelsea funeral director does well with Hague blue, while the Tea Rose is a rose-tinted spectacle, a show-stopper of a copper casket with a pink tint and matching pastel pink interior with rose motif. One innovative design feature is Memorysafe, a slide-in compartment which, like the glove compartment of a car, is a place that you can stow sentimental items for the journey, including mementos and photographs – although, personally, I think memories are more safely stowed in the hearts and minds of the living.

When, in 1963, Jessica Mitford penned *The American Way of Death*, her classic critique of the American funeral industry, she believed that Blighty was a bastion of tradition, and would remain impervious to American-style marketing and merchandise. Such are the changes in the British way of death that she is probably turning in her grave. In the updated version of her book, she continued to pile blame on to the funeral trade, but did not take on board the changing consumer climate. For the traditional English conservatism is changing. In fact, a nation of shopkeepers is also a nation of shoppers, and although some of the changes in the funeral trade are industry-led, others are consumer-led. Although compared with our American cousins we still err on the side of understatement, we are now prepared to put more into our funerals, and this is opening up merchandising opportunities for the funeral director. Increasingly, in death as in life, we are starting to see ourselves as consumers entitled to choice, service and value for money. In 1996 the Dead Citizens Charter and the Charter for the Bereaved were two unrelated campaigns based on the belief that consumer rights don't end with last rites. The worm has turned. At last a sector of trade which for years inverted the cardinal rule of retail – the funeral director, not the customer, is always right – is having to rethink its practices. Historically, price, like the dingy façades of old, has been far from transparent, but in response to a new generation of customers prepared to shop around, the funeral director is having to steel himself to the telephone quote. This is nothing short of a social revolution.

Indeed, funerals are slipping into a lifestyle framework that replicates other sectors of the retail industry. The choice of what you buy and where you buy it has expanded to accommodate all tastes and budgets. This is a radical social change compared with what was available even five years ago. From the organic collective to the convenience store, there are equivalents in shopping for funerals. The green generation can go for the cardboard coffins sold by the alternative DIY funeral specialists. Those with more money than time can go to the American big brand funeral directors (dubbed 'McFunerals' when they first arrived), or they can buy British with the big brand high street equivalent of the American conglomerate, Co-operative Funeral Services. Die-hard traditionalists, who like the corner shop approach, can go to the core of the British funeral trade, the old-style bona fide family firms of funeral directors, which – contrary to public perception – still represent the backbone of the British funeral trade and maintain the biggest market share. Here, what you get in personal service more than compensates for limited choice. If, on the other hand, trends rather than traditions are your preference, the internet is increasingly an option. The sex trade does not have exclusive rights on harvesting the new technology for commercial ends. 'Pick your own' funeral sites are cropping up all over the web, offering potentially rich pickings for those working with the Grim Reaper.

For busy people, the death supermarket is the most unusual application of the convenience concept, for death is eternally inconvenient. In 1995 Britain had its first exposure to this type of bazaar when the Regale Funeral Store opened in Walthamstow, London, opposite a bookmaker. With neon strip-lights, trolleys and even an angel logo, Regale looked like a normal supermarket – except that with regard to on-site facilities, instead of the bakery and crèche there was a state-of-the-art embalming theatre and facilities for lying in state. Apart from small garden tools sold for tending graves, the merchandise was mainly morbid. As a one-stop funeral shop, there were mix-and-match options for coffins and caskets, and a mock Garden of Remembrance displaying a range of memorials including sundials and bird baths with compartments for cremated remains. Yet the idea failed to take off. Even though the coffins were discreet, sectioned off like the gardening section at a DIY store, treating death as a self-service shopping experience like B&Q was a consumer concept too far for the British public, or perhaps just premature. Regale closed in 1998. Perhaps part of the problem was that, while we are all standing in the same queue for the final check-out, this is one case where we don't mind waiting our turn.

The French, though, are different. For the death supermarket that flopped in London was a French import altered only in name. In France it has thrived. In the early 1990s Michel Leclerc, renowned hypermarket-owning monopoly-breaker of petrol prices, took on the funeral trade. He pioneered the concept. In just four years he opened sixty large stores and twice that number of smaller agencies, acquiring an impressive one-third share of the French market. His shops are open seven days a week, from eight 'til late, and are full of trolley-filling temptations for the bereaved. Shelves groan with coffin attachments, tomb trimmings and mini-memorials with motifs of playing cards, skiers and motorcyclists. Hobbies feature heavily in the iconography. One memorial is inscribed '*De ses amis boulistes*', but while honesty in obituaries is a growing trend, honest memorials are less common; there isn't yet one sporting a motif of a television and a re-mote control to cater for the large numbers of couch potatoes in our midst. The overriding impression is of the worst type of mass production, the cheap and not-so-cheerful – fake flowers, plastic plaques, labels saying 'UV and frost resistant', everything manmade and with a false promise of per-manence.

I feel ambivalent about the funeral as a commodity, bought and sold in such an uncompromisingly mundane manner. With Madonna – the pop singer, not the mother of Jesus – in the background, a young sales assistant in cowboy boots and tight jeans slouches at a desk, negotiating the sale of a burial plot. The gist of what she is saying is that the proposed grave has room for four family members, with big reductions if single occupancy changes within thirty years as a result of another member of the family moving in. Special offers, discounts, reductions: the store is incredibly un-sentimental about what you get for your francs. The branch I visited sells around twenty funeral packages a week at prices that are about 30 per cent cheaper than the competition. Business is brisk. No wonder the angel em-blazoned on its carrier bags has such a satisfied grin on his face.

Superstores are not the only way of marketing death. There are niche markets, too. For the style-conscious, Heaven on Earth in Bristol is Britain's first death boutique. There is nothing new about *doubles entendres* and death in conversation, but the novelty of this shop is the way it extends the *double entendre* to objects and increases the functional meaning of the parapher-nalia of body disposal. A coffin is not just a coffin, it's a CD and video holder, a wine rack, a spice cabinet or – the most popular line – a 'Heaven on Earth Chest as a Bookcase'. Another bestseller is the coffin presented as a window seat covered with cushions. From around £300 you can arrange to have a chest stencilled with a variety of designs, including a bird of prey and Art Nouveau motifs. If stencilling cramps your style, for a little more money you can have a customised chest. A housewife from Aberdeen wanted a Red Arrows coffin so Paula, whose shop it is, had to consult the RAF to check on colour schemes and specifications. In the background there are monks on tape, around the shops an extraordinary profusion of products: faux fur mourning armbands, funerary vases as toothbrush holders, pasta jars for cremated remains, coffin rings as towel holders, and coffin paperweights complete with brass plaques for engraving. Apparently it's too much for some people, who walk in and walk straight out, but others are clearly more enthusiastic. 'Mind blowing' and 'Cosmic' are the last two entries in the visitor's book. Beside the cash register is a small ceramic pot with a label saying 'MY DAD'S ASHES ARE IN HERE'. Paula explains: 'He was in one of those coloured spaghetti jars over there but a woman came in saying she really wanted it and as it was the only one in that colour, I poured my father into a small pot. I offered to wash out the jar he'd been in but she said, "Don't worry" and left with a bit of my dad.'

Paula's flippant façade is reserved for the 'Life' side of her business, which is about persuading people to treat coffins as furniture and to buy ahead. She also helps people to arrange funerals, however, and with the 'Death' side of her business she is respectful and compassionate. Like her stock, in fact, she is dual-functional.

For those with a keenly developed social conscience, a green death-style is now well within reach. Just as organic is being pushed as a brand and is particularly fashionable in the marketing of food, eco-friendly funerary products are all the rage. Those in the know recommend the Swiss Ecology Peace Box, which sounds more like a solution to global conflict than a cardboard container. Just as buying organic vegetables means there is not much to choose from between the earthy spuds and the hairy carrots, cardboard coffins come in less variety than caskets, but even within this sector there are signs of expansion and innovation. The point is less choice than price, practicality and concern about the planet. The prices are compelling. At just over £50 the flat-pack Woodland Coffin is unquestionably a bargain, but even when assembled it doesn't quite look finished. A tad more sophisticated is the Brighton Casket from the same firm, which is 100 per cent cardboard, but less rough and ready. Both these models have removable lids for viewing, and both can be bought over the phone and delivered to your door within a couple of days.

Those who take the collective concept very seriously may be interested in the fact that the Brighton Casket comes in a pack of five or ten with considerable savings and the same delivery time. The bulk buy could be turned into an opportunity for communal coffin painting, perhaps even a party where people bring a paintbrush rather than a bottle and everyone mucks in. If cardboard is too down-to-earth for you, an aesthetic alternative is the Mawdesley Willow Coffin. This charming hand-woven wicker coffin has something of the old-fashioned hamper about it, complete with hinged lid and toggles; it suggests countryside and panamas and haystacks. With flowers intertwined through the lid and sides, you could easily emulate William Morris rustic chic by way of death style. In 1896 Morris's coffin of unpolished wood was borne on a red-wheeled hay cart decked with alder boughs, bulrushes, moss and a wreath of bay leaves. It made such a charming, albeit sad, spectacle that one of the mourners commented, 'It was the only funeral I have ever seen that did not make me ashamed to have to be buried.'

Recently I had a glimpse of the future in death design when I witnessed 'a new development in the history of the coffin' with the unveiling of the Ecopod. This deeply pleasing tactile coffin has been six years in the planning, and is billed as 'a design for the new millennium'. With no harsh angles or lines it certainly breaks the mould of conventional coffin geometry. It is a coffin that does not look like a coffin. The curves of the Ecopod echo those of a bulging pea pod. The display model, painted in gold and lined with feathers, as if several boas had been unfurled (one presumes from free-range birds) was stunning, and drew gasps of admiration. It is rare to elicit a reaction where people want to curl up in a coffin! The standard range comes in four colours, with a choice of ornamentation including Aztec Sun, Rose Garden and Flying Doves. It includes a calico mattress. It is made of recycled, biodegradable materials and signifies the next stage in the evolution of the cardboard coffin, with its more sophisticated blend of practicality and aesthetics.

The makers of the Ecopod have addressed the need for 'greater ecological responsibility' and this does seem to be a mentality that will gain ground in the consumer experience of death, in much the same way as it has in other consumer areas. 'Eco' is echoing through the funeral trade, not as a passing phase of public taste but as a serious issue for the industry. The advent of radical new forms of coffin is challenging the supremacy of the conventional casket market in much the same way that the rise of organic food is challenging the cellophane-wrapped, polystyrene-packed convenience variety of supermarket fresh produce. This burgeoning sub-culture of alternative approaches to the merchandise of death has implications for the mainstream funeral trade, but as yet it is a long way from being a threat. The groundswell of opposition to GM foods in which the Grim Reaper is being used as an image of protest, and the direct action of crop destruction, all indicate a mood of change which is very gradually moving towards the mainstream and creeping into the culture of death.

This sort of transformation is not new, however. At the beginning of what is not just a new century but a new millennium, the *fin de siècle* phenomenon is particularly charged. It is especially pertinent in the history of death, for the radical changes in the merchandising of death, such as those which we are experiencing now, echo currents of change, which intensified towards the end of the nineteenth century. In each case, the dynamics involve consumerism, costs and backlash, but with significant differences in the direction and impetus for change. The changes towards the end of the twentieth century are about an expansion of consumer choice, and assertion of consumer rights, and represent a backlash against that bland brand of the production-line funeral which characterised the post-war British way of death. We want to make more of death. By contrast, the changes that occurred towards the end of the nineteenth century saw collective energy directed towards curbing rampant consumerism. They were a reaction to excess, to over-the-top mourning rituals, and unnecessarily elaborate funerals. They wanted to make less of death.

Before embarking on a comparison of two centuries of consumerism and death, it is perhaps helpful to paint with a broad brush a sketch of both the nineteenth- and twentieth-century British ways of death. Only in this context is it possible to appreciate how dramatic the changes that started in the 1980s really are. In plotting the evolution of the contemporary consumer model of death, embalming and planning and paying for your own funeral in advance are useful co-ordinates. They are the most distinctive developments to have taken place within the notoriously change-resistant British funeral trade within the last one hundred years. They neatly frame the narrative of twentieth-century death, for embalming was introduced at the beginning of the twentieth century and pre-paid plans towards the end. The psychological distance travelled is immense. The advent of embalming signified a shift to denial and distance from death, a key differential between nineteenth- and twentieth-century attitudes. The development of the pre-need market signifies a more practical rational approach to the inevitable, which promises to be an important difference between this century and the last. Indeed, 'click and buy' coffin shopping services on the internet indicate a psychological shift which, if it continues, could mean that coffins become part of our household clutter, commonplace beside the skis and barbecues in our grandchildren's garages.

Importantly, embalming marked the death knell of domestic death. When the undertaker assumed the role of technical magician with skills and secrets that necessitated the disappearance of the body from the family home, his status was much increased and the culture of death irrevocably changed. The promotion of undertaker to funeral director with an increased range of professional services signified death's transference from a context of community to one of commerce. When death ceased to be a chore for the laying-out women it became hard, impersonal and practical – a matter of money for men. This comprehensive delegation of death to funeral directors is a uniquely twentieth-century phenomenon. In the nineteenth century, the bereaved enlisted the help of the undertaker to supply the necessary trappings for the funeral, but not until the twentieth century did undertakers take such a central role. An etiquette book of 1893 written by Lady Colin Campbell suggests that family involvement was the norm both for the care of the body – 'the necessary offices' – but also with most of the funeral arrangements:

> The arrangements for the funeral are generally directed by the head of the family who expresses his wishes to an undertaker, and leaves the superintendence of the minor details in his hands.

Having said this, she does suggest that the bereaved exercise caution, keeping a close eye on the proceedings, 'or undertakers may carry out *their* ideas, which are too frequently for ostentatious display and the very reverse of simplicity'.

The move towards downplaying death predated the twentieth century. The First World War greatly accelerated the process. The war irrevocably changed the culture of death, and comparisons of pre- and post-war etiquette books illustrate the move towards downsizing funerary ritual. After the war, one gets the sense of society cut adrift from the old protocol, consciously shifting from *memento mori* to *carpe diem*. A guide to form published by *Vogue* in 1935 powerfully conveys this transitional mood:

> In neither men nor women of distinction today does one find the old-fashioned deeply respectable, long drawn out etiquette of sorrow, when one stayed in mourning for years on end, hardly emerging after the loss of one relation before another one dropped off. The awful devastation of war taught us to look upon death after the manner of Hamlet: 'Aye Madam, it is common,' the lot of any of us at any moment, a fact to be faced almost with defiance. Black would be the livery of the world unless the spirit of those left behind rose against it. And it is, after all, life that signifies, not death, no matter how we grieve for our departed.

The abandonment of mourning contributed to the disappearance of death from everyday life. Yet if the bereaved no longer donned black in the same spirit as they had before, they were also in a vacuum as regards appropriate behaviour. Without the clarity of the old protocol, however rigid it may have been, death was becoming increasingly problematic. *Vogue*, for example, felt that for a widow,

> the opera from the social circle of a box would be most unsuitable. But to go quietly to a concert with a friend in the afternoon or to the opera in seats might surely be allowed to a music lover after the first few months of almost prostrating sorrow are over.

There is a sense of a silence descending on death, a climate in which death is not only becoming less visible with the decline of formal mourning dress, but also unmentionable. This is conveyed in another post-war etiquette book in which the author, Constance Burleigh, advises mourners to control their emotions and 'not to harrow with painful questioning those ill fitted to bear it, for morbid curiosity is so cruelly ill-bred'. When visiting the bereaved, 'the caller should not be the first to mention the recent loss, even though this means it is not spoken of at all'.

With the exception of a show of unity for celebrity funerals, public acknowledgement of death for private loss became increasingly taboo, and the emergence of death as taboo corresponds to the rise of the funeral director. Our increasing fear of death created a monopoly for the funeral trade which remained unchallenged until the 1990s and, within an unusual matrix of mystery and money, a lucrative market burgeoned worth approximately £1 billion and representing an average yearly figure of 600,000 funerals. The fear persists that to talk of death is to risk invoking it. By degrees in the twentieth century, this collective reticence consigned death to the area of crisismanagement, something we only deal with when we have to. Like locksmiths, funeral directors belong to that murky sub-culture of human calamity that lurks in the listings of Yellow Pages, those numbers we hope we'll never have to call. Alongside pest control and flood damage repair, locksmiths and funeral directors pedal services which involve an uncomfortable combination of commerce and distress, where the buyer is *in extremis*. In much the same way that having a calm talk about cost is the last thing on your mind when you are locked out of your home at three in the morning, most people don't shop around or quibble about money when there is a dead body in the house.

Complaints about cost dog the funeral trade. It is almost as if we cannot accept the concept of anyone making a living out of death. The funeral trade is perhaps the second oldest profession, and yet while we look tolerantly upon the collision of market forces and sex, we cannot bear the literal profit and loss inherent in the death trade, the idea of bereavement as business. The most comprehensive information about funeral costs is supplied in the annual survey of the Manchester Unity Friendly Society, one of the few organisations to conduct regular research into funeral costs. It provides an invaluable source of reference, including a checklist of questions to ask funeral directors. It is available to the public. I recommend stowing away a copy beside the household appliance instruction books and other infrequently consulted publications in the domestic library – a sort of last-aid manual. Published for the past thirteen years, this survey relies on the mystery shopper method and therefore is one of the most accurate. People are urged to shop around, because even within the same geographical region there can be startling differences. For example, in Nottingham one funeral director quoted a rate for a funeral which was one of the cheapest in the country, while another funeral director in the same neighbourhood quoted nearly double that, a rate which was one of the most expensive in the country. The cost of burials has risen by 25 per cent in the last two years. In April 2000 the average cost for a burial was £2,048, and £1,215 for a cremation.

Jessica Mitford was convinced that RIP meant rip-off, and many people agree with her. To those who ceaselessly complain about the price of funerals, however, my response is 'What about weddings?' It is strikingly illogical to have such a mercenary attitude to one rite of passage, while at the same time showing a flagrant extravagance for another one which increasingly is not a once-in-a-lifetime event. People persist with their belief that the funeral trade is exploitative, but don't seem to bat an eyelid about the caterers, photographers and car hire companies whose price lists and quotes rocket the moment you admit you're arranging a wedding rather than a party. The public seem to have no problem with putting down deposits for tents and wedding dresses, when as a matter of course funeral directors extend credit to complete strangers and commonly allow a gentlemanly ninety days before pressing for payment. I've been to workshops on the bad debts that plague the trade (£20 million of funeral accounts were written off in 1998), but you never hear about this, because exploitation makes better copy than good will and sustains the myth of avarice. Funeral directors commonly carry out the funerals of children at no charge, showing a level of compassion which is not evident in private medicine, which is perhaps equally a 'distress purchase situation'.

The funeral trade is hounded by accusations of opportunistic greed. Yet less often is it considered what they actually do. Being instructed in April to retrieve a body from a house where there is a Christmas card in the letterbox, the paddling-pool drowning of a toddler in the garden – these are things I've heard funeral directors talk about. Increasingly, too, there are violent deaths – the boy beaten to death for refusing a friend a cigarette, the suicides of young men – these are funeral directors' daily round. They also say how, more and more, they see that cruel reversal in which parents bury and burn their children, and octogenarians come in to arrange the funerals of their forty-something offspring. We rarely pause to think about those who play an active role in personal tragedy every day. It is easy to forget the heartache part of the job, for while every job has its headaches, there are few jobs that test the emotions to quite the same degree. Funeral directors all say that the deaths of children get to them, even if they are not parents themselves.

Rather like medicine, the funeral trade seems to run in families. Many is the man heading a successful firm with several branches who in his youth made a toboggan from coffin off-cuts, helped his father to clean the hearse, and saw dead bodies. I've even encountered a mortuary technician whose father was a pathologist and who, when growing up, used to make coffins out of plasticine when his friends made animals. To a greater extent than the media lead us to believe, funeral directors tend to work in family businesses. The bloodlines are long. A. France & Son Ltd of Lambs Conduit Street, Holborn, who today have a reputation as society funeral directors to smart Catholics, have a family connection to funeral directing which spans three centuries. In the nineteenth century, as France and Banting, they were royal undertakers and co-ordinated the funerals of both George III and George IV. More recently, they performed the honours for cookery writer Jennifer Patterson: the Brompton Oratory refused her wish to have her crash helmet on her coffin, and so – with echoes of the grand, aristocratic funerals of the past – Mr Frances's son carried it at the funeral like the baton of the deceased.

As a 211-year-old family firm, Leverton & Sons Ltd are similarly distinguished. As royal warrant holders they were responsible for many of the arrangements for the funeral of the Princess of Wales. Unofficially, they are funeral directors to the famous and have been known to throw journalists off the scent by fibbing about the funeral venue. Given the thriving market for mourning television, there is a growing demand for graveside grief shots. Kenyons formerly held the Royal Warrant, but when the American conglomerate SCI took over the firm, the warrant was withdrawn amidst fears the company might exploit royal associations with unseemly marketing practices. If the American exploitation of presidential deathstyle is anything to go by, this fear was valid. The manufacturers of caskets chosen by the families of US presidents have not been shy to capitalise on the connection. 'The Presidential' is described as 'the Rolls Royce of the casket world':

> A very prestigious casket, of the finest quality. Selected for President Truman, President Kennedy, and Mrs Jackie Kennedy Onassis. Made of Solid Mahogany finished to the highest standard, with finest velvet interior. Clearly recognised as one of the finest handmade caskets in the world.

Public relations have always been problematic for the funeral trade, which have yet to recover from the bad press they received from Charles Dickens and others in the nineteenth century. As 'bedmakers to the dead' undertakers will never be in the ranks of professions that anyone is ever pleased to see. Needing, not wanting, is the basis of customer contact. Funeral directors have been knocked for years. In 1747 they were equally unpopular.

> They are a hard-hearted generation and require more money than brains to conduct their business. I know no one qualification peculiarly necessary to them, except that is a steady, demure and melancholy countenance at command. (R. Campbell, *The London Trademen*, 1747)

In fact, they need no qualifications at all. Although it takes years and exams to qualify to drive a London cab, anyone can be an undertaker – anyone can hire a lock-up shop and become an instant undertaker. No licence is required to store bodies.

In the mid-nineteenth century, a successful London undertaker said of his colleagues,

> In nine cases out of ten the undertaker who has much to do with the corpse is a person of cadaverous hue and you may almost always tell him where you see him. (Edwin Chadwick, 1843)

In my experience of funeral directors, some of them, but by no means all, do indeed give away what they do with a cold handshake, a candle-wax complexion, but most of all with a way of speaking, a solemn voice as slow as a cortège. They also are prone to using phrases that sound like advertising captions, the type of thing you see written on free pens or calendars: 'Big Enough to Cope, Small Enough to Care'; 'Better to Know Us and Not to Need Us, Than Need Us and Not to Know Us'. It is as though, banned from advertising in the media, they speak their own campaigns *sotto voce*. For all the flack they get when dealing with bereaved people, their particular brand of comfort, with its clichés and euphemisms, works. Most of us don't really believe the guff and the jingles that go with the commercials, but we buy the products. It's the same with commercial consolation. Even if we don't really believe 'Absent from the Body, Present with the Lord', it's a harmless lie to buy into if it helps.

I've spent quite a bit of time with funeral directors, trawled the trade fairs, chatted over biers, seen the latest coffin collections at the biannual Paris show – the funeral trade's equivalent of the Motor Show – I've even been asked to the Hearse of the Year Show. My impression is that the average British funeral director is in fact a fairly reticent salesman, who is less happy with the pressure to get into the hard sell and software that an increasingly competitive market requires, than he is to get on with his job of helping families in distress. For that is where a good funeral director's skills lie. They work for the living, not the dead. In the main, they do well by the families they serve. They receive far more letters of thanks than complaints.

In a commercially conscious world, however, image counts. Many funeral homes are being made over. The dusty net curtains and dead flies are being consigned to history as the funeral directors are waking up to the possibilities of public relations. They are transforming their premises with soft pastel paint schemes, even softer sofas, and price lists. This is progress, for it was only in 1995 that the trade got its knuckles rapped by the Consumers' Association for 'breathtaking complacency' after its researchers found that the majority of funeral directors they approached failed to supply clear information about costs, and in many cases scribbled down rough estimates on scraps of paper or the backs of business cards. Given that pre-need is the way ahead, funeral homes want to encourage people to 'drop in' to plan and pay for their own funeral while hale and hearty. With the number of single childless households booming, funeral planning could become the twenty-first century version of the bottom drawer trousseau. Bridget Jones can't count on a wedding, but a funeral is a certainty, and when the time comes she will find plenty of scope to do it her way.

Slowly, the funeral trade is kicking off the traces of tradition. The quill pen and ledger mentality is being replaced by electronic systems. More women are being employed in what was formerly an all-male trade, enhancing the sense of modernisation. New facilities are being added in response to the needs of increasingly multi-cultural communities. Carpet burns caused by Chinese Buddhists burning messages for the deceased on his premises inspired one London funeral director to cater more fully for such specialist requirements; he has now introduced purpose-built ritual rooms. Across the board, funeral directors are changing their approach from telling people what they can have to listening to what people want. In what was quite literally a sign of the times, one funeral director even put up a notice 'Gay-friendly' in his window. It would be more honest if others put up signs saying 'We don't do AIDS funerals', because, to their great shame, that is the case with some of the more ignorant funeral directors, who remain caught up in a timewarp of prejudice and fear.

In Britain, it was businessman Howard Hodgson who ushered in the era of Death and the Salesmen. He was a major force behind extending the scope of the funeral director by expanding ancilliary services such as memorials and flowers, and by launching the 'Dignity In Destiny' pre-need plan. A third-generation son of a traditional family undertaker and a gilded son of Thatcher's Britain, he gave a cottage industry a wake-up call, and introduced twentieth-century business strategy to a dusty, fusty sector which was essentially stuck in a nineteenth-century mentality. Old-fashioned and fragmented, the industry was ripe for change, and in Hodgson's view it had its own lack of business acumen to blame for many of its problems. He could see the economic factors that were hampering the traditional small family business. In his autobiographical business book *How to Become Dead Rich* (1992), he outlines the context:

> The cost of a funeral in 1950, for a hearse, coffin, two cars, church service and grave was £27 10d. The average weekly wage was only £3, so my oft-quoted maxim that a funeral cost nine times the post-war working wage, whereas in the 1980s it was only three times, is correct.

From first-hand experience of his father's firm Hodgson identified a problem which was universal – namely, fixed overheads and fluctuating funeral rates. The potential solutions – a sudden upsurge in the deathrate, or drumming up more funerals – were both unfeasible. An alternative approach was consolidation. It was this concept of turning rivals into partners, resulting in persuasive economies of scale, that was the secret of his success. He could see that there were far too many firms in competition and sensed that many would be only too happy to call it a day. In nitty-gritty terms, his tactics were rationalisation and centralisation. They worked. He built up an empire which, at its peak, was responsible for 65,000 funerals a year. As well as earning him the soubriquet 'the Lord Hanson of the funeral trade', this success made him a vast personal fortune. As a study of entrepreneurial nerve his career is exemplary. He transformed his family business from near-receivership to a publicly quoted company valued at £90 million.

Hodgson's own personal style was equally revolutionary. With his Jermyn Street shirts and Knightsbridge haircut he challenged the conventional image of the undertaker: the man in black with a sober suit and quiet tie, a fob watch perhaps his only accessory. Hodgson looked like a male model and posed like one, notably for the *Sunday Times,* standing in a cemetery in a camel cashmere Crombie and trilby, like a glamorous gangster after a shopping spree in Savile Row. He also loved the limelight. By putting an industry more used to being in the shade into the headlines, the Sunday supplements and on the television, he single-handedly raised the profile of the funeral trade and gave it a new lease of life.

The revolution which Hodgson started entered another dramatic phase when, in 1994, the American conglomerate Service Corporation International (SCI) – the largest funeral group in the world – entered the British market by acquiring Hodgson's former companies, the Great Southern Group and Plantsbrook. The headline 'Invasion of the Body Snatchers' sums up how welcome their arrival was to the British funeral trade. Their 'Catch 'em with a tear in their eye' reputation preceded them and resulted in a spate of sensational media coverage. Tales of dubious sales practices abound, such as the 'SCI stroke' which a former salesmen alleges was a standard part of training; with this method in the casket selection room, the salesman merely points fairly swiftly at each of the less expensive caskets, but touches and strokes in a lingering way the more expensive model he wants the client to buy. Undercover films shown on British television have further fanned the flames of sensation and contributed to a storm of publicity – which is really in a teacup, given the fact that SCI have not 'Disney-fied' the English funeral trade. The publicity they receive is disproportionate to the actual size of their stake in the market – around 13 per cent, compared with 25 per cent controlled by Co-operative Funeral Services and 62 per cent by the independent sector. To ensure that you are not dealing with SCI masquerading as an old-style independent family firm, simply ask whether the funeral director is a member of SAIF, the Society of Allied and Independent Funeral Directors. This is the equivalent of a clove of garlic and a cross for sorting out bona fide British firms from bought-up ones trading on traditional loyalty without declaring their new ownership.

Hodgson's influence has extended to the funeral trade at large. The fact that, standing in a bright exhibition hall buzzing with people, I had the chance to buy my own funeral from a funeral director whose line in public relations patter was only marginally less impressive than his line in coffins, is proof of Hodgson's lasting legacy. Post-Hodgson, pre-need is the part of the business that the funeral trade is most keen to develop. Faced with a stable death rate until the babyboomers start to die, it is its most effective way to generate revenue. Also, by taking the transaction away from the context of crisis, in theory it represents opportunities for advertising that remain out of bounds in the 'at need' market. Happily, to date our commercial breaks have been spared the type of adverts conjured up by Monty Python with 'Arthur Sodgen of Prestatyn, the Fastest Funeral Director in Wales' who promised customers 'free wine glasses with every certified stiff'.

Yet those of a sensitive disposition had a close call recently with the proposed ads for Burymeright, an online pre-need funeral service. In one of their ads, to the theme music from *This is Your Life*, a figure clad in black emerges from the mist with four pallbearers. When the camera pans to the coffin, we see that it has been sawn in half. Simultaneously the caption 'Magician's Assistant' appears. Next, a hand zips up a body bag and then two men in donkey jackets are seen throwing the same bag into a grave as the title 'Dustman' appears on screen. In the final sequence, the coffin of a game-show host moves along a crematorium conveyor belt followed by a set of matching luggage, wine and a cuddly toy. As the theme music fades, the words 'burymeright.com – go your own way' appear on screen. As far as the ad regulators were concerned, Burymeright got it all wrong with such an overtly flippant approach to funerals, bringing too much black comedy to a subject conventionally handled with care. Their irreverent approach to pre-need was deemed unfit for human consumption. It was banned from being shown in cinemas, although it can be seen on their website.

Yet this reticence is odder than it might initially appear. It seems extraordinary, given how uninhibited the mass media are about sex, that they remain so inhibited about death. Even in healthcare advertisements people look well, and jaunty jingles – 'You're Amazing – We Want You to Stay That Way' – dispense with unwelcome associations. It was not until 1992 that the first-ever transmission of an advertisement for the funeral trade was broadcast on television. It was, of course, for pre-need and suitably subtle in the way that silver-haired senior citizens arranging flowers tend to be. The only hitch occurred when it was realised that one advertising slot had inadvertently been booked around a programme called *Highway To Heaven*. The slot was duly cancelled.

For most people in this country it remains anathema to think of a funeral as anything other than a distress purchase. The idea of planning and paying for our own funeral ahead of time is very much the exception rather than the rule. Currently only 3 per cent of funerals are 'pre-need' sales. This is strikingly low compared to elsewhere in Europe, where pre-need accounts for around 70 per cent of sales in Belgium and the Netherlands, and around 50 per cent in Spain. In this country the seeds of change may have been sown, but they have yet to germinate. One method of trying to chip away at this mental block is to employ marketing methods which play on the universal tendency of people at funerals to speculate on the wishes of the deceased. At weddings people tend to speculate whether it's what the bride would have wanted if she had had her own way, but at funerals when people don't know what to say, they are likely to declare that 'it's just what he'd have wanted'. The Dignity Plan – brought to Britain in 1996 by Service Corporation International – appealed to this tendency with a print campaign which emphasised the idea of funerals tailor-made to the buyer's wishes, so that there would be no doubt that the funeral was what the deceased wanted. 'There's a spot overlooking the 18th green where my ashes will be scattered, mingled with those of my hickory shaft putter', one advertisement went, 'for people who turn up there will be cocktails in the club house or mulled wine if it's winter.' There does seem to be more than a whiff of the American way about this particular commercial, conjuring up an image of a cortège of golf buggies and of mourners in plaid slacks and spike shoes covering bits of their friend with earth, rather as if replacing a divot. It would certainly not be par for the course at Wentworth. With more foresight and market research SCI might have appealed to the hearts of Englishmen with something like 'The Ashes', at Lords has happy memories for me, and there's a spot by the Members' Stand where I want mine scattered. For people who turn up there will be tea in the pavilion.'

Again, there is a poignant contrast here with nineteenth-century practice. The thrust of the marketing of the modern pre-paid funeral is based on securing peace of mind and sparing relatives inconvenience. In this regard, the modern version varies greatly from its nineteenth-century equivalent, which was motivated by real terror of a pauper burial. As a result of the Anatomy Act of 1832, the bodies of those who died in poverty could be given over to anatomists. Previously, the legal supply of corpses for anatomy schools had been provided by the victims of public execution, but there were not enough felons and murderers to satisfy demand, and the rapacity of the Resurrectionists caused the government to bring about a change in the law to regulate the supply.

Body-snatchers and 'corpse kings' were the bogeymen of the early nineteenth-century psyche. Such illustrious characters as Joseph Naples, who called himself '*Resurgam homo*' and kept a grim log book of his work, haunted the dreams of the poor. Protection of the dead became an obsession that spawned a commercial market with 'mortsafes' and metal coffins much in demand. An advertisement by a funeral director from this period shows the concern: 'Improved coffins – the fastenings of these important receptacles being on such principles as to render it impracticable for the grave-robbers to open them.'

In an idiosyncratic twist of the law resulting from the theory that the body cannot be possessed, body-snatching was not illegal. The law itself, therefore, was an accessory to the crime. By contrast, the theft of grave clothes, coffins and their fixtures constituted a criminal offence. To foil body-snatchers, a range of elaborate contraptions was devised, including iron coffins and high-security hearses, 'so that the body cannot be stolen out during a journey into the country as has happened to the common hearses'. A promotional pamphlet by the Royal Patent Burial Company in 1818, a firm specialising in this type of merchandise 'for the safeguard of the dead', provides a detailed account of a widespread practice, although one senses that its sensationalism owes much to salesmanship. It suggests that the 'abominable traffic' is such that 5,000 corpses are taken annually from graves and vaults to supply hospital lecture rooms and private medical schools in London and Edinburgh. Even country churchyards were unsafe. Rarely visited from one Sunday to the next, they provided plenty of scope for grave robbers:

> If the mould of a new grave be disturbed, it is easily accounted for; the Parson's cow is feeding there, or the pigs have been routing about it, or the school boy has been heedlessly playing over it, and thus suspicion passes over. But the country churchyards prove very productive for the Grave Robbers.

It goes on:

> Indeed sometimes the dashing vehicle which was designed to carry the dogs to the hunt, is employed to bring up the dead to London.

Although the rich could afford the trappings of security and could pay people to guard their graves, the body-snatchers struck where they could. In January 1822 the *Observer* newspaper reported that

> the inhabitants of the village of Hammersmith were thrown into a state of considerable excitement last week in consequence of the body of Mr Alexander Wilson, a private Gentleman of King Street, having been stolen from his house by a gang of body-snatchers.

In the macabre market for corpses, the fresher the better; there was a premium on bodies secured prior to burial. Burke and Hare, commonly thought of as grave-robbers, were in fact body-snatchers, and although their fame has resulted in the assumption that Edinburgh was the capital of the corpse trade, business was brisk elsewhere. Grave-robbing and body-

snatching were rife in London, where some of the more enterprising entrepreneurs even went so far as to export bodies by boat to Scotland, cam-
ouflaging the cadavers in cargoes of blacking and cured pork.

Although fear of falling into the hands of the anatomists permeated all
sectors of society, the Anatomy Act meant that the poor were most at risk.
Their fear of dying in the workhouse and ending up on a dissecting slab
was the reason for the nineteenth-century version of the pre-need funeral.
For many working-class people, funerals were organised and financed
through burial clubs, which were at their most popular from the 1840s until
the development of the welfare state around the time of the First World
War. The origins of burial clubs lie deep in the past – with short-lived local
self-help organisations in the seventeenth and eighteenth centuries, or perhaps even with laymen's religious confraternities that flourished on the eve
of the Reformation – and were later formalised into co-operative friendly
societies, a few of which still survive, albeit in altered form.

Friendly societies varied in size, ambition and formality. They had two
main purposes: payment in case of sickness or inability to work, and payment to a member's widow in the event of his death. This expenditure was
funded out of small cash payments made weekly or monthly by club members. In time, some friendly societies built up substantial sums which were
then invested in order to generate larger returns. The sum paid to a member's widow was not specifically ear-marked to cover funeral costs; rather,
it was to function as funeral money and a sort of low-level life insurance all
in one; the widow could presumably spend the money as she wished.

At its simplest, a burial society might consist only of a circle of friends,
neighbours and colleagues. When one of the circle died, the others were
each expected to chip in with a set amount towards the funeral. On a
slightly more sophisticated level, burial societies might collect dues regularly, hence building up a fund from which burials could be financed so as
to avoid the delay in gathering up the requisite money. Most of these
groups did not last long, in part because – once the 'circle' was growing old
and dying off – no young person would want to join and be left with lots of
expense and the prospect of outliving the rest of the group. On the other
hand, some schemes – but far from all of them – allowed families to insure
against the deaths of their young children. In this case, given infant mortality rates, young parents were more likely to 'benefit' from the scheme than
were older people. Local burial societies were disproportionately popular
in the north-west, particularly in Lancashire. In 1874, Preston and its district
had a population of about 86,000, but 108,120 burial society memberships –
a sign that some people double- or treble-insured – an activity which was il-

legal, but which at the same time demonstrates the almost compulsive anxiety to avoid a pauper's burial.

The other means by which working-class people financed their last rites were the large-scale 'collection societies', which were basically a form of burial insurance. Most were based around Liverpool and Glasgow; several were affiliated with the Roman Catholic church. In 1874, there were approximately 550,000–650,000 adult members of these societies. The largest, the Royal Liver Friendly Society [sic], had 600,000 members; the second largest, the Liverpool Victoria Legal Society, had 200,000. They were large, impersonal and critics claimed they were run mostly for the benefit of their employees, rather than the members, who had almost no say in their administration. Canvassers (who might take a 25 per cent cut of receipts) sold policies door-to-door, targeting the very poor and playing on fears of body-snatching and the social stigma of not receiving proper burial. Of premiums collected, anywhere from 40 to 55 per cent might be spent on 'administrative costs'. There was no oversight whatsoever, and abuses were rife: refusal to pay out claims, encouraging people to miss single payments in order to invalidate policies, and outright embezzlement of funds. Yet it is striking that more people took up these policies than participated in the more broad-based friendly societies – powerful evidence that people were more willing to pay money to secure a decent burial than, say, to insure themselves against ill health and resulting unemployment.

Predictably, the governing classes found various aspects of these arrangements deeply worrying. There were complaints that friendly societies regularly spent some of their funds on liquor, both for drinking at the monthly meetings, and as a funeral expense; the boozy 'wake' was an aspect of north-western working-class culture which found little resonance amid the corridors of Westminster. Politicians also worried that friendly societies sometimes made unsafe, unsecured investments, and that their activities were not sufficiently scrutinised or regulated.

More sensationally, it was also alleged that poor families were murdering their children in order to collect the funeral insurance for them. While the Parliamentary Select Committee on the Friendly Society Bill of 1854 found that there was so little evidence of this that there was no need to legislate with reference to it, the following year's Act raised the level of funeral benefit to £6 for an infant under 5 years, and £10 for a child aged 5–10. Yet in 1865, Edwin Chadwick claimed to have come across child murder for burial money during his investigations into the causes of destitution. The story ran and ran. In 1874, a Royal Commission studied the issue yet again. The Commissioners summoned coroners from the north-west to report to them; while seventy-five pronounced themselves unable or unwilling to comment, forty-five replied that they were aware of evidence of child murder for funeral money. For instance, Mr Aspinal, the coroner for Liverpool, said that he had not the slightest doubt that an immense amount of parental neglect, of a most scandalous character, went on in Liverpool, and that 'I am really most disposed to think that the neglect is greater than it would be, on account of the prospect, at the end of the child's term of lingering, of the club money.' The Commission further noted that in Liverpool, there was a marked rise in the rate of mortality just after the age of one year – in other words, just at the point where an infant first became eligible for burial society membership. The Commission also found instances where infants had been signed up to more than one burial society. Despite this, however, it does not appear that the resulting Friendly Societies Act (1875) was directed in any very clear way against this problem. Perhaps, in the age of the cult of domesticity, this was simply a very poignant and powerful way in which to suggest that industrial, urban poverty was making the poor ever more 'unnatural' and inhuman, and hence increasing the perceived need to regulate them.

Fears about mistreatment of the dead have not gone away. Even today there are still faint echoes of the bad old days of body violation and anxiety about anatomists with an interest in procuring corpses to harvest. The Alder Hey hospital case in Liverpool, in which it became clear that the organs of hundreds of children had been retained by the hospital without their parents' permission, highlighted the deficiencies of modern law, whereby body parts may be used for the advancement of medical science without the consent or even the knowledge of relatives. The law presumes consent. Although rationally we have no need to worry about actual corpse theft, the compulsion to protect the body remains strong. It is reflected in contemporary casket catalogues where specifications resonate with the language of security: '20-gauge steel', 'hermetically sealed', 'a zinc interior case for extra protection', and even one model, The Edwardian, that offers what must be the ultimate assurance: 'Each casket has its own key.' An iron coffin in an age of grave-robbers is an example of an obvious connection between what people buy and why, the simple mechanics of supply and demand. But in considering death as a consumer experience, there are not always such rational connections between the supply and demand relating to a massive variety of merchandise. My all-time favourite example was unearthed in America by Jessica Mitford in the form of burial footware – the sublime Fit-a-Fut Oxford shoe, available in calf, tan or oxblood.

Death styles have altered not only in their detail, but in the deep urges informing them. In the nineteenth century the primary motivation in burial, as in much else, was conformity. In contrast, the growing trend at the start of the twenty-first century is individuality. Where Victorian protocol exerted massive pressure on people to behave like other people, today the pressure is to be different, to express oneself. This is the age of the customised coffin, the 'personal message from the grave' funeral video; funeral directors also report that more and more people want to be buried in their own clothes. There is a growing preoccupation that every detail of the funeral should be in character. In the nineteenth century the priority was doing the right thing, which meant buying the right things. Consciousness of status informed the scope of these decisions. Where our ancestors spent money to be like other people or – even better – to show superiority to other people, increasingly we are spending money to assert our difference. Doing the right thing has become doing your own thing.

Sandwiched between nineteenth-century conformity and twenty-first century individuality is twentieth-century uniformity. This is characterised by the impersonal, production line cremations that became standard in the post-war period, and represented a classless practicality that was a legacy of the war in society at large. In *Funeral Formalities and Obligations* (1936), the author R. Willoughby conveys the post-war zeitgeist:

> Whereas a few years ago there was a popular feeling that unless the cortège was of a lavish nature, there was the stigma of disrespect for the dead, we are now more practical minded, and the plainer the funeral within the limits of decency the better for all concerned.

In this climate, the funeral director supplied the ceremonial equivalent of standard issue to an undiscerning consumer who was content to have what everyone else was having. Until the self-assertion of the 1980s, rightly called the 'me decade', this was, in the main, the British way of death.

Of course, changes of attitude are gradual, and in spite of the recent trend towards consumerism relating to self-expression, status consciousness remains significant as a motive for spending money on a funeral. It resonates not only in the names of caskets – the Royale, the Baronet – but also features in the marketing of merchandise in the murky area of 'funeral requisites'. 'Funeral requisites' is a front for the things that no body needs – clothes, a frilled satin mattress and matching pillow – but that the funeral trade wants you to buy. And how do you persuade funeral directors to sell and customers to buy clothes for coffin wear, and bedding whose 'pillows never ruffle'? You appeal to status. So these shiny, synthetic garments are given grand names, as if the less functional the product the fancier the name necessary to market it. In one catalogue alone, I came across San-dringham, Sovereign, Monarch and Ambassador – the latter a rather natty 'velvet' creation with 'cravat front', a sort of cut-price Noel Coward. It could be set off to perfection with a matching tasselled brocade cap of the sort Norman Parkinson used to wear.

Snobbery, an ache to ape blue-blooded funerary practice, has long been the lifeblood of the death trade. It is bound up in the beginnings of the trade and is still present in the popular concept of a 'good send-off': a horse-drawn hearse, floral tributes the size of snooker tables, a pricey casket with as many specs as a luxury customised car. The funeral trade was founded in the seventeenth century on the middle-class wish to emulate the pomp and panoply of heraldic funerals – funerals that were strictly regulated by the College of Arms, and the exclusive preserve of the aristocracy. The first undertakers were entrepreneurial opportunists who eventually succeeded in undermining the authority of the College of Arms and broke their monopoly, putting the trappings of funerary spectacle within reach of lesser beings with the money to pay for it. In 1735 the College of Arms complained about 'undertakers, painters and others' who had 'presumed to marshal direct the proceeding of solemn funerals without regard to the right of arms and likewise employ mean persons to carry trophies of honour at such funerals'. Commercialised undertaking had been born.

Status consciousness seems to be a psychological trait with a long history. Bronze Age graves have been found containing grave goods – batons, fine daggers and items for the purposes of display – showing a concern in death to reflect the station and attributes of the warrior and hero. In the eighteenth century, anticipating the market for 'funeral requisites' with her concern about what to wear for her big day, Alexander Pope's Narcissa shows that death as a sartorial problem (and satirical subject) has a long tradition: 'One would not; sure, be frightful when one's dead – Betty give this cheek a little red.' Narcissa does not want to be seen dead in wool. At the end of the seventeenth century a Burial in Wool Act was passed to promote the British wool trade with fines if other materials were used. This was a blow to the vanity of many women. Lady Brompton, in Richard Steele's play *The Funeral: Grief a la Mode* (1700) pleads: 'Harkee hussy, if you should, as I hope you won't, outlive me, take care I ain't buried in flannel; 't would never become me I'm sure.' Narcissa similarly would prefer to pay and display herself in something finer:

Odious in woollen! It would a saint provoke,

(were the last words that poor Narcissa spoke)
No, let a charming chintz and Brussels lace
Wrap my cold limbs, and shade my lifeless face.
(Alexander Pope, *Epistle 1, Epistles to Several Persons*,
in *Moral Essays*, 1734)

Narcissa was in fact based on the popular actress Anne Oldfield whose last words when she died in 1730 were a request not to be buried in wool. According to her biographer William Egerton (*Faithful Memoirs of Mrs Anne Oldfield*, 1731), her death-wish was granted:

> Mrs Oldfield was nicely dressed after her Decease; being by Mrs Saunder's Direction then laid in her coffin. She had on a very fine Brussels lace Head, a Holland shift with a Tucker, and double Ruffles of the same Lace, a pair of New Kid Gloves, and her body was wrapped in a winding sheet.

If human psychology has disposed people to want to show their status in death, then the eighteenth century provided unprecedented opportunities to acquire the material things necessary so to do. The mass production that characterised the industrial revolution was a catalyst for a consumer revolution. In a frenzy of getting and spending, people for the first time experienced the novelty of purse power, and the thrill of buying what they wanted, rather than simply what they needed. Suddenly, ordinary people were able to emulate those of higher social status by buying consumer goods. The concept of affordable luxury inherent in such goods as Wedgwood's 'Queensware' applied equally to the paraphernalia of death. In London, Southwark became a centre for the production of coffin furniture, Whitechapel a centre for coffin-makers and the manufacture of elaborate outer cases for coffins, while Spitalfields became capital of the 'black stuff' industry, which made now-obsolete funeral trappings such as horse velvets, cloaks, palls and so forth. Birmingham was also an important centre for the trade when new industrial processes made it possible for metal workers to mass-produce coffin fixtures and fittings.

Fashion fuelled the consumer boom, and what was most fashionable was most desirable. Even death was not exempt from the vagaries of fashion. In fact, the rise of fashion magazines with coloured plates made women more fashion-conscious than ever before, and this extended to mourning dress. Fashion even affected men's hairstyles. The author of *Notices Historical and Miscellaneous Concerning Mourning Apparel* (1850) writes

For instance with those who wore hair powder (which was introduced here from France early in the 18th century) its use was during the first stage of mourning discontinued; and even the tiewig, then worn was studiously dressed out of curl. Hair powder on being taxed by Mr Pitt soon went out of fashion.

Fashion and death jar horribly, and although in the nineteenth century the merchandising of mourning dress became bound up with fashion, thankfully good sense prevailed towards the end of the century. Interestingly, the editors of *Vogue*, the main mouthpiece of fashion and dress, were unequivocal about the dubious mix of fashion and mourning, and in their book of etiquette said of mourning that 'it should not have the look, even for the young, of being what shopkeepers call "the very latest thing". The last word in fashion is not the word for a widow.' Over and beyond fashion, however, a constant influence in the merchandising of death is custom and a sense of 'form'. These factors have exerted a different kind of pressure on people to buy certain things.

Protocol was the hub of the nineteenth-century funeral trade. The middle classes paid handsomely for a diluted version of an aristocratic funeral. Their principal concern was respectability, and this was at the core of the buying and selling of the merchandise of mourning and funerals. Poor Joe Gargery in *Great Expectations* (1860–61) shows the force of social pressure when he admits to Pip he felt compelled to enlist the services of Trabb and Co.:

> I would have in preference carried her the church myself, but it were considered wot the neighbours would look down on such and would be of opinions as it were wanting in respect.

The extraordinary changes in people's physical mobility following the development of the railways correlates with a surge of social mobility. The nineteenth century was the era of the upwardly mobile, of acquisition, aspiration and emulation. It was the golden age of the self-made. Triple-shell coffins, mutes, elaborate hearses, extensive distribution of hatbands, scarves and cloaks for mourners, impressive mourning coaches where the longer the line of empty coaches the greater the kudos – all were symptomatic of an epidemic of the social disease of snobbery. *The Times* railed against these middle-class delusions of grandeur in a leader in 1875:

> It is within the last half century that prodigious funerals, awful hearses drawn by pretenatural quadrupeds, clouds of black plumes, solid and mag-

nificent oak coffins, instead of the sepulchral elm, coffin within coffin, lead brick graves and capacious catacombs have spread downwards far beyond the select circle once privileged to illustrate the vanity of human greatness.

Martin Chuzzlewit's son was not alone in wanting his father's funeral to be 'perfectly profuse in feathers'. This mentality is evident in accounts of the funerals of 'Liverpool Celebrities', as described in a curious funeral anthology of distinguished burghers and businessmen of the city which vividly conveys the concept of the funeral as parade and spectacle. One of these civic celebrities was Sir John Bent (d. 1857) of Rake Lane, a brewer and former mayor who had been knighted by Queen Victoria after a visit to the city in 1850. 'No man in Liverpool stood higher in the estimation of all classes than that said gentleman.' The funeral cortège consisted of a hearse and three mourning coaches, the Mayor's carriage and eight other carriages. Interment was in a private vault in a prime position in Toxteth Park New Cemetery in a coffin 'of the finest oak with gilt furnishings and handles'.

> Messers Woolwright and Company of Bold Street acted as the undertakers, and having confided to them the entire management of the ceremonial proceedings we need not say in naming so eminent a house that the arrangements were faultless, the appointments perfect and everything comme il faut.

For another distinguished citizen, Sir William Brown (d. 1864) of Cabbage Hall, particular effort was made with regard to the horses.

> The hearse and eight mourning coaches were each drawn by four horses; and the style in which the equipages were turned out, the whole of the thirty-six horses being fairly matched elicited admiration from a large number of the spectators.

Although having sprung from humble beginnings as the son of a well-known builder, the late Alderman Dover was keen to have a grand ending.

> By great natural abilities and determination of character he rose to a position of influence and respectability. He was emphatically a self-made man ... Following the hearse containing the body, which was in a shell and polished oak coffin with brass plates, were three mourning coaches, the family carriage of the deceased, closed, the mayor's carriage and fourteen private carriages (without occupants).

The appetite for impressive funerals created a lucrative market for those in the dismal trade. The options for pomp and pageant are evident in undertaker's price lists. One London firm offered seven different funerals, ranging from the one-horse option at £3 5s. to the 12-horse, top end of the range funeral at £53. The details of these packages show the emphasis on display, both at the higher and lower end of the market:

> Funeral costing £3 5s. – Patent carriage, with one horse; smooth elm coffin, neatly finished, lined inside with pillow &c; use of pall, mourners fittings, coachman with hatband, bearers, attendants with hatband, &c.
>
> Funeral costing £53 – Hearse and four horses, two mourning coaches with fours, twenty-three plumes of rich ostrich feathers, complete velvet covering for carriages and horses, and an esquire's plume of best feathers; strong elm shell, with tufted mattress, lined and ruffled with superfine cambric, and pillow: full worked glazed cambric winding sheet, stout outside lead coffin with inscription plate and solder complete: one and a half-inch oak case, covered with black or crimson velvet set with three rows round, and lid panelled with best brass nails: stout brass plate of inscription richly engraved: four pairs of best brass handles and grips, lid ornaments to correspond: use of silk velvet pall : two mutes with gowns, silk hat bands and gloves : fourteen men as pages, feathermen and coachmen with truncheons and wands silk hatbands &c use of mourners' fittings; and attendant with silk hatband &c." (Cassell's *Household Guide*, 1870)

The commercial imitation of the aristocratic funeral set an expensive standard for the middle classes in the nineteenth century. Indeed, it represented a form of social bondage. People felt compelled to buy into it, and yet ironically they were largely unaware of the original symbolism of what they were purchasing. This ignorance was demonstrated in a cross-examination between Edwin Chadwick and an undertaker, Mr Wild, for Chadwick's 1843 government report on the practice of interment in towns:

> Question – Are you aware that the array of funerals commonly made by undertakers is strictly the array of a baronial funeral – the two men who stand at the doors being supposed to be the two porters of the castle with their staves, in black; the man who heads the procession, wearing a scarf, being a representative of a herald-at-arms; the man who carries a plume of feathers on his head being an esquire, who bears the shield and casque, with its plume of feathers; the pallbearers, with batons, being representatives of knights companions-at-arms; the men walking with wands being supposed to represent gentlemen ushers, with their wands; are you aware that this is said to be the origin and type of the common array usually provided by those who undertake to perform funerals?

Answer – No, I am not aware of it.

Question – It may be presumed that those who order funerals are equally unaware of the incongruity for which such expense is incurred?

Answer – Undoubtedly, they are.

Again, it comes back to the power of the wish to conform. Elsewhere in Chadwick's illuminating report he asks Mr Wild about costs:

Question – Are the ordinary expenses and inconveniences of funerals generally severely oppressive to persons of the middle classes?

Answer – Very generally; it often occurs that a poor widow is crippled in her means through life by the expense of a funeral.

Asked if savings could be made, Mr Wild concedes that 'For about 50 per cent less they could be done'. The desire to appear respectable by adhering to mourning and funeral protocol outweighed all other concerns, even later financial hardship. The shackles of custom were simply too strong to escape, as Mr Wild tells Mr Chadwick when Chadwick asks:

Is not much of the accompaniments of funerals, which as at present conducted are deemed part of the solemnity, questionable in effect as well as appropriateness? Is it not the effect of custom, rather than choice or wish of the parties?

Mr Wild – Merely customary; the term used in giving orders is to provide what is customary.

On a similar note, a campaigner for funerary reform, the vicar of All Saints, Pontefract, was particularly incisive about the nineteenth-century social climber for whom a funeral represented a summit to scale from which one may look down on one's peers:

What makes the parade of wealth at funerals so particularly odious is, that it is the carrying out our propensity to 'stand on tiptoe' and overtop our fellows, even in the sacred and humbling presence of death; we want to make the poor corpse assert his superiority over other common corpses. Hence, the board of feathers, the four horses with their gloomy trappings, hence the mutes with their fatuous solemnity; hence – greatest mockery of all! – the long train of empty carriages, and then as if to rebuke all this lies the speechless, passionless, clay unheeding of this funeral pomp, unconscious of the pageantry intended to do it – or perhaps the survivors – honour. (Joseph Hammond, *Funeral Reform*, 1875)

It is important to put the nineteenth-century middle-class leaning towards impressive funerals into perspective, for there is a common misconception that the Victorians were 'obsessed with death' and revelled in flashy funerals. In fact, it is not the funeral that characterises nineteenth-century excess, so much as the weight of mourning protocol. Although there was a love of the funeral as spectacle in the first half of the century, soon after Queen Victoria ascended the throne in 1837 there were the first murmurs of funerary reform and calls for moderation. Victoria's strong identification as a widow has created an erroneous view in the eyes of posterity that her subjects were similarly pathologically morbid. They were not, although there were some eccentrics like the Earl of Portsmouth who evidently had 'an invincible penchant for funerals – "black jobs" as the Mad Lord used to call them'. Throughout the second half of the nineteenth century there was a shift in mentality from elaborate funerary spectacle to funerary simplicity. Those promoting funerary reform became increasingly impassioned in their bid for less expensive and elaborate ceremonies. Their campaigns were given credence by the tendency among eminent people to have less elaborate funerals than had formerly been the case. For example, in 1845 *The Times* applauded the funeral style of one of the Princess of Wales's forebears, Earl Spencer, who was buried at Althorp with only one mourning coach and an 'absence of parade or ostentatious ceremony'. The fact that those who determined what the 'done thing' was now did less, encouraged the shift towards downscaling what had been at one time ludicrously over-the-top funerals.

The Duke of Wellington's funeral in 1852 provides a useful dividing line between funerary profligacy and the move to moderation. It was the apogee of extravagance, costing £100,000. The bargain send-off Nelson got cost a mere £15,000. As a state funeral for a hero it was by its very nature designed to be a hugely impressive spectacle – a tribute to a victorious imperial power, as much as to an individual person. Ironically, the ducal death style was infinitely grander than Wellington's Spartan lifestyle had been, given his preference for sleeping on a soldier's camp bed with a thin horsehair mattress and a leather pillow. Contemporary accounts of the incredibly complicated funeral arrangements make highly entertaining reading. At times solemnity threatened to turn into farce. For example, things did not get off to a propitious start when it was discovered that the enormous quadruple state coffin would not fit into the Duke's room:

> Before the state coffin could be introduced into the Duke's room it was found necessary to remove the little camp iron bedstead, the common deal wardrobe, chest of drawers, the table and three chairs which constituted the whole furniture of the room. The floor of the apartment was covered

with black cloth, and upon a frame covered with velvet stood the coffin oc-
cupying the greater part of the narrow apartment. (Charles Maybury
Archer, *Complete Guide to Funeral of Duke of Wellington*, 1852)

Things did not get easier during the actual funeral when owing to the
height of the hearse special arrangements had to be made to manoeuvre it
through Temple Bar.

As the car will be some feet higher than the top of the gate at Temple Bar,
which is only 17 feet high, advantage will be taken of the halt occasioned by
the civic authorities falling into the procession to lower the body of the car
by machinery so as to allow its passing through. (Charles Maybury Archer,
1852)

Wellington's funeral was literally the height of funerary opulence, and a
national triumph. The coffin was covered in crimson velvet; a splendid pall
made by seventy workmen cost 500 guineas. This must have looked breathtaking against the black hangings of a specially arranged funeral chamber
in Chelsea Hospital where the Duke's body lay in state prior to the funeral.
The grandeur was further enhanced by the presence of pairs of soldiers
with arms reversed standing in niches all along the funeral chamber. The
otherwise dark chamber was lit by eighty-three enormous candelabra,
catching in their glow the glittering, silver star-studded canopy over the
bier, and a cloth of gold that draped the dais where the coffin lay. All this afforded the mourners a spectacle 'the magnificence of which surpasses anything that has hitherto been seen in this country by way of funeral
decoration'. The chamber remained open to the public for some weeks
after the funeral and the whole event captured their imagination. A commemorative issue of the *Illustrated London News* was credited with boosting
circulation from 130,000 copies sold in 1851 to 150,000 in 1852. It was the last
of its kind, a great state funeral for a national hero, lavish in every particular, from the finest Genoa horse velvets, to the elaborate coffin which, like
a set of Russian dolls, consisted of four cases. The first, containing the body,
was an inner plain deal coffin; then a larger oak coffin; this in turn was
placed within a hermetically sealed leaden coffin weighing 25cwt; and finally, there was a splendid outer shell of solid Spanish mahogany sporting
the type of handles used on royal coffins.

What is striking is the extent to which the use of material has become
obsolete in contemporary funerary ritual. We have no equivalent to the
dramatic drapery of death which played such a crucial role in nineteenth-
century funerary and mourning rituals. The modern funeral is barely black

at all, but in the nineteenth century the cost of the coffin was dwarfed by the expense of ancillary black materials. These accoutrements of mourning were at the heart of the nineteenth-century funeral trade. Black material was the priority of the nineteenth-century consumer, a tyrannical protocol that even dictated when the funeral took place, for until the necessary outfits had been acquired for the family it could not begin. Black material was the basis of the *magasin de deuil*, the mourning warehouses which flourished in this period. The sheer amount of funerary haberdashery, hatbands, gloves and scarves for distribution to mourners and the strict requirements of mourning dress were the budget buster for the bereaved. Black material was the basis of the Courtauld empire. Fortunes were made on the back of black, but also lost. When, for example, Princess Ameila, daughter of King George III, died, hence necessitating public mourning, the fashion trade and specifically coloured ribbon manufacturers were plunged into crisis and had to close mills. Similarly, when Queen Caroline died, there were 'sacrificial reductions' on coloured chintz. From time to time public appeals were made by the cloth industry to lessen the length of nineteenth-century public mourning by way of damage limitation, for a whole season's fashions could turn into a sad stockpile if a member of the Royal Family died, suddenly turning society black.

Historically, guidance about how to behave with death has come from Court. Old habits die hard, as shown by the way in which the British people instinctively looked to the Queen for navigation when the Princess of Wales died, although it is a sign of the changing times that many were more than willing to criticise her behaviour. The influence of the Court in the past has been two-fold. It has informed the funeral styles of status-conscious people, and on the death of a monarch it has required the British people to rally as subjects and participate in official national mourning. Traditionally, on the death of a monarch, instructions for 'Court and General Mourning' were issued by the Lord Chamberlain's office, whereby the general public was expected to wear black as a mark of respect, but for much less time than those at Court. In fact, the black suits of the Eton school uniform as recently worn by Prince William date from mourning dress for his ancestor George III which for some reason was never abandoned. Lord Holland described the widespread mourning for Princess Charlotte in 1817, where from Dover to London people had 'signs of mourning on their persons'. The startling effect of the return to colour after the universal public mourning for Charlotte is vividly conveyed by the American ambassador, who in February 1818 observed that 'It was like the bursting out of spring.'

It is hardly surprising that in 1817 the nation as a whole was so well-prepared to rise to the occasion of a royal death. More than marriage, death was the axis around which nineteenth-century British society spun. It was continually visible. The paraphernalia of death played a crucial role in society. In the acquisitive climate of upward mobility mourning dress flourished. Its heyday was the period 1840–1880. It was a complex code, clothes denoting not only the wearer's relationship to the deceased but also their social status according to the style of accessories and the quality of the fabric: 'Bombazine would have shown a better sense of her loss', as Mrs Gaskell had a character say in *Cranford* (1853). But the most important factor governing mourning etiquette was the duration of time it was worn, with strict rules dictating what was worn for whom, and for how long.

The strictures should not be underestimated. Second wives were required to don mourning clothes for three months when their husband's first wife's parents died. The grades of mourning extended from six weeks for a first cousin to around two years for a widow in varying combinations of crape. For a year and a day, 'full mourning' was generally a dress of paramatta covered with crape. After six months this was 'slighted' to a black silk dress trimmed with crape, and at eighteen months crape could be dispensed with. At two years, colour was sanctioned, although one magazine advised that 'it is much better taste to wear half-mourning (grey, violet, mauve) for at least six months more: many widows never wear colour again'. Mrs Sherwood, an American writer and observer of English society, gives a good description of the social exclusion signified by this 'tyrannical custom':

> By many who sorrow deeply and who regard the crape and solemn dress as a mark of respect for the dead, it is deemed almost a sin for a woman to go into the street, to drive or to walk for two years, without a deep crape veil over her face. Many people hold the fact that a widow, or an orphan wears her cap for two years to be greatly to her credit. (Mrs Sherwood, *Manners and Usages*, 1884)

When Prince Albert died suddenly from typhoid in 1861, Queen Victoria opted to wear mourning for the rest of her life. Her widowhood defined her later years, and her ostentatious mourning seems to have permeated the national consciousness, for the English enthusiasm for mourning dress became tantamount to obsession. Mrs Sherwood noted that

> Everyone who has seen an English widow will agree that she makes a hearse of herself. Bombazine and crape, a widow's cap and long thick veil, such is the modern English idea.

The essence of mourning dress was non-reflective materials – even gilt buttons were proscribed. In *Dombey and Son* (1847–8), Dickens gives a superb account of the texture of the widows' weeds:

> Black bombazine of such a lustreless deep dead sombre shade that gas itself couldn't light her up after dark and her presence was a quencher to any number of candles.

For the twentieth-century consumer, the coffin dominates the funeral. In catalogues and casket selection rooms it represents the single greatest expense and a challenging choice, with endless possibilities for social aggrandisement inherent in the consumer's particular decision on fixtures and fittings. For the nineteenth-century consumer, the choice of black stuff was similarly loaded. A sample from a list of dresses in a mourning warehouse catalogue provides a vivid sense of the complexity of black material: black alpacas, black baratheas, black brilliantines, black cobourgs, black french merino, black imperial cloths, black paramattas. Black material was a whole language; it is a fabric we no longer speak.

Some have argued that the cost and urgency involved in acquiring mourning dress greatly exacerbated the distress of the bereaved. The vicar of Yaxley, a member of the anti-mourning movement, paints a grim picture of the dear departed putrefying at the family home while the local tailor and dressmaker struggle with impossible deadlines. For tailors and dressmakers in the country, the funeral generated an awesome workload – six black suits ordered for completion within as many days, twenty dresses in the same time.

> The same message is brought from both the tailor and the dressmaker: the work can't be done in time. The time is therefore extended, by the funeral being put off 'til the seventh or even the eight day after the decease, all the while that the dead body may be crying aloud for earth. (Revd W.H. Sewell, *Sewell's Practical Papers on Funeral Reform*, 1883)

If black material represented hard labour for seamstresses and tailors, it was a heavy yoke for those compelled to buy it and wear it.

For women especially, black was a heavy sartorial burden, in some cases a life sentence. It also represented a form of sexual apartheid, for the merchandising of mourning imposed upon women a purdah whereby they were not even allowed to attend the funerals of those they mourned. Olivia Bland, author of *The Royal Way of Death*, anchors this tradition in Georgian England, specifically the funeral of George III's youngest and much-loved daughter Princess Amelia, who died aged 27 in 1810 and whose funeral was distinctive for its absence of royal female mourners. Women, in effect, were stitched up by mourning protocol, bound to buy clothes to show their bereavement, but banned from funerals lest they show their feelings in public in an unseemly way. Etiquette guides of the period demonstrate this discrimination. A guide to Court etiquette (*Court Etiquette by a Man of the World: A Guide to intercourse with royal or titled persons to drawing room, levees, courts and audience,* 1850) states clearly that

> as these pages may sometimes be perused by foreigners it is right to add that women are never to be seen in the funeral cortège of any person in the rank of a gentleman. Rare instances of the infraction of this rule by eccentric people must not be mistaken for examples of usage.

Queen Victoria, the most famous widow of her age, proved a model of good form and did not attend the funeral of her beloved Albert. Cassell's *Household Guide* states that

> it sometimes happens among the poorer classes that the female relatives attend the funeral; but this custom is by no means to be recommended since in these cases it but too frequently happens that being unable to restrain their emotions they interrupt and destroy the solemnity of the ceremony with their sobs, and even by fainting.

Women were allowed to express grief through the socially sanctioned language of mourning dress, but not with their own voices or emotions. In 1875, George Phillips, in a funeral reform pamphlet, was pro the 'presence of women who lost untold comfort from not being present at the solemn, edifying and elevating service.' Only by the 1890s did it become common for women to attend the funeral service, if – as Lady Colin Campbell put it – 'they feel strong enough, and can keep their grief within due bounds, let not the thought of what is customary prevent them from following their lost one to the grave'.

Where central London today is studded with flashy, one-stop wedding shops selling miles of white material for the bridal big day, in the nineteenth century department stores dedicated solely to mourning dress flourished. The latest funeral fashions were eagerly awaited. Peter Robinson's Court and General Mourning, known as 'black Peter Robinsons' supplied the rich and fashionable with every conceivable variation on a theme of black. When it opened, Messrs Jay & Co. of Regent Street was described as 'presenting another great improvement among the many offered by the facilities of our modern retail trade, to the metropolis and its vicinity'. It received a glowing review in the *Ladies' Blackwoods* magazine (1850):

The shop front of which the outward style is that of great neatness and suitability to its purpose as an Establishment for general mourning, exhibits a large and choice assortment of every material proper for the exclusive uses intended whilst an ample store of goods within and a commensurate attendance (male and female) of the most unexceptionable description, superintended by Mr Jay himself, together with handsome show rooms on the principal floor stocked with articles of all kinds needful for the demands of mourning costume in all its gradations and assuredly of the first quality, constitute the feature and advantages of a highly respectable undertaking which to our judgement lacks not anything of the best ability and fitness necessary to its completeness or of the peculiar attention, delicacy and good taste which should unquestionably distinguish a boutique of this stamp and character.

Provision was made for mourning underwear and mourning swimwear and – lest the hard of hearing cause a gaffe with a shiny eartrumpet – a special mourning version in black vulcanite was available. Magazines like *Maids, Wives and Widows Magazine* and *Sylvia's Home Journal* featured mourning plates to inspire their readers, and a sizeable part of their editorial was dedicated to dilemmas of mourning etiquette. Men were also required to do the right thing. Amidst graphic accounts of death in gung-ho tales of derring-do, an editorial in *Young Men of Great Britain* (1875) advises readers on how to avoid getting lost in what to modern eyes is a bewildering maze of mourning rituals:

Fashion does not interfere with the habiliments of sorrow in the way that it does with garments of other kinds. In fact there is very little room left for it to display its fickleness. The depth of mourning is of course dependent entirely upon the closeness of your relationship with the deceased. If you are invited to the funeral of a person who is no relation to you, you should dress entirely in black, with a moderate band on your hat and black gloves. The latter are generally provided at the house, whence the funeral procession starts, but it is always best to be provided with some yourself. Make no display of grief, but be as quiet, gentlemanly and attentive as you can. About a week after the funeral you should leave a card at the house. A mourning card sent to you does not imply that you are invited to the funeral, as it is a common practice now to send these cards out to a large circle of friends. If you receive a card returning thanks for kind inquiries, you call again and you will then be expected to enter and see the family. Upon this occasion you should put on slight mourning if you happen to be an intimate friend of the family.

Reading this makes one aware of the absence of any comparable guidance in contemporary editorials. When was last time you read a fashion feature about what to wear for funerals? In modern life there is almost a complete – and nearly unprecedented – absence of protocol for death. There is an absence of information on what to wear, what to do, what to say, right down to what it is appropriate to feel.

This was notable when the Princess of Wales died. In the ensuing chaos, a form of 'emotional correctness' was evident when some people's behaviour did not conform to the expectations of the majority. People flounder on all counts, and it is an astonishing indictment of a so-called huggy-feely society that death, a notable rite of passage, should be so widely ignored compared to birth and marriage. Another striking example of the lack of a social context for modern death was the reaction of young people when Kurt Cobain, the lead singer of the rock group Nirvana, committed suicide. The number of teenagers in turmoil following his death, and the way they vented their distress in letters to the *New Musical Express*, provoked the publication to take the unprecedented step of involving the Samaritans in framing the magazine's response.

But despite the social strictures and conventions which allowed it to thrive for so long, the nineteenth-century funeral trade eventually overreached itself. Towards the end of the century there was a backlash against flagrant consumerism. From the 1870s the anti-mourning movement flourished, and calls to curb undertakers' excesses and to simplify funerals featured prominently in newspapers and pamphlets. *The Times* was at the forefront of this clamour for change:

> Latterly funeral pomp has exceeded itself, and while the world is living faster than it ever did, and fashion indulging in wilder caprices, death in a kind of rivalry joins the race of extravagances. Funerals are more oppressive, mourning more costly, and both are really more revolting to the true instincts of grief. (*The Times*, 2 February 1875)

The Victorian public had lost patience with Mr Mould's approach to the trappings of death: 'Oh do not let us say that gold is dross when it can buy such things as these.' The Ecclesiological Society called for their abolition altogether:

> The race of undertakers must either be most utterly and radically reformed: or if this should be found impossible, abolished. Some few exceptions there are: but as a body their extortions, their hardheartedness their injustice, the indecency of their behaviour their abominable arrangements, do indeed bring us back to the old heathens' saying and make a

modern funeral of 'all horrible things the most horrible'. Their present trade is driven by taking advantage of mental agony to extort exorbitant prices. How is the widow in the first burst of grief to haggle about hat-bands and scarves and mourning cloaks and black kid gloves with men whose hearts are as hard as the nether millstone?

It was not only in his novels that Dickens expressed his disapproval of funeral extravagance. In the *Uncommercial Traveller* (a collection of essays originally published in the journal *All the Year Round*, 1860–69) he wrote, 'Once and twice, have I wished in my soul that if the waste must be, they would let the undertaker bury the money, and let me bury the friend.' He was also clear about his personal preferences for his own obsequies and did not want to be driven to the grave 'in a nodding and bobbing car like an in-firm four post bed-stead, by an inky fellow creature in a cocked hat'. The mood of rebellion extended to mourning restrictions and in 1875 a woman's journal spoke out against mourning dress for children: 'The little children do not understand it and it is absurd to invest them with the signs of grief they cannot feel.' Grown women similarly rebelled against the tyranny of mourning. In *Manners and Usages* (1884) Mrs Sherwood mentions an Eng-lishwoman who had had enough. 'Indeed so overdone are mourning cere-monies in England – that Lady Georgina Milner of Nuneappleton in York, a friend of the Archbishop, wrote a book against the abuses, ordered her own body to be buried in a pine coffin and forbade her servants and rela-tives to wear mourning.' Cultural permission for change came indirectly via the Court, and specifically the Princess of Wales, who notably es-chewed wearing crape when she was in mourning for the Duke of Clarence. A fashion journal noted: 'There has been a decided stand against wearing crape for some years past, but the Princess of Wales gave it the *coup de grace*.' Another small but symbolic Court-driven change was when in her Jubilee year Queen Victoria consented to wear silver jewellery. By wearing a shiny metal object the Queen, a stickler for mourning tradition, broke the rule of matt black non-reflective surfaces and signalled to women that they were free to leave the literally lacklustre world of widowhood. The Queen's strong identification as a widow added an extra weight of symbolism to her death in 1901. It was as if widowhood died with her, and certainly from this time there was a rapid decline in the formal rituals of death and a dilution of the solidarity of the old system. Increasingly, there was a sense that life went on, notably in 1911 with 'Black Ascot', when it was decided not to let the death of Edward VII ruin the Season. In 1936, when George V died, the more relaxed stance was conveyed by an article in *Vogue* which advised readers not to make 'ostentatious' adjustments to their normal routine 'unless closely connected with the Royal family'. In 1952, when George VI died, orders for General Mourning were not issued. In sartorial terms, at least, British subjects were freed.

The phasing-out of mourning turned death from a social experience with a common code of conduct into a private, anti-social experience to be coped with alone. One of the functions that mourning fulfilled was identification of the bereaved. By being set apart in black a woman was granted padding from normal life – something which is arguably an advantage not available to bereaved people today. Mrs Sherwood wrote that

> Mourning dress does protect a woman while in deepest grief and against the untimely gayety of a passing stranger. It is a wall, a cell of refuge. Behind a black veil she can hide herself as she goes out for business or recreation fearless of any intrusion.

It is ironic that what passes for the last word in cocktail party chic, a staple of the social butterfly's wardrobe, is the little black dress, when for years the big black dress was a powerful symbol of social segregation. Black gradually outgrew its primarily practical function as the uniform of grief and became the focus of style and more fashion-conscious treatment. 'Have you noticed how very smart mourning is nowadays? Crape is adapted to the most fashionable forms of costume such as zouaves and tight fitting out door coats', commented *Drapery World* in 1897. Not even fashion, however, could help a material so closely associated with Victorian widows' weeds, and sales plummeted in the early part of the twentieth century. In a poignant sign of the times, Courtaulds, having built a thriving business on the manufacture of mourning fabrics, redirected their energies to the production of synthetic materials such as rayon for mainstream fashion.

Some commercial concerns, however, made the effort to rise to these new challenges. Undertakers recognised the need to adapt and set about marketing new wares. They started to appeal to the mood of reform and turn it to their advantage. A telling example of this occurs in the catalogue of the Derby Mourning and Funeral Warehouse, St Peter's Street, Derby. The undertaker Thomas Lloyd, proprietor, advises his readers of his new range of goods and services, and how he has

> at a great outlay, added to his establishment a hearse built on the funeral reform principle without plumes; also mourning coaches to correspond. Flemish horses warranted quiet (used only for funeral purposes with competent coachmen). Special estimates are given for this class of funeral where bands and scarfs are dispensed with.

Anticipating the modern market for Green funerals and cardboard coffins, an important scion of the reform movement at the end of the nineteenth century concerned cost-effective funeral goods, marketed on the grounds of their benefits to public health. These included 'The Necropolis coffin of compressed pulp', Mr Stretton's bier which 'may be wheeled into the church and then placed over the grave', 'the Tortoise Tent Company's graveside tent for the protection of mourners in inclement weather' and 'Johnson's grave memorials which are within reach of the very poor'. The reform movement was so successful, and simplicity so widely accepted as preferable to ostentatious display, that in 1894 the *Lancet* was able to assert that

> it is unnecessary now to attack burial on the grounds of its expense in funeral paraphernalia. Funeral reform is an accomplished fact in most parts of the kingdom and the funerals of the past generation are almost as extinct as a dodo.

The rhythms of change in the nineteenth century replicate the rhythms of change towards the end of the twentieth century. At one level, both relate to what John Berger called the 'dehumanisation of capitalism'. Ever since the rise of the high-production, high-consumption economy in the eighteenth century, the British way of death has involved people attempting to make death meaningful in different ways by spending money on a funeral. Sir Francis Seymour Haden, one of the luminaries of funeral reform, touches on this when he describes the history of the coffin. Having posed the questions of when and why coffins, he answers that

> when the pretension which attends the acquistion of wealth without intelligence suggested its use; when it was desired to keep the body for days for the purpose of giving it an ostentatious funeral, when the prosperous hosier or vintner aspired to the fashions and follies of his betters; when time was needed not to honour the dead but to open the pestilent vault and prepare the obsequious mourning; when in the jargon of the undertaker in short (the covert irony of which it was not given him to understand) funerals came to be 'performed' in this country, and when a week was wanted to arrange the pagaent which was to set out with the blazon of a mock heraldry and to return with a dozen of the performers now dangling their legs from the but now vacated hearse. (Haden, *Earth to Earth*)

But past a point, commerce corrodes communality. When the funeral becomes principally a matter of merchandising it ceases to be a satisfying rite of passage. Secularism, which started to intrude on the nineteenth-century way of death, became like hogweed in the twentieth. We are in a similar predicament to the one confronted by our Victorian ancestors, for a 'click and buy' model of modern death suggests that we are in danger of developing as much of an out-of-balance consumerism as they experienced.

It is not just confined to the death ceremony. A useful comparison can be made between coffins and wedding cakes. Both are expensive items created for short-term use, both are central items on display at ceremonies, and each – in the cutting of the cake, and the lowering of the coffin – are at the centre of the defining moments in these ceremonies. Mirroring the explosion of choice in coffins, wedding cakes have also been caught up in a consumer revolution. Social anthropologist Simon Charsely has written that

> For the cake trade the eighties was a complicated decade with a major change invisible at its beginning sweeping the country by its end. The old specifications was not abandoned but a number of enthusiastic specialist confectioners around the country exploited the opportunities for affluence to produce bigger and better. New styles of icing were developed, using an increasing variety of techniques and the intricate, and therefore costly, designs of earlier periods were sometimes copied. (*Wedding Cakes and Cultural Meaning*, 1992)

Chocolate mousse cakes, ice cream cakes, cakes decorated with personal biographical details of the protagonists – anything goes. So it is with coffins and the other trappings of contemporary funerals. Increasingly, consumerism is creating tension between form and content. But what our ceremonies mean should concern us more than what they cost. Suffice to say that we have much to learn from other cultures. We desperately need new forms of social cohesion to restore a better ratio of commerce to community. Where once shared faith conferred meaning on ceremonies, increasingly the church is used like a stage set for our ceremonies. Part of the problem is knowing what to put in the place that was once filled by widespread, shared religious faith. It is a problem we have yet to solve. The cult of self-obsession comes at the cost of a sense of community, and money is not a sufficient substitute.

THE CHANGING
LANDSCAPE
OF DEATH

HE SUMMER OF 1998 WAS HOT. WHILE MY FRIENDS decamped to Europe to flop by pools, I embarked on an unusual tour of duty to judge the final round of entries in the Cemetery of the Year Competition. Burial grounds are rarely sun-traps. A legacy of nineteenth-century landscaping means there is plenty of shade under tall trees; impressive monuments dating from the days before height restrictions cast cool, long shadows. In Carlisle Cemetery the rabbits appeared to have a Mediterranean temperament. Charmingly, they took to rustling their way up the inside of yew trees to sunbathe on the upper branches.

The competition, the first of its kind, was the brainchild of three scions of the funeral trade: the Confederation of Burial Authorities, the Memorial Awareness Board and the National Association of Memorial Masons. In organising what was essentially a public relations exercise, their objective was to restore a sense of pride in the nation's cemeteries and to raise the profile of these much-neglected communities of the dead, many of which have been abandoned by the living and have fallen into disrepair. In urban areas especially, theft and vandalism are a problem, the memorial mason's lament being, 'Find me the memorial that can withstand the Newcastle vandal.' Unkempt graves and a policy in some burial grounds of 'lying down' precarious memorials, so they look like toppled dominoes, further contribute to an aura of dereliction.

Few visitors to the average municipal cemetery are likely to share Shelley's exuberance when he commented, 'It might make one in love with death to think one should be buried in such a place.' As cultural snapshots, the impression of abandonment is a powerful expression of the contemporary preference for keeping death at a distance. Overgrown graves are a sorry testament to the fragmentation of contemporary society and the short-term interest of relations in the earlier offshoots of the family tree. When was the last time any of us visited our grandparents' graves, let alone those of our great-grandparents? In poignant contrast is the burgeoning trend towards commemorating domestic pets; in a telling sign of the times, their graves tend to be far more regularly visited than those of their human peers, and are even seasonally decorated with Christmas wreaths and Easter tokens, indicating ongoing interest. One of the most memorable I've visited is near the small town of Holywell, near Flint. At first sight it looks like an ordinary cemetery with floral tributes and memorials. Only on closer inspection is the illusion of normality dispelled. In hand-carved letters on one panel of a niche in the columbarium I read: 'OUR GERBILS PIXIE AGED 2, 29.7.97, DIXIE 24.2.98 AND WHISKEY 13.6.98 GOD BLESS'. (A niche costs £125, a gerbil about £2.)

Fortunately for those taking part in the 1998 Cemetery of the Year competition, pet burial grounds were excluded, so the standards were not as exacting as they might otherwise have been. The first duty of the judges was to study the written entries. The different styles of submissions revealed the diversity of entrants. From Kensington and Chelsea came an executive portfolio, and from Hull a video – a brave choice of promotional tool, for there is not generally much action in a cemetery. The Friends of Shepton Mallet Cemetery sent happy snaps of fund-raising jamborees, and tips on how to evict badgers from squatting in graves by installing a one-way flap which lets them out but not back in again. The hard work and uphill struggle implicit in cemetery maintenance was most forcefully conveyed by Yeovil and Yeovil Without, where four staff had put their backs into clearing 23,815 overgrown graves in the Victorian section. When you consider the effort it takes to tackle six-foot high garden hedges, you can appreciate the physical exertion involved in cutting back the undergrowth, which in some parts reached twenty feet. On an erratically typed and much-corrected page, their entry was touchingly apologetic: 'We have to watch our budget very carefully as you will probably have noticed by my letter hence no posh videos just photos taken by yours truly (no secretary either).' Evidently they are quite literally Yeovil and Yeovil Without.

The two categories of the competition were for 'open' cemeteries, where new grave spaces are still available, and 'closed' cemeteries, where the emphasis is on upkeep. Entries ranged from Gray's Elegy-style picturesque churchyards in rural locations such as Bolton Percy near Tad-caster in the Vale of York with forty graves, to busy municipal cemeteries with on-site crematoria such as Carlisle, where there are 60,000 graves. With such a diversity of size and wealth, the aim was to select winners both on the basis of atmosphere and on whether the cemetery was an inviting space, not just for the bereaved but the casual visitor, too. The wildly con-trasting settings made the judging process particularly challenging. At Bolton Percy, dedicated horticulturist Robin Brook has transformed a ne-glected parish churchyard into a profusion of colour and foliage, like a cot-tage garden with graves. In stark contrast to this rural idyll is Hedon Road Cemetery in Hull, sandwiched between an industrial estate and a prison. In spite of this unpromising location it yielded one of the highlights of the competition, a wonderfully original columbarium for the discreet and imaginative interment of cremated remains. Built in 1902 when cremation was very much a minority interest, its date of origin adds to its interest as an innovative piece of design. Reminiscent of a grotto in a gothic novel, with rampant ivy clinging to craggy walls that look like a natural rocky out-crop, it is in fact made of mud and straw, and irreverently referred to by cemetery staff as Boot Hill.

After a month on the road I returned to London for Judgement Day. In the offices of the Memorial Awareness Board we had the difficult task of agreeing on the winners. Some judges ranked facilities much higher than aesthetics, and provision of 'lavatories and litter-bins' scored higher in their assessment than imaginative planting schemes. One judge's managed-and-manicured ideal was another's nightmare of maintenance gone mad. Where someone praised a cemetery which encouraged flora and fauna, an-other opinion held that it gave a poor impression of insufficient mainte-nance. If someone cited a teddy bear-shaped memorial as a positive example of freedom of expression, with equal conviction another judge used it as an example of a crime against aesthetics and an argument for cen-sorship. Appropriate wording is increasingly contentious. Given some re-quests such as 'Look Out Heaven Here She Comes' as an affectionate commemorative inscription for the matriarch of the house, one can under-stand the difficulty in arbitrating so as to satisfy the wishes of the bereaved while conserving heritage, particularly in old churchyards, where abbrevia-tions and nicknames are harder to accommodate without altering the over-all atmosphere.

After much deliberation we were unanimous in voting for the winners, which were announced at an awards ceremony at the Joint Conference of Burial and Cremation Authorities in Eastbourne. Contrary to public perception, those in the 'cem and crem' profession like nothing more than a party, perhaps taking to heart more than most of us 'Eat, drink and be merry, for tomorrow we die'. Consequently, some delegates seemed a little jaded after their enthusiastic efforts with the line-dancing entertainment the night before, and the fact that a few looked like death warmed up suggested that at the accompanying Tex Mex feast the tequila had flowed. The evening entertainment and the Cemetery of the Year awards were light relief in an otherwise serious agenda of papers on major issues affecting the disposal of the dead, ranging from the medical uses of radioactive materials to the law on exhumation.

Anticipation mounted as all eyes were fixed on the podium. The Deputy Mayor and Lady Mayoress jangled into position. Then came handshakes and applause as the winners were announced. In the 'open' section Carlisle was the winner, with Carmountside in second place. In the 'closed' section Hull took first place and Almorah in Jersey came second. Bolton Percy was given a discretionary award.

Although built in 1855, with magnificent monkey puzzle trees and Portuguese laurels also dating from that period, Carlisle cemetery is a paradigm of the progressive cemetery in the way that it addresses consumer choice, catering equally to conventional and conservationist interests. Ken West, bereavement services manager, is one of the most innovative people in the British funeral profession, and his visionary attitude to cemetery management means that Carlisle has won plaudits and awards from both the mainstream authorities and the Natural Death Centre. The cemetery hums with life. Besides the bereaved, you may bump into school children doing quizsheets, bird watchers seeking out wintering redwings and visitors following the Walker's Guide. In a variety of ways, the cemetery has been adapted to contemporary requirements to become an integral part of the community. It was the first cemetery in the country to have a woodland burial section in which oak tree saplings are planted instead of headstones. Commitment to conservation is carried through in a host of initiatives, ranging from a hedgehog hospital to a butterfly walk. There are bat boxes and tawny owl breeding areas, and old grave plots have been designated for the increase of the vole population. A fawn was born amidst cowslips and orchids in the wildflower area. In another conservation section there are kingfishers and a beck full of sticklebacks.

The right to choose is taken very seriously at Carlisle, resulting in the widest range of options for both graves and memorials. This includes traditional kerb-set graves, recycled graves, woodland graves and graves with headstones for cremated remains. There is a more liberal approach to memorials than in many cemeteries. For example, for a young Michael Jackson fan there is an image of the singer, and on another memorial is the unusually forthright inscription 'Grumpy Grandad'. The contemporary secular climate is also shown by a Barbie doll left as a tribute on a child's grave. As a further sign of the times, the yew clippings are collected and sent off to make the anti-cancer drug Taxol.

Carmountside cemetery in Stoke-on-Trent similarly reflects contemporary needs. There is no more sensitive subject than the death of a child, which is why the Butterfly Garden of Remembrance is so impressive. Established in 1997, it is designed from a child's perspective, with child-height features such as a birdbath and a wendy house for 'items of personal remembrance' such as teddy bears. These have become a contemporary symbol of condolence for children, both in the form of soft toys left at the scenes of tragedies (notably Dunblane), and as stone memorials. This sympathetic design, intended to afford consolation to the bereaved siblings of babies and other children, is striking in a society which, for most of the twentieth century, excluded children from death rites. An important legacy of the Princess of Wales's death was the way in which it accelerated the readmission of children to mourning rituals.

In a different vein, Almorah cemetery in Jersey, a closed cemetery, is a testament to the successful preservation of the past. As superintendent of cemeteries for the parish of St Helier, Robin Clapham, oversees some 70,000 mortal remains in 30,000 burial plots. He has given the five cemeteries under his care a new lease of life with open days, and has capitalised on the potential of Almorah's heritage with the conversion of a chapel into a study centre, and the transfer of information from graves and monuments on to the internet. This is of particular interest to Canadians, for Almorah was a staging-post for the Cabots who helped to settle Canada, and about 5,000 Canadians a year come in search of information about their ancestors.

Built by private enterprise in 1854 when Dissenters were forbidden burial in Church of England burial grounds, Almorah's incumbents are Catholics, non-conformists, French Protestants and Jews. The backdrop of the sea and the sweeping views of the St Clement's coastline create a stunning aspect, further enhanced by wild strawberry bushes and fine Victorian memorials exemplifying a freedom of style that is hampered by modern planning restrictions. The upturned bow of a boat commemorates the loss of the *Stellar*, in which a group of dignitaries drowned on a day-trip from Portsmouth. Another memorial commemorates a child's self-sacrifice:

William Francis Le Geyt aged 12 years and 14 days
kind hearted noble minded gentle brave
to grasp Alf from the flames his life he gave.

If conservation of the past, respect for self-expression and sustainability are perennial problems in contemporary cemetery management, two issues are even more urgent – memorial safety and grave reuse. Although compared to deaths on the roads it is a small statistic, it is still shocking that in the last five years two children have been killed by falling memorials – most recently a six-year-old at a cemetery in Harrogate, Yorkshire. In response to growing concern about the stability of the 'plinth and plate' style which characterises the majority of modern memorials, cemetery managers are being encouraged to use a 'topple tester' to assess stability. Although both theoretically and legally, the upkeep of a grave and memorial is the responsibility of the person who purchased them, in practice health and safety issues mean that the landowners of the burial grounds are in the front line for claims. Desertion by relatives over time and the landowners' loss of contact with them is the reason for cemeteries' seemingly heavy-handed approach to memorial safety, whereby managers flatten tilting memorials and even deny public access to areas where memorials are giving cause for concern.

Dwarfing all other concerns, however, is the issue of burial space. This has assumed the status of crisis – not only in London, where three areas (Hackney, Tower Hamlets and Camden) are already full, and many more inner boroughs will run out of space in an average of seven years – but also in urban areas nationally. The severity of the problem is being exacerbated by early indications that public preference is shifting back to burial after years in which cremation was by far and away the more popular option. The trend for interring cremated remains in cemeteries, as opposed to scattering them, also suggests a reappraisal of the significance of a fixed place of rest. Yet in spite of the cemetery authorities' best efforts to convince the government of the urgent need to address the sensitive subject of grave reuse and to revise nineteenth-century laws, the Home Office is recalcitrant. Consultation papers, long promised, have yet to materialise. There are few indications that in the near future there will be changes in the law which would sanction the disturbance of human remains for the purposes of grave reuse. Fear of public opinion is no excuse either, for the most recent poll on the subject, conducted by the University of Nottingham in 1995, found that in principle 62 per cent of people supported the reuse of graves, while 35 per cent opposed it. Government sensitivity about reuse is an anomaly, given that it is legal to disturb human remains for other reasons such as property development and road widening. This happened on a large scale in the spring of 2000 in London, when 1,500 victims of the Blitz were unceremoniously exhumed by mechanical diggers and bagged in plastic binliners to make way for a luxury block of flats. This type of legal disturbance of human remains seems brutal, compared to the comparatively civilised procedures which the experts would like to see introduced in this country to create more space for new burials in existing burial grounds.

The method that those championing reform want to see legalised is called 'lift and deepen'. This technique, which is widely practised in Europe and Australia, involves reopening an old grave, removing the earlier remains and digging the grave more deeply before re-interring the earlier remains at the bottom in such a way as to allow room for new burials on top. But at the time of writing, the 'double-decker' system remains a theoretical solution to the British burial crisis, and is a long way from being sanctioned by the Home Office. As with many other aspects of the history of disposal of the dead, we lag behind our French neighbours who have taken a more progressive approach to the disposal of the dead in towns. In France it is legal to exhume a body after a minimum of five years in order to create more space.

Bound up in the government's reluctance to address the sensitive subject of grave reuse is the powerful concept of the sanctity of the grave, and the emotive phrase 'rest in peace'. In this regard, it is fascinating to compare the contemporary burial crisis with that which preceded it. The nineteenth-century burial crisis, like that of today, concerned exactly the same issue of how to accommodate the urban dead, yet exposed vastly different perspectives of the ontology of the grave and the appropriate treatment of human remains.

Before the establishment of cemeteries, the dead were interred in and around churches. Looking back to the state of these overcrowded city churchyards is not only a powerful reminder of our ancestors' proximity to death compared with our distance, but it also gives us a benchmark for contemporary squeamishness. A notable aspect of a secular society is the extreme importance attached to the treatment of the corpse. Without the concept of the soul, we perceive ourselves more materially defined by our bodies, and the idea that we *are* our bodies is a powerful factor in determining our expectations of how dead bodies should be treated. There is a disparity between our tolerance for the live body being treated like an object in the care of the medical profession, notably in the high-tech world of intensive care, and our expectation that the dead body should be treated like a person, an individual. This was illustrated recently when a space shortage in the mortuary facility of a hospital in Bedford resulted in bodies being temporarily laid on the chapel floor. Pictures of this caused a national outrage, and the hospital manager was forced to resign. This sensitivity is striking given that bed shortages regularly impose indignity on the living patients, who often wait on trolleys in cramped corridors without any privacy. What we endure with the dehumanising aspects of modern medicine, we compensate for in what we demand from the funeral directors. For while we put up with the impersonal professionalism of modern medicine, we insist that the dead body is accorded individual care, personal comfort – consider the mattresses and pillows in coffins – and privacy, and this carries through from the funeral home to the grave and style of interment. (A significant development in the evolution of contemporary sensitivity is a new respect for neonatal remains and an increased concern for their humane disposal.). These concepts are the privilege of the time in which we live, for the dignity accorded to the dead and the sanctity of the grave that we take for granted in the twenty-first century could not be counted on by the bereaved of the nineteenth century. Far from it – the inhabitants of towns were subjected to conditions that are completely alien to our contemporary frame of reference.

In 1819 an article in the *Quarterly Review* noted that 'In large towns and more especially in the Metropolis, it has become more difficult to find room for the dead than for the living'. The article gives a vivid account of mortal congestion:

> There are many churchyards in which soil has been raised several feet above the level of the adjoining street, by the continual accumulation of mortal matter; and there are others in which the ground is actually probed with a borer before a grave is opened! In these things the most barbarous savages might reasonably be shocked at our barbarity.

The sheer bulk of human remains in relation to the space available to contain them spawned a macabre market in human bonemeal. 'Many tons of human bones every year are sent from London to the North where they are crushed in mills contrived for the purpose and used as manure.' But English agriculture was not the only beneficiary of the burial crisis. Shipping also capitalised on the problem with a bizarre use of ballast:

> A curious expedient has been found at Shields and Sunderland: the ships which return to those ports in ballast were at a loss where to discharge it, and had of late years been compelled to pay for the use of the ground on which they threw it out: the burial grounds were full; it was recollected

that the ballast would be useful there, and accordingly it has been laid upon one layer of dead to such a depth that graves for a second tier are now dug in the new soil.

As we have seen, the sanctity of the grave was also under threat from another quarter, in the form of grave-robbers. Desecration of the grave was merely the start of the indignity that the bereaved feared might befall the dead. This pamphlet gives a truly horrific account of further mutilation:

> It is very shocking to the feelings, that after the body has undergone investigation by dissection, the lacerated flesh should not again be buried; it is cast into cess pools, where thousands of rats feed on it; but it is thought that these destructive animals cannot live long on it; for at one very considerable surgical theatre they have tried almost all carnivorous birds, and hardly any can live on it but vultures, and numbers of those birds are therefore kept on purpose to devour the human flesh. How dreadful to reflect that a beloved relative or a respected friend should be torn from their vault or grave, and after being mangled by dissection, should be devoured by vermin and birds of prey.

This grizzly account of a fate worse than death is the prelude to the sales pitch:

> But though till lately no efficient means have been adopted to prevent the minds of survivors being wounded by the apprehension of such shocking practices, they may now obtain an effectual preventative, by the adoption of the Patent Iron or Metallic Coffins, which cannot be broken open and are equally secure in the vault or in the grave. His Royal Highness the Prince Regent has given the Inventor of this admirable plan the exclusive use of it, under his own hand and seal, for fourteen years; and if graves still continue to be robbed of their dead, the fault will entirely rest with the Public themselves.

If the possibility of premature resurrection of a loved one by the grave-robber's spade was an uncomfortable threat hanging over the nineteenth-century bereaved, they seem to have given less thought to the disturbance by the gravedigger's spade. Until the surgeon George Walker forced them to pay attention to the conditions in urban burial grounds, the general public did not seem to have given much thought to the daily desecration in their midst. This is illustrated by an article in the *Lancet* of 30 November 1839:

Bodies are deposited in the churches, vaults, church-yards and cemeteries with becoming decency, but no one stops to enquire through what process they subsequently pass, and the public seem to take it for granted that the dead will lie harmlessly and tranquilly until 'the resurrection of the just' provided the interference of the anatomist be averted.

The truth was that in order to accommodate the dead and to ensure that the demand for 'empty' graves could be supplied, the proprietors of grave-yards resorted to a barbarous style of 'management'. The *Lancet* noted:

It is in fact quite evident that a wholesale system of resurrectionism was carried on, under the technical term 'management', by the very parties who were most loud in their cries against the 'bodysnatchers' engaged in their more precarious but more useful trade.

The generally drab municipal cemetery, keeping death at a safe remove and out of sight, is something we take for granted, yet in the history of death the 'white belt' concept is a relatively recent development, and its impact should not be underestimated. Distancing the dead from the living by establishing cemeteries on the outskirts of communities was a radical development. It marked the start of the transference of power in the disposal of the dead away from the Church, and in this way it initiated the first of a series of dramatic splits which have altered the course of death rites and resulted in a fragmentation that is definitively modern. The history of death in the last two centuries is defined by schisms – churchyard and cemetery, church and crematorium, grave and scattered remains, body at home and body removed to funeral home, body and memory. These schisms represent a systematic process of distancing that has not only altered the physical topography of death, but has also involved a mental re-mapping.

In terms of social history the relocation of the dead achieved by the cemetery movement was a peaceful revolution, an unusual revolution where those for whom the cause was being fought were already dead and where the revolutionaries represented the Establishment. It was a civilised but devastating overthrow of the old order embodied by the Church of England. It was a slow change, dating from the point at which politicians started to address the burial crisis and thereby embarked on a collision course between Church and state. The intimations of unrest at a high level are evident in 1842 when, as part of Sir Edwin Chadwick's inquiry into the health of towns and the sanitary condition of the labouring classes, a select committee was appointed to investigate the burial crisis. The committee's objective was to consider the expediency of framing some legislative enactments (due respect being paid to the rights of the clergy) to remedy the evils arising from the interment of bodies within the precincts of large towns or of places densely populated.

This sentence contains the beginnings of territorial conflict between lay and religious authorities, and it indicates how the burial crisis encouraged death to be seen increasingly through the lens of public health.

The nineteenth-century burial crisis was precipitated by dramatic demographic changes. As industrialisation gathered momentum, men moved where they could work with machines in mills, factories and foundries. The mass migration to cities was to have a colossal impact on the necro-geography of England. Between 1801 and 1851 the population of towns soared. Blackburn grew from 12,000 to 65,000 and Bradford from 13,000 to 104,000. The population of London jumped from below a million to over two million inhabitants. At the heart of the new industrial economy was manpower. Where once he had worked the land in small agricultural communities, man now harnessed energy from a machine in a line of machines in a factory. He became a unit in a relentless large-scale cycle of production. Output soared. In 1740 the country's iron production was 18,000 tons; by 1850 this had risen to 2.5 million tons, half the global supply. Coal production rose from 2.5 million tons in 1700 to 16 million in 1830.

For the human cogs grinding away in the vast industrial machine, living conditions contributed to disease and premature death. The sheer density of people generated by the influx into towns meant unimaginably cramped accommodation. Government reports from the first half of the century describe a sub-culture of cellar life in Leeds and Manchester, with factory workers sleeping six and seven to a bed, intermittent water supply and deplorable provision for sanitation where, as a matter of course, one privy might serve up to forty houses. Inadequate sanitation, coupled with a lack of understanding of the complexities of preventative medicine, meant that infectious disease was the main cause of death. In densely populated areas, outbreaks of illness spread like wildfire. In 1854 an outbreak of cholera from one pump in Broadwick Street, Soho, claimed 500 lives in ten days. In her richly informative book *The London Burial Grounds* (1896), Isabella Holmes describes wells, pumps and conduits not merely near, but actually located *in* churchyards. She relates how, during a cholera epidemic, the vicar of St George's in the East, the Revd Harry Jones, attached a placard to the pump in the churchyard used by his parishioners which read 'Dead Men's Broth'. She also describes how, for Charles Dickens, the sound of pumps at work in churchyards conjured up the voices of the dead protesting, 'Let us lie here in peace; don't suck us up and drink us.'

Overcrowding in life spilled over into overcrowding in death, as the profound demographic changes brought a particularly challenging form of congestion to daily life in the form of overcrowded intra-mural burial sites. Urban churchyards soon became choked with corpses. In *Nicholas Nickleby* (1838–9) Dickens describes how the dead 'lay cheek by jowl with life: no deeper down than the feet of the throng that passed there every day and piled high as their throats', while in *Bleak House* (1852–3) a churchyard is a dreadful, vermin-ridden place. The problem of over-population is even more lurid in *The Cemetery*, a brief appeal to the feelings of society on behalf of extra-mural burial. This long, anonymous poem (1847) is well worth reading in its entirety for its admittedly melodramatic but detailed account of the problems caused by the burial crisis:

> Hark! Creaks the mattock on a coffin lid,
> and earth gives up her injured dead unbid.
> Wrought loose as mole-hill 'neath th'oft ent'ring tools,
> Each op'ning grave, a banquet meet for Ghoules,
> Bids yawn in livid heaps the quarried flesh;
> The plague-swoln charnel spreads its taint afresh.
> A womb of death, not yet effete with bane;
> But every victim draws a lengthening train.
> Death with such widely wasting sickle sweeps,
> Man can scarce house the harvest as he reaps.

This was not poetic licence. The physical bulk of the dead population in relation to the capacity of ground to contain it was a grim equation. George Walker claimed that in Spa Fields burial ground in London '80,000 corpses had been put in space fitted to serve 1,000'. The fact that the most prolific commentator on the burial crisis focused on London tends to eclipse the suffering beyond the capital. In this regard, George Milner a director of the Hull General Cemetery Company, gives an interesting and, compared to Walker, a cool, calm and collected account of conditions in Hull. In 1846 Milner wrote, 'No town is in greater need of a cemetery than Hull.' He reviewed registered deaths in the Hull district over eight years. From 1838 to 1845 in a population of 41,130, he found that 9,113 deaths occurred. In the context of statistics for the whole borough, with an estimated population of 70,000, he put the number of deaths in the same ratio at 15,509. He then invited the reader to postulate on the cumulative impact of these figures:

Were we to carry our calculations backward only for fifteen, or twenty years the numbers would become startling, and we should involuntarily exclaim – what has become of the remains of those dear friend who have been called away and what must become of our own earthly tabernacles, when the enemy of our nature shall let fly his shaft against us. (*On Cemetery Burial, or Sepulture, ancient and modern*, 1846)

The overriding impression is of a metropolitan infrastructure straining under sheer weight of numbers, and of both the dead and the living being packed into a steadily shrinking space. The appalling conditions are a recurring theme in much writing of the period. A poem by H. K. White conveys the grim reality of shallow graves in the city:

> And who would lay
> His body in the city burial place
> To be thrown up again by some rude sexton,
> And yield it narrow house another tenant,
> Ere the moist flesh had mingled with the dust,
> Ere the tenacious hair had left the scalp,
> Exposed to insult lewd, and wantoness?
> No, I will lay me in the village ground;
> There are the dead respected.

There is a sense of a rapidly widening gulf between town and country, and the peaceful pastoral mood and imagery of the grave in Gray's 'Elegy', 'with each in his narrow cell forever laid', becoming emblematic of an irretrievable rural idyll. In this respect, the burial crisis is an important and arguably under-rated consequence of urbanisation.

The sense of living far removed from nature and from the rhythms of rural life emerges strongly in contemporary accounts of the city, as urbanisation starts to corrode the stability of religion and tradition – both powerfully cohesive elements in rural communities, and central to death rites. The debased urban death style of the lower stratum of society was a source of great concern to Chadwick, who worked tirelessly through the General Board of Health and the Poor Law Commission to effect reform. His reports give a dismal picture of the mêlée in the metropolis and the 'profanation arising from interment amidst the scenes of the crowd and bustle of everyday life'. He describes irreverent crowds of curious onlookers muscling in on newsworthy funerals, such as those of suicides, murder victims and children killed in street accidents. He also describes dispirited vicars complaining about the volume of funerals, which led to unseemly scenes with funeral parties queuing for their turn, converging and harassing each other. Continually, the funeral was disrupted by 'the reckless din of secular traffic'.

Above and below ground, the dramatic influx of people towards cities was affecting the quality of life. The living struggled to co-exist with the dead. Of the considerable coverage given to the burial crisis in the nineteenth century, Walker was the most influential commentator and ardent campaigner. He embodies the philanthropic spirit of the time, and his lurid accounts of bodybugs crawling from coffins and mourners slipping on human remains captured the public imagination and put burial reform high on the government agenda. His first and most powerful polemic, published in 1839, was the result of a personal survey of around fifty urban graveyards. The title sets the tone: *Gatherings from Graveyards; particularly those of London with a concise history of the modes of interment among different nations, from the earliest periods; and a detail of dangerous and fatal results produced by the unwise and revolting custom of inhuming the dead in the midst of the living.* In a style rich in gothic horror and exuberant disgust he conveys the physical perils of proximity to putrefying bodies, but also the damage to mental and moral well-being:

> Burial places in the neighbourhood of the living are, in my opinion, a natural evil – the harbingers, if not the originators, of pestilence; the cause direct or indirect of inhumanity, immorality and irreligion.

He gives gut-wrenching accounts of the density of human remains as gravediggers struggle to make room for a new interment:

> It often happens that every opposing obstacle is cut through and that the legs the head or even the half of a body are frequently dissevered. Thus among all classes of society, those who have been loved during this life, and to whose remains the last affectionate duties have been paid are – after they have passed perhaps for ever from our sight, though they may dwell in our remembrance – subjected to the most disgusting indignities. Even the enormous fees paid in some places cannot secure for our dead undisturbed repose.

Walker's findings were corroborated before the parliamentary committee in 1842, and in 1846, in order to promote burial reform further, he founded the National Society for the Abolition of Burial in Towns. A donation of £5 secured life membership of this organisation whose target audience was 'the Press and the friends of physical and moral regeneration'. To this end, Walker delivered a series of lectures on metropolitan graveyards in which he described 'practices that would disgrace if not disgust a cannibal'. His catalogue of unscrupulous behaviour included the sale of coffin plates and handles, and coffin wood being used as firewood. In one case a penitent woman threw away her kettle 'as she could not fancy the water in consequence of its having been boiled with wood from a coffin'. To prevent this abuse, Walker suggested that 'a considerable reduction in the price of coal will destroy one of the temptations to violate the tomb – a practice most shocking and injurious to all concerned'.

More horrific was the commonplace violation of corpses, as when skulls were used to play skittles in St Ann's, Soho. But abominations sank to new depths in the notorious Spa Fields burying ground in Clerkenwell.

> The gravediggers in this ground have committed the most fearful and un-heard of atrocities on the bodies of the dead. The long hair of the women has been cut off and sold to the hair-dressers; 'rails' (teeth) have been taken from every corpse affording them of sufficient quality to stimulate their cupidity; whilst the materials in which the bodies of the dead had been clothed by the hand of affection have been in hundreds of instances torn off by these midnight prowlers.

The same burial ground was the subject of a sensational work published by Walker in 1846 entitled *Burial Ground Incendiarism: The Last Fire at the Bone House in the Spa Fields Golgotha or the Minute Anatomy of Gravedigging in London*. In addition to being sold as fuel, coffins were also burned in bulk to make more space. At Spa Fields an illicit fire in the bone house became a serious conflagration when a gravedigger mistakenly poured pitch instead of water on to the flames. The engine keeper of the parish of Clerkenwell had to break down the door with a crowbar.

Ordinary people witnessed scenes of depravity. At St Matthews, Cheapside a young woman called Elizabeth Norris gave an eyewitness account of human remains being 'kicked about' like rubbish:

> She observed a thigh bone with flesh upon it, as broad as her hand, and a foot in length; a spinal bone also with flesh attached to it, a silk handker-chief stained with blood, evidently used to tie up a person's jaw; and a woollen mattrass, still bearing the impression of a human figure.

Even more distressing, the bereaved often saw the mutilated and brutalised remains of people they knew. In one burial ground, 'amongst a heap of rubbish, a young woman recognised the finger of her mother who had been buried there a short time previous'.

A letter to *The Times* in 1838 elaborates on these fears.

Sir,
Passing along Portugal street on Saturday evening, about ten minutes before seven, I was much shocked at seeing two men employed in carrying
baskets of human bones from the corner of the ground next to the old
watch house (where there was a tarpaulin hung over the rails to prevent
their being seen and where they appeared to be heaped up in a mound) to
the back of the ground through a small gate.

Where this leads to I do not know but I should be glad through the
medium of your invaluable journal to ask why is this desecration?

Sir, I feel more particularly than many might do, as I have seen twelve of
my nearest and dearest relatives consigned to the grave in that ground; and
I felt that perhaps, I might at that moment be viewing, in the basket of
skulls which passed before me, those of my own family thus brutally exhumed.

At all events, for the sake of the community at large it should be en-
quired into.

Before the nineteenth century, a few lone voices had heralded the need
for new burial arrangements, highlighting the health hazards of burying
the dead among the living in densely populated areas. Isabella Holmes
makes reference to a sermon preached by Bishop Latimer in 1522:

I do marvel that London being so great a city, hath not a burial place without; for no doubt it is an unwholesome thing to bury within the City especially at such a time, when there be great sicknesses, and many die
together.

In the seventeenth century Sir Christopher Wren was ahead of his time in
mooting the idea of establishing cemeteries on the outskirts of the City of
London. In 1721 Thomas Lewis published a pamphlet entitled *Churches No
Charnel Houses; being an inquiry into the profaneness, indecency and pernicious
consequences to the living of burying the dead in churches and churchyards.* He
condemned this as a practice 'begun through pride, improved by superstition and encouraged for lucre'. It was not until the nineteenth century,
however, that worsening conditions reached crisis level and extra-mural
burial became a matter of universal concern.

It seems ironic that an age which throbbed with the power of the factory and the foundry, and which prised from nature the liberating force of
steam, was for so many years complacent in its approach to dealing
efficiently with the most natural processes of human waste and human

remains. The standard view of the nineteenth century is of an age of expansion and progress, of an empire being built through the sheer might of a small island's ideology and technology. The steam locomotive, the railway, the beginnings of petrol production in 1850 and, towards the end of the century, Faraday's advances with electricity expanded possibilities for commerce and tourism, and revolutionised human mobility. Yet less often considered is the flipside of this boom – the sludge beneath the surface of Georgian and Victorian enterprise. The by-products of industrialisation were congestion and contamination, a slurry of sewage in rivers, and churchyards clogged up with corpses

In descriptions of this period there is a powerful sense of pollutants leaking and seeping into the air and water, of the city as a collapsed lung gasping for clean air. It is fitting that one of the pioneers of the cemetery movement should state the need for cemeteries to be 'breathing places', for in creating a context in which the need for burial reform is most urgently felt, the olfactory sense is the one to which Victorian writing most frequently appeals. Periodicals, novels and newspapers are permeated with the stench of putrefaction. In 'City of London Churches', an essay in *The Uncommercial Traveller*, Dickens writes that 'Rot and mildew and dead citizens formed the uppermost scent in the city'. Attending church he breathes in 'a strong kind of invisible snuff, up my nose, into my eyes, down my throat. I wink, I sneeze, I cough.' He continues, 'Not only do we cough and sneeze dead citizens, all through the service, but dead citizens have got into the very bellows of the organ, and half choked the same.' The 'pestiferous exhalations of the dead' were at the core of Walker's campaign, and he underpinned his arguments with scientific proof detailing a series of extraordinary experiments on destructive vapour in graves carried out by a French scientist, Dr Haguenot, in Montpelier in 1744.

> First experiment Dr Haguenot had the grave opened, – a very fetid odour issued from it, which impregnated linen, thread, even glass bottles and clothes, with a cadaverous odour.
>
> Second experiment – Lighted paper, chips and tarred rope, placed at the opening of the grave, were entirely extinguished.
>
> Third experiment – cats and dogs were thrown into this grave, were strongly convulsed, and expired in two to three minutes – birds in some seconds.
>
> Fourth experiment – the mephitic vapour from the grave was collected and preserved in bottles, and six weeks afterwards submitted to the same experiments; it had lost none of its destructive properties.
>
> These experiments were made in the presence of a Committee of

scientific gentlemen and demonstrate the danger arising from cadaverous vapours, and consequently that of interment in churches.

The fixation with the toxicity of the dead was reinforced by evidence that people had been harmed. Walker described the startling impact of inhaling noxious gases from a coffin on his colleague Mr Sutton. Sutton's alarming symptoms included

> vomiting accompanied with frequent flatulent eructations, highly fetid, and having the same character as the gas inspired. He reached home with difficulty and was confined to his bed during seven days.

One of the most famous cases of 'fatal miasmas' was reported by the *Weekly Despatch* in 1838. Under the headline 'Two Men Suffocated in Grave', it describes how two gravediggers were killed by noxious gas in the base of a deep pauper's grave. One of them was literally knocked out by the smell: 'He appeared as if struck by a cannon ball, and fell back and appeared instantly to expire.' This was not journalistic sensationalism. One of the most respected voices on cemeteries was the writer John Claudius Loudon. In his seminal work *On the Laying Out Planting and Managing of Cemeteries and on the Improvement of Churchyards* (1843) he spells out the harmful effects: 'to inhale this gas, undiluted with atmospheric air, is instant death and even when diluted, it is productive of disease which commonly ends in death'.

The stench of the dead was a staple topic of public discussion in the pages of numerous publications, and the prosaic aspect of human mortality – that is, an excess of dead flesh in urban areas – became a preoccupation verging on obsession. It was the principal theme of Chadwick's government report, which in turn was backed up by compelling evidence from witnesses who vividly conveyed the strained relationship between the living and the dead. A society woman who lived near a congested churchyard described the problem of noxious neighbours who were particularly objectionable when the wind was in a westerly direction:

> The smell was very peculiar; it exactly resembled the smell which clothes have when they are removed from a dead body. My servants would not remain in the house on account of it, and I had several cooks who removed on this account. (Edwin Chadwick, 1843)

The nineteenth century reeked and, as time went on, exasperation about this escalated. Dr Lyon Playfair, postmaster general to Queen Victoria, even attempted to quantify the problem. He estimated that for the year

1849 the smelly dead of London – all 52,000 of them – generated 2,572,580 cubic feet of noxious gases. Bad smells culminated in the Big Stink of 1858, when the Thames became a fetid cesspit and the curtains in the House of Commons had to be doused in chloride of lime so that MPs could breathe more easily. But the definitive expression of concern must surely be that expressed in an article in *The Builder* in 1843, which gives the impression that the author is holding his nose and covering his mouth with a handkerchief as he writes:

> This London, the centre of civilisation, this condensation of wisdom and intelligence, this huge wedge and conglomerate of pride, buries – no, it does not bury but stores and piles up – 50,000 of its dead to putrefy, to rot, to give out exhalations, to darken the air with vapours, faugh!

In France the problem of what to do with the urban dead had been addressed much earlier. Lurid accounts of meat and milk going off in the neighbourhoods of city churchyards, and reports of sickly children with a peculiar pallor attributed to proximity to human remains, had given cause for alarm. As early as the mid-eighteenth century, the abuses of interment in cities were the subject of legislation which resulted in the closure of city graveyards and in the case of the Cimetière des Innocents in Paris, manual relocation. From December 1784 to October 1787, 1,000 carts of bones were removed to catacombs hewn from old quarries on the outskirts of the city. An estimated six million Parisians were stacked floor-to-ceiling in eerie corridors. A seam of skulls ran through the arrangements of tibia, fibula and thigh bones like cake filling. This configuration did not meet with the approval of the *Quarterly Review* (1819).

> It would have been better to put them out of sight and wall them up in quarries than to arrange them in patterns along the wall – skulls and thigh bones, like muskets and pistols in the small armoury at the Tower. Such exhibitions cannot have a salutory tendency; they foster that disease of mind in which melancholy madness has its foundation; they harden brutal natures, and are more likely to provoke the licentious to impious bravadoes than to reclaim them.

Although the Paris bones are better known, more spectacular arrangements, although on a much smaller scale, are to be found at the ossuary near Kutná Hora in the Czech Republic. In 1870 when František Ritna was commissioned by the Schwarzenburg family to rearrange the inhabitants of a fourteenth-century bone house, he pushed artistic licence to the limit. Great garlands of skulls hung around the walls like paper decorations, the

Schwarzenburg family crest was reworked in the bones of anonymous dead serfs, and a huge skull-and-bone chandelier looked like a macabre mix of rococo ornament and gothic horror.

It was with the establishment of the great Parisian cemetery of Père Lachaise in 1804 that the French set a new standard for the civilised treatment of human remains and safe burial practice. The first of four cemeteries, it was designed to utilise the skills of the architect, the sculptor and the horticulturist. The resultant blend of fine monuments in a pleasing landscape created a new aesthetic for the topography of death which was subsequently emulated by many English and American cemeteries. Père Lachaise is widely regarded as the prototype of the garden cemetery, although as it appears today there is little sense of leafy Arcadia and more of an upmarket residential enclave, a millionaires' row of high-security mausolea. The discreet exclusivity of this silent estate took a dive in 1971 when Jim Morrison, lead singer of The Doors, moved in after dying in Paris, aged 27, as a result of a reckless cocktail of drink, drugs and asthma medicine. At his grave, a perpetual stream of teenage pilgrims light up cigarettes, rather than candles, while votive gestures include a message scratched on a nearby grave: 'Jim we want to have your babies.'

If Jim lowers the tone, in the early days of the cemetery the founder, Nicholas Frochot, took great pains to acquire several celebrity corpses. This was a savvy marketing ruse, for interring Molière, Jean de la Fontaine and the celebrated lovers Héloïse and Abélard convinced status-conscious Parisians that Père Lachaise was the place to be seen dead in. It also became a fashionable destination for casual visitors, which did not win the approval of the more conservative English. 'The Pleasure Ground Treatment of Cemeteries in France' was the subject of an editorial in the *Quarterly Review* in 1819:

> The Parisians have acted like themselves in making shew catacombs and *cimetières ornés* ...It would hardly happen in the neighbourhood of London that we should have a Guide to the Burial Grounds, as a fashionable promenade; that parties would be made to visit them; nor, though grief is proverbially dry, that taverns and drinking houses should be established close beside them, for the accommodation not only of these parties of pleasure but of the mourners also!

This article, published in the year of Queen Victoria's birth, underestimated the English. On 12 June 1831, *The Times* reported the public response to the new catacombs at St Martin's: 'Crowds of ladies perambulated the vaults for some time, and the whole had more the appearance of a fashionable promenade than a grim depository of decomposing mortality.' Notwithstanding the 1819 article's disapproving tone, it acknowledged the superiority of French death style: 'The monuments in the new Parisian cemeteries are generally in good taste, better than is usually found in England.' French flair was also evident in some inspired individual responses.

> We are told that a former possessor of Ermenonville planted dead trees in his gardens, *pour inspirer la philosophie*. But the oddest display of this kind was exhibited by a certain M. de Brunoi, who put his park in mourning for the death of his mother and had barrels of ink sent from Paris that the *jets d'eau* might be in mourning also.

While the cemetery movement forged ahead in France and America, England was lackadaisical – as Walker lamented, 'a silent and unmoved spectatress of some of the most offensive and dangerous encroachments upon the security and sanctity of the resting places of her dead'. While Parisians appreciated the elegant sophistication of their new cemeteries, Londoners experienced almost farcical scenes as entrepreneurs capitalised on the worsening crisis by running private burial grounds at competitive rates and employing bogus priests.

> In Butlers burial ground, (Horsleydown), for instance the person who read the burial service (of the Church of England) wore a surplice, but he was merely an employee of the undertaker, who also acted as porter.

> In Hoole and Martin's ground a Mr Thomas Jenner was employed to officiate at funerals for £20 a year! He also read the burial service of the Church of England, but he was by trade a shoemaker, or a patten-maker whose shop was close by. (Isabella Holmes, *The London Burial Grounds*, 1896)

Although public health was the driving force of the burial reform movement, in England there was another scion of the cemetery movement whose influence tends to be eclipsed by the public health lobby. Rather as today the green movement are establishing woodland burial sites which reflect their lifestyle, and are outside the jurisdiction of the established Church, in the early part of the nineteenth century the non-conformists started to press for burial sites that were not affiliated to the Church of England. An increasingly powerful population of non-conformists was responsible for a wave of new cemeteries which opened before the public health campaign gathered momentum. Importantly, they also pioneered the concept of the joint stock cemetery system, whereby new cemeteries were financed by the sale of shares. The first burial ground that could properly be termed a cemetery was the Rosary in Norwich, which was licensed in 1819 to provide burial for anyone who could afford the fee. Soon afterwards, non-conformist burial grounds were cropping up throughout the country. The best known is Rusholme Road, Manchester, which opened in 1820. Also significant are Westgate Hill Cemetery, Newcastle (1825) and the Glasgow Necropolis (1831), a spectacular hill-top city of the dead, full of grand monuments.

Although London was worst affected by the burial crisis, it lagged behind other British cities. Influenced by the non-conformists' approach, barrister George Carden played a prominent role in forming the first commercial enterprise to open a cemetery in London. At one stage a wildly ambitious proposal was put forward by the architect Thomas Wilson in the form of giant pyramid to be erected on Primrose Hill with space for five million bodies. It was to be as high as St Paul's Cathedral, with a base as big as Russell Square, an observatory at the top and, in the architect's words, it would provide 'a *coup d'oeil* of sepulchral magnificence unequalled in the world'. By comparison, the General Cemetery Company executed a more down-to-earth proposal when they opened Kensal Green in 1833. Although it is often referred to as the British Père Lachaise, Kensal Green has more of a feeling of *rus in urbe* than its namesake. Similarly, it acquired considerable social cachet as a result of some celebrity interments. When two children of Mad King George, Princess Sophia and Augustus Frederick, Duke of Sussex, were interred there, its reputation for the status-conscious was sealed.

Such was the success of Kensal Green that other private enterprise cemeteries quickly followed: West Norwood(1837), Highgate (1839), Abney Park (1840), Brompton (1840), Nunhead (1840) and Tower Hamlets (1841). Enthusiasts of nineteenth-century cemeteries regard these as 'the magnificent seven'. Years of neglect have taken their toll on these great cemeteries, yet the palpable sense of decay enhances their aesthetic appeal, particularly in the catacombs. These cool corridors are amongst the few places left in life where you can smell the concentrated mustiness of time that you normally experience only fleetingly when suddenly opening an old trunk. In the algae-coated corridors of Brompton catacombs, 1,200 distinguished Victorian were 'deposited' between 1841 and the late 1890s. Where the oak outer cases have rotted away, you can glimpse the thick lead linings of the coffins which must have been extraordinarily heavy for the men who bore them down the wide flight of stairs. At Kensal Green a hydraulic catafalque provided a much more dramatic method of conveyance from chapel to catacomb. Like an elaborate disappearing trick, complete with the magician's material of black velvet, the coffin vanished from the sight of the mourners. John Claudius Loudon (who now lies at Kensal Green) explains the mechanics:

> This machine, while it lowers the bier through the floor, moves at the same time two horizontal shutters, which gradually close the opening in the floor as the coffin descends from the view of the spectators in the chapel; by the time they have arrived in the area below, the bier is already at the bottom, while the coffin on it ready to be removed to the vault. The great advantage of screw movement for the descent of the bier is that the motion can never be otherwise than slow and solemn, and that it cannot run down in case of the handle being set at liberty.

The fund-raising efforts of the Friends of Kensal Green mean that 'this admirable contrivance' has now been fully restored at a cost of £41,885.83 compared to the original total cost of £400, and is now a highlight of their regular catacomb and chapel guided tours. Such dignity and theatre seem infinitely preferable to the modern practice at the crematorium, with the sound of Celine Dion singing her Titanic number as, similarly doomed never to return from her maiden voyage, the coffin disappears – a clumsy commotion in a synthetic sea, as peach Dralon waves ripple and close. *Finus Coronat Opus* – not.

In nineteenth-century cemetery society, death – far from being a great leveller – divided people mercilessly according to their monetary capability. Cemetery prospectuses reveal a wide difference in prices according to first-second- or third-class requirements. Cassell's *Household Guide* advised readers that 'interment in a brick vault is the most costly, and is only suited for those in comfortable circumstances'. Vaults at Highgate and Kensal Green were the most expensive at £49 7s. 6d. and, while a shelf in a catacomb may have seemed a much better deal at both Highgate (£17 10s.) and Kensal Green (£19 5s.), 'it must be remembered that additional expense attends interments in vaults and catacombs owing to the regulations which require lead coffins to be used'. Price lists and options read like railway fare descriptions: 'adult single interment in third-class ground', 'single interment in second-class ground', or 'private brick grave in a first-class portion of the ground'.

This comparison with rail fares takes on a different dimension in the railway funerals pioneered by Brookwood Cemetery in Woking. The *Spectator* announced

The novelty of the railway train is to have the newer novelty of the funeral train. Once a day the black line will leave the metropolis for Woking, the station will put on a funeral aspect and death will take its turn amid the busiest traffic of life. (14 November 1854)

The forty-minute journey departed from a private station at 121 Westminster Bridge Road, Waterloo, at 11.20 every morning, and trains terminated at either the north station for non-conformists, or the south station for Anglican funerals. Rather as today VIP airline passengers can go to the final departure gate more quickly than economy class, a prospectus for the London Necropolis Company suggests a similar approach to their RIP customers.

Funerals must arrive at the London Terminus in the case of the first class 10 minutes, those of the second class 20 minutes and those of the third class 30 minutes at least before the time of starting of the train, and the coffin will then be immediately transferred into the railway hearse carriage, and the Company will conduct the remaining portion of the funeral. Other funeral trains will be added when required by increased traffic.

For the mourners on return tickets, the first-, second- and third-class fares were 6s., 3s. 6d., and 2s. respectively. For the silent passengers on one-way tickets, instead of coffin class, they travelled either first, second or third class at the respective rates of £1, 5s and 2s. 6d. In his riveting book *The Brookwood Necropolis Railway* (1992), historian John Clark highlights the degree of importance attached to class distinction by quoting Mr Wyndham Harding, the secretary of the London and South Western Railway:

We should have to lift by the simplest possible machinery the coffins of the poorest class and put them in to a great carriage constructed for the purpose ... If one were to come to the better class, we should have to do it in a different way. We should have to take them up one by one, and to allow mourners to see the coffin put in if they chose to, and to do it in a more circumspect manner than with regard to the paupers, merely attended by the Parish Officers.

The railway funerals did not catch on. The London Necropolis Company failed to prosper, and although there was ample scope in the extensive acreage and efficient access via the reliable services of the South West Railway, it certainly did not fulfil its original ambition of accommodating a considerable proportion of the dead denizens of London. Of the 52,000 or so number of deaths per year in the capital, Brookwood's annual rate of burial averaged only 3,200.

One of the more disquieting aspects of the nineteenth-century burial crisis is the way in which disposal of the dead became prey to commercial enterprise. Sustainability remains a challenge for the contemporary cemetery, but thankfully today there is less of a climate of entrepreneurial opportunity and speculative trade surrounding the way in which we dispose of the dead than there was in the days when the London Necropolis Company was trying to make a profit. Then, the delicate balance between sensitivity and economics was less well gauged. The conflict of interest was the subject of a *memorandum* of the Sanitary Association in 1852.

> The Companies (with one or two exceptions) scarcely get a living return for their capital: and they are constantly tempted to forego their religious scruples for the sake of their money interests – having indeed no other alternative than the sacrifice of their duty or their dividends.

It continues,

> No wonder that the Woking Necropolis Company entering on such a career of ruinous competition offended the public decency, a few days since by proposing to deposit the corpses entrusted to it for burial, in the dry arches under the South Western Railway, and thence to transport them to their final resting place in the horse boxes attached on the other railway trains. No wonder that in one of the Eastern burial grounds, the person officiating as minister has been accustomed to assume at one time the vestments of a Church of England clergyman, and at another the garb of a dissenting minister, according to the religious denomination of the applicants for his clerical service. All these, and many similar evils of a moral and religious kind, grow out of the pecuniary difficulties inseparable from the fragmentary burial arrangements ...

This criticism reverberates in the present, for as recently as the autumn of 2000 the incoming president of the Institute of Burial and Cremation Authorities, Ian Hussein, called for consolidation and stressed the urgent need to establish a national body with responsibility for running all the country's cemeteries.

A more emotive expression of concern about the intrusion of the worldly into the realm of the sacred occurs in *The Cemetery*, the long poem mentioned earlier:

> Yet yield no joint stock undertakers room,
> Nor let the sexton traffic in the tomb.
> In hands that grasp at worldly gain, the trust
> Is ill reposed of consecrated dust;

Where on full length prospectus flaunts unfurl'd
A railway company to th'other world;
A speculation in the last of cares,
Where pestilence shall raise the price of shares.

The London Necropolis Company's use of a train to take the dead to a commercially run cemetery a long way from the living is a good metaphor for the way that distance and money in the guise of progress changed the pattern of disposal of the dead. The train to Woking, like the hired hearses that drove people to crematoria a long way from their own neighbour-hood, undermined the close-knit community and the custom of parish bur-ial. Instead of the local funeral procession and the cohesion of a community rallying around the bereaved, death was shunted into the private realm. Instead of the cycle of kinship and the comfort of knowing that, in death, you would lie by those who had known you, the dead were henceforth anonymous and in the company of strangers. The congregation united by baptising, marrying and burying was divided, death was isolated as a rite of passage, and the deceased was driven into extra-mural exile, accompanied by smaller units of kith and kin.

The Sanitary Association objected to the practical implications of this change:

> The change from intra mural to extra mural interment involves the annual transport of 52,000 corpses, attended by between a quarter and half a million mourners, ten times as far as they now go for burial. This ten-fold prolongation of funeral transit, with the consequent increase of conveyance costs, is one of the chief difficulties to be dealt with in any scheme of extra mural sepulture.

Outweighing cost was the social and psychological impact of distancing the dead in cemeteries. William Hale, Archdeacon of London, eloquently expressed his fears on this theme.

> As respects the poor, their being compelled as they now are, to carry their dead to a long distance, attended by the smallest number of friends and relations, is destructive of that solemnity which was wont to attend the walking funeral from the poor man's residence to his Parish Church; and the dimunition of the number of mourners, now necessary to avoid expense, is a narrowing of the exercise of the best feelings, as it causes the fewest tears of the fewest relations to be shed over the grave. The solemnities of death used to unite all the members of the family in paying respect to the dead, and recognising the ties of nature by which they were bound, but

journeys to distant cemeteries and all the noise and rapidity of the railway, dissipate serious thought, and make burial the work of business rather than of religion. Modern Cemetery burial appears to me injurious to religion, in the exact proportion in which it separates the Parishioner from his Parish and from the place of worship and of weekly if not of daily concourse.

In the vast body of support for the sanitary advantages of cemeteries, Hale's impassioned arguments *against* the cemetery movement are striking. Expressed in a pamphlet entitled *Intramural Burial in England Not Injurious to the Public Health Its Abolition Injurious to Religion and Morals* (1855), it is an extraordinary counter-argument, a lone voice spelling out the radical damage to society threatened by the Burial Act. Before focusing in more detail on Hale's arguments, it is perhaps helpful to sketch the legislative background to his objections.

Although in 1842 the select committee had concluded that the crisis was so severe that no time should be lost in applying for a remedy, they did not respond with any urgency. It took a cholera epidemic of 1849, which claimed 14,500 lives in London alone, to provide the impetus for government action, and it was not until 1850 that the first law was passed, starting a steady stream of legislation about burial of the dead. When the problems arising from commercial enterprise started to be recognised, the 1850 law was refined and enlarged upon by the Metropolitan Burials Act of 1852. It is this Act which set the pattern for cemetery management today and provoked Hale's ire. Put crudely, it represented a victory for bureaucracy over belief. Crucially, it granted authority for the closure of overcrowded churchyards and responsibility for the provision of cemeteries to local burial boards, which anticipated contemporary local authorities.

The general consensus was that the new law represented progress. Charles Greene, clerk to the Burial Board of St Pancras, spoke for many when he described it as 'a liberal piece of legislation quite in accordance with the spirit of the times and the age of sanitary improvement in which we live'. Death was now primarily and officially a public health issue. This was even played upon in advertisements such as that placed in a friendly society magazine by the London Necropolis Company: 'The only Cemetery Company which combines in its practice a proper regard to public health and public decency'.

In this context of support and approval, Hale presents a compelling alternative view to the idea that the cemetery is a civilised concept. In fact, he argues the opposite, and spells out the dangers of burying the dead in places where society has no concourse, 'Deserts of the dead as have been

THE CHANGING LANDSCAPE OF DEATH

formed at Woking Common and Kensal Green'. Central to his argument is the idea that alienating the living from the dead encourages them not only to forget the dead – 'to bury the dead in places apart from human habitation is to overwhelm their memories in darkness' – but to forget death. The notion that the cemetery helped to promote a culture of death denial resonates with significance for the modern reader and, with hindsight, Hale's slim publication is both prophetic and moving.

> I cannot any longer forbear giving vent in public to feelings, which I have expressed to many friends in private; and endeavouring at whatever cost, to avert from my Church and country as great an evil as can befall us – neglect of the dead, and loss of their example.

Although religious conviction informs his arguments and his stance is outrage about the enforced closure of churchyards, the sense of a social fabric being torn badly strikes a chord. The congregation, the key unit of community, was decimated by the segregation of the dead in impersonal cemeteries. Similarly, the motivations he attributes to those advocating removal of the dead from the midst of the living remain relevant.

> The one great object of all the opponents to Intramural Burial appears to be the entire separation of the mansions of the dead from the houses of the living: the modern Hygenist advocating the measure for the sake of the public health, and the modern Epicurean, because nothing is so painful to him as the thought or the sight of death.

Hale refutes the health arguments on which the cemetery movement was based and, in the best spirit of Victorian campaigners, he backs up his views with scientific evidence. His colleague, a professor of chemistry at King's College, at his request conducted experiments in which he buried organic matter in a lead box and also directly in the earth, and then analysed the gases emanating forth. The evidence was inconclusive: 'His answer at that time to me was that gaseous chemistry is too much in its infancy to enable us to come to any result.' Hale rounds on the public health lobby, accusing them of blinding the public with science and misleading them.

> It is an easy thing to use scientific terms such as miasma and gases and deleterious emanations and if you talk scientifically, or appear to do so, you may easily persuade simple-minded persons to distrust their own experience, and though they are not aware of anything being wrong to make them begin to think it may be so.

The complaint resonating through his appeal that the evidence is too insubstantial to warrant radical government action such as the compulsory closure of churchyards.

> Having for many years conversed with men of science, chemists, physiologists and physicians, I never heard any chemical principle alleged, or argument from analogy brought forward, from which it could be concluded, that the atmosphere of our churches or our churchyards is unwholesome or dangerous to health, which would not equally prove that all places are unwholesome, or what is probably the real truth, that there is no place however generally healthy, no substance however generally nutritious, that is not found to be to some person, under some circumstances an exciting cause of disease.

Again, what makes reading Hale so interesting from a contemporary stance is that his views are whispers of issues which are amplified today. With health scares multiplying daily, our relationship with the environment is becoming increasingly fraught. It is also becoming increasingly influential in determining how we deal with the dead. The implications of a border dispute and the sense of 'God's Acre' being trespassed on by sanitarians – today, environmentalists – are highly relevant to the modern map of death.

To appreciate the extent to which the boundaries have changed, one only has to glance at a plethora of historical pamphlets written by clergymen. These indicate how authoritarian and strictly territorial the Anglican Church was in the nineteenth century compared to the grey area it occupies today. The titles say it all: for example, *Children That Have Been Registered and Dying Without Having Been Baptised are Not Entitled to Christian Burial* and *A Clergyman's Defence of Himself for Refusing to Use the Office for Burial of the Dead Over One Who Destroyed Himself.* The impression of patrol and rigidity is in striking contrast to contemporary flexibility, as evidenced by the advent of the Christian woodland burial site, where, for instance, recently the Revd Peter Owen Jones concurred with the request from an atheist nihilist parishioner to inter her without ceremony or the help of a funeral director.

Importantly, the cemetery movement brought a secular aesthetic to death. The garden cemetery concept created a landscape of earthly delights, a place of recreation and contemplation at once worldly and otherworldly, for as much as they afforded solace for the bereaved, in the early days the new cemeteries provided shareholders with healthy dividends. They were visited regularly both by the casual visitor and by the bereaved, and at one time it became fashionable to send photographs of graves to relatives and friends. Guidebooks read like travel brochures. The official handbook for Kensal Green, published in 1843, suggests that, like the perfect resort, whatever the weather it's worth a visit, presenting as it does 'a smiling countenance as well amidst the gloomy winter as in the sunny days of blooming summer', and that it 'allures us to enter its sacred precincts both by the floral charms within and the view afforded thence of the extensive and pleasing scenery without'. Abney Park in Stoke Newington, known as the Campo Santo of the non-conformists, had a magnificent arboretum, ponds of water-lilies and a vast variety of trees and shrubs, which were labelled as if in a botanical garden. Mrs Stone, writing in 1858, enthuses, 'a more beautiful and luxurious garden it is impossible to conceive'. The overwhelming impression in contemporary descriptions is of landscapes designed to alleviate death's sting. Of the picturesque setting at Brookwood, a prospectus of the London Necropolis Company assures readers that 'they will hardly fail to acknowledge that even death is not bereft of consolation'.

In the twentieth century there has been an almost catastrophic disregard for the aesthetic aspect of the cemetery: low-cost maintenance has been the priority. This could not be more different from the vision of the pioneers of the cemetery movement, particularly the Scotsman Dr John Strang, the force behind the great necropolis at Glasgow and author of *Necropolis Glasguensis* (1831), and the landscape designer John Claudius Loudon. They believed that the cemetery was as much about the civilised disposal of the dead as about exerting a civilising influence on the living, a landscape literally cultivated for moral instruction. The sense of Nature's capacity for consolation being realised by the gardening skills of man is powerful in a description of a walk through Woking cemetery, featured in a friendly society magazine in 1863:

> The various plots of roses and the blooming flowers give to the heath-like appearance of the place a very pleasing effect which might be greatly and easily improved in beauty by the Company planting a few score of quick growing trees, as poplars, willows etc., at certain distances, and as the railway could help them, about a dozen truck loads of rich mould could be obtained at little expense.

The emphasis on the horticultural aspect of the garden cemetery and the design and execution of planting schemes seems to encode an attempt to keep death under control. The twentieth-century lawn grave, designed for the municipal mower to speed around, is a less inspired version of this, signifying a bland practicality. Along with the regimented rows of rose bushes it symbolises a sad attempt to keep death tidy.

The landscape was the backdrop for commemorative monuments with a richly symbolic vocabulary: broken columns for life cut short, inverted torches for life extinguished, butterflies for resurrection, the serpent with its tail in its mouth for eternity. By comparison, the modern commemorative idiom is as slang – sand-blasted pictures of pop stars and cars, mawkish messages often on mass-produced memorials made of corned-beef granite of the kind that is also found in abundance in shopping malls in Hong Kong. Displaying the same zeal with which, in life, they spent their money to show their social standing, the prospering Victorian middle classes developed a taste for flamboyant, extravagant monuments to affirm their standing in death. Echoing the freed-slave syndrome in the early Roman Empire, when slaves who had gained their freedom erected extravagant monuments to flaunt their newly found status, Victorians relished using their wealth to assert their status. The height of some of their monuments – towering obelisks and tall angels – present a neat metaphor for their upward mobility. Walking around Kensal Green, you get a strong impression of an era when the self-made stormed the once-impregnable barriers of birth and rank that had historically dictated English death style in every detail, from the position of your tomb either in or outside the church to the design of the tomb itself. Not for celebrity circus performer Andrew Ducrow the discreet escutcheons and modesty of those to the mausoleum born – his monument is a wildly eccentric and egocentric mishmash of motifs, including beehives, sphinxes, angels and shells. It also features in stone his showman's hat and gloves, and is inscribed 'erected by Genius for the reception of its own remains'.

The trend for aggrandisement by memorial came in for criticism. The Sanitary Association objected to the

> above ground scandals of the trading cemeteries; such as for example the offensive prominence given in one cemetery to the monument of a public prize fighter, in another to the gigantic mausoleum of a patent medicine vendor, who had been prosecuted in his lifetime as a scandalous quack; and in a third case to the number of empty monuments, run up on speculation among the real tombs, for sale to the highest bidder.

But it was not just for being *arriviste* and transgressing social boundaries that nineteenth-century monuments were attacked. It was for destroying the sense of aesthetic unity. Again, this is vividly conveyed in *The Cemetery*:

> Allow the tomb its privacy – yet rate
> The grave-ground as the manor of the state.

Here taste should range, caprice should find control,
Forms individual tend towards the whole.
Not he alone, the mourner's watch who keeps,
Claims int'rest in the tomb o'er which he weeps;
Bid public criticism the sceptre claim,
Lest one man's sorrow be the general shame.
Nor clip too close the pinions of design,
Else will the rich evade thy rigid line,
And e'en in sorrow finding vent for spleen,
Shame art and squander cash at Kensal Green.

Amongst the silent citizens of dust
Yield due allowance, claim forbearance just.
None to himself alone may live or die,
None here as though alone he lay, may lie,
Let each design some central feeling warm,
The monuments a congregation form.

This poem highlights the changes in commemorative style that happened as a result of the cemetery movement. Where the consecrated ground of the churchyard had a weight of meaning as God's property and was subject to jurisdiction dating back to the thirteenth century, in the new cemeteries Mammon tended to take precedence. The change in system – from a burial ground where ideological kinship had imposed a strict sense of order to the position of the dead to one where the forces of individualism ran largely unchecked – was dramatic. Traditionally, the geography of the churchyard had powerful symbolism. For example, it was believed that those buried on the north side would at the Day of Judgement rise later than their more favourably located brethren. This belief is alluded to in an epitaph in Epworth churchyard, Lincolnshire, dated 1807, which was quoted in the *Westminster Review* in 1893.

And that I might longer undisturbed abide,
I chorsed to be laid on the northern side.

The cemetery movement heralded a more materialistic order. Commemoration was primarily social, size mattered, and the imagery was predominantly secular, with inscriptions leaning towards the sentimental more than the devotional – 'Not Lost But Gone Before', 'The Flower Fadeth', and a host of buxom stone angels looking more winsome than ethereal. Concern about the infiltration of the worldly into the religious context is expressed in an etiquette book of the period, which objects strongly to a memorial which recorded that the deceased was 'the largest single-handed brewer out of London':

> A marble monument, however fine the sculpture and costly the material, with an inscription such as this, is far more offensive and outrageous to true taste than the wooden memorial of the ignorant rustic, sculptured with painted bones and decked with death's-heads in all the colours of the rainbow. (Lady Colin Campbell, *Etiquette of Good Society*, 1893)

Monuments expressed individuality in a variety of ways: in scale, design, and the choice of stone (grey granite from Bodmin Moor, pink granite from Aberdeen, white carrera marble from Italy). They told stories – manner of death, descriptions of life events and occupations. For example, in Charlton cemetery is a memorial dated 1855 for a son lost at sea, on which the latitude and longitude of where he drowned are inscribed. Elsewhere motifs personalised memorials. For example in Chiswick Old Cemetery is a granite carved pith helmet and Union Jack made for an Empire builder who fought the Zulus. But less adventurous lives were also set forth for posterity. For example, at Abney Park, there is a memorial dedicated

> To Mary Hillum who died in the same house in which she was born, scarcely ever slept out of the house in the whole of her life never travelled either by omnibus or railway and was never more than fifteen miles from home.

The overarching impression of nineteenth-century memorials is of sentimentality and melodrama, weeping maids and endless draped urns – a trend which, in the opinion of *The Builder* magazine (1859), spun out of control at Highgate cemetery so that 'at last the object supposed to be covered presents a shapeless and unsightly mass'. This is in striking contrast to the restraint of the eighteenth century, which spawned a commemorative style of elegance and grace exemplified by neo-classical motifs, cartouches and sarcapoghi. It is as if an emotional anaesthetic had worn off. Suddenly memorials emphasised personal loss and engaged the viewer at a much less sophisticated level. An example of the monument as melodrama is that erected to Princess Charlotte in St George's Chapel, Windsor. It makes a direct emotional appeal. Against the backdrop of a vast, partially drawn curtain, bare-breasted and with arms outstretched like a prima donna taking a curtain call and keen to address the upper circle, the princess is shown gazing upwards, en route to heaven. She is flanked on either side by angels, who gaze at her like adoring fans. In the foreground, the outline of her dead body is draped in a large sheet surrounded by other draped figures, like furniture under dustsheets.

In simplistic terms, the index of psychological orientation to death as revealed by memorial styles over five centuries evolves from direct confrontation in the sixteenth and seventeenth centuries, to euphemism – angels ousting skeletons – in the eighteenth century, to sentimentality in the nineteenth century, and finally denial in the twentieth century. This is a pattern replicated in trends in mourning jewellery. Churchyards and cemeteries provide a visual record of how far society has moved from consciously remembering death with macabre motifs of *memento mori*, to consciously trying to forget death and tempering the horror of mortality with increasingly euphemistic imagery. Sixteenth- and seventeenth-century memorials reminded the viewer that he would die with skull-and-worm realism – a good example is the skull-studded monument for Dean Fotherby in Canterbury Cathedral – and graphic bunk-bed tombs where the fleshy occupant of the top bunk seems unaware of the mouldering version of himself beneath. This macabre imagery developed in the context of a society underpinned by a shared belief system and absolute faith in the afterlife. By contrast, memorials in today's municipal cemetery downplay death – a popular inscription is 'Death is Nothing at All'. The stone is often treated like a greeting card, as shown by recent requests for inscriptions such as 'Good Night Handsome XXX' and 'Take Care'.

A key element in the changing imagery of memorials – and, by extension, the meaning of death – is the rise of individualism. As man's sense of self has changed over time, so has his view of death. The greater the celebration of individuality, the sharper death's sting has become. Loss of identity is an insupportable concept, and this is central to the compulsion to commemorate. It is interesting to compare statements on individuality by two great thinkers in different centuries. In the eighteenth century, the French philosopher Jean Jacques Rousseau wrote:

> I am made unlike anyone I have ever met. I will even venture to say that I am like no one in the whole world. I may be no better but at least I am different. (*The Confessions*, 1781)

In the twentieth century Carl Jung stated in *Man and his Symbols* (1964):

> All the corpses in the world are chemically identical but living individuals are not.

Both comments concern individuality but are made in strikingly different psychological contexts, of optimism and pessimism respectively.

At the heart of Rousseau's thinking was a positive view of man's place in the world, an idealised vision of man in harmony with nature emulated by the style of his tomb on a private island in an idyllic landscape at Ermenonville. Romanticism flourished in the eighteenth century and spawned a fashion for mannered melancholy including mock ruins, gothic novels, and books extolling the virtues of paying visits to tombs. In 1778 Lady Miller's account of the delights of Italian catacombs inspired Sir John Soane to follow in her footsteps and make a tour of Italian catacombs, columbaria and mausolea. At the same time, George Wright urged his audience to take 'a serious walk in a place of skulls'. This was an elegant era for death. The urn was a recurring motif – not only on a pedestal as a favourite tomb style of the smart set, but as a popular decorative design used by Josiah Wedgwood on many products from salt cellars to jewellery. In death, individual lives were celebrated in epitaphs displayed on cartouches in churches. At this time railings started to be used to surround outdoor tombs, conferring a sense of both protection and private property.

In stark contrast to this confidence is the crisis of fragmentation and introspection in the twentieth century. Edvard Munch's painting *The Scream* (1913) and Samuel Beckett's bleak absurdist vision of the world as an 'old muckball' are but two examples of the pessimism left in the space that God once filled. In a world of mass death where man's sense of himself as his own destroyer has added a new dimension to self-awareness, death has become for the majority an unmanageable and unimaginable prospect. Instead of contemplating death, man has done everything in his power to forget it. There has never been an era comparable to the twentieth century for giving man such a demoralised and reductive view of himself – blasted to oblivion in no man's land, a shadow on scorched earth at Hiroshima, a canister of ashes scattered to the wind or poured down a grating.

An important aspect of our attitude to death is the way in which we define our abstract relationship to the dead. This is evolving in interesting new ways, causing us to re-evaluate the function of a physical memorial which marks the place where a body lies. In the twentieth century, commemoration and remembrance tended to be social rather than religious. One consequence of a loss of faith and decreased church attendance is that the once-powerful cohesion between the extant congregation and the silent one that its members were destined to join was fragmented. Loss, separation and rupture started to exacerbate death as a crisis, where once the belief in salvation, reunion and repose – and, most importantly, the doctrine of the resurrection – had diminished the sense of ending and even made redundant the need for a physical memorial. The evolution of memorials and commemorative architecture signifies the substitution for a collective system of dealing with death where the emphasis was on the soul, with an individualistic system which placed more importance on memory.

In our mind's eye, reinforced by the weight of tradition, our idealised mental picture of the landscape of death tends to take the shape of a memorial over an individual grave. This is interesting, because until well into the sixteenth century, with the exception of the nobility, the majority of people were buried in unmarked graves or in graves with simple wooden markers. Memorials assumed a different order of significance after the Reformation, when there was a dramatic psychological shift in the perception of the relationship between the living and the dead. A belief system founded on the connection of the living to the dead gave way to a less reassuring sense of death as a separation. This important change of emphasis from the plight of the deceased – specifically, the repose of the soul – to the plight of the living left behind with their grief paved the way for contemporary attitudes to bereavement.

Until the mid-sixteenth century, the living believed they could influence the passage of the soul of the deceased. They acted as spiritual caretakers and with prayers and masses sought to hasten the soul's departure from Purgatory. The dead, however, had to pay for this service, and believed that the more they paid, the better their post-mortem life would be. Endowments providing prayers and services of intercession were known as chantries, and as well as dedicated chapels there were priests whose sole responsibility was the health of dead men's souls. Purgatory exerted a powerful influence. People paid handsomely for prayers on their behalf, bequeathing funds for obits or masses to be said on the anniversary of their death days. This financial insurance for salvation generated huge wealth for the Church. It was not uncommon for people to bequeath their entire estate 'to the health and salvation of my soul' and leave their family nothing. Clearly, the more people praying for you, the better, and as an incentive to get a good head count at a funeral, doles of fees and food were provided. The cost of dying, it seems, is not uniquely a twenty-first century problem. This practice continued until various parliamentary acts from 1529 onwards made it illegal and the Crown seized chantry endowments.

The constructive and communal practice of prayers for intercession alleviated death of some of its more terrifying, isolating aspects. While the emphasis was on the soul, there was less concern for the body or the sanctity of the individual grave. Individual coffins were not used until the end of the seventeenth century, and mass burial and the reuse of graves were common, with disturbed remains either being rearranged in the same grave or removed to charnel houses. The macabre arrangements of bones in chapels in Europe, such as in the Cappucine church of Santa Maria della Concezione in Rome – arrangements which jar contemporary sensibility and provoke feelings of violation – stem from a time when respect for the individual body was of secondary concern to the welfare of the soul. The cultural shift from the hope of intercession to monuments and grieving marked the start of the process in which death has become increasingly personal, emotional and problematic.

With fascinating resonance, the contemporary use of the internet – specifically the virtual reality cemetery – fulfils a similar function to the chantry chapel. Instead of sustaining the dead by praying for the repose of their souls, the proliferation of cyber-cemeteries and the number of visits correspond to a process whereby a relationship with the dead is sustained by memory. Web 'hits' are the contemporary version of obits. The more hits you get, the more you're remembered, and the better your chance of avoiding oblivion, the twenty-first century equivalent of Purgatory. The duality of the internet as a private tool for access to a community is not so different from the role of the praying individual in a congregation. Importantly, just as the site of the body was insignificant for those using the chantry chapels, the proliferation of virtual reality cemeteries corresponds to a trend towards unmarked graves in the new wave of woodland burial grounds. It also lends itself well to a society where cremation, with its lack of emphasis on a permanent resting place, is still the norm.

One of the most striking features of the twentieth-century landscape of death was the construction of crematoria. It is interesting that where our nineteenth-century ancestors feared that the body might disappear from the grave and devised a system to inter it safely and healthily, we devised a system to get rid of it. Where their landscape of death was shaped by digging, protecting and marking the actual site with stones, ours has been shaped by burning, scattering and writing a line in a book or planting a rose to commemorate less directly. If the nineteenth-century burial crisis which resulted in the evolution of the cemetery was a physical crisis, the crisis which resulted in the construction of crematoria and a similarly radical re-mapping of death was psychological. If one crisis inspired action from the top of society down, the cremation movement happened from the grass-roots level up. Yet the intersection of both developments was environmental concern. Our relationship to the environment is assuming an increasingly important role in shaping the topography of death. Contamination of the air and earth, miasmas, effluvia and now dioxins are important co-ordinates in establishing our bearings on an increasingly secular map.

'CLEANLINESS VERSUS CORRUPTION'

YOU DON'T OFTEN GET THE CHANCE TO HAVE A CREAM TEA at a crematorium. But business was brisk in the refreshments tent at the City of London Cemetery and Crematorium open day. At first sight it looked like a garden fête: fathers in shorts and shades carrying babies and cameras, grandmothers and cheese sandwiches suffering in the heat. But there were tomb tours, a horse-drawn hearse, a gravedigging display and, instead of a band, there was a medley of funeral favourites on the Yamaha in the crematorium, where the Samaritans were drinking Liebfraumilch from plastic cups.

The star attraction of the afternoon was the behind-the-scenes backstage tour of the crematorium and the chance to peek behind the final curtain. James Bond waking up in the furnace in *Diamonds Are Forever* put many off cremation for good. Nowadays, cremation accounts for 80 per cent of London's funerals. In 1902, the year the City of London Crematorium was constructed, thirteen cremations took place, compared to the current daily average of twenty, although they have capacity to carry out forty-seven cremations in one day, if need be. Allan Lee, one of seven staff, was a cheerful guide. 'We get lots of film crews these days and the radio. It's definitely death's turn to be in the spotlight.' Everything you wanted to know about incinerating people and didn't like to ask was asked and answered. Pacemakers, although only the size of coins, cause explosions if left in the body. Lithium batteries are the reason for this volatility, which in 1996 caused thousands of pounds'-worth of damage at a crematorium in Morden, Surrey. It remains contentious as to whether it is the responsibility of the doctor or the funeral directors to remove them. All medical implants are collected and buried separately. Magnets are used to remove metal residues left by dental fillings, hip replacements and coffin nails. After a quick spin in a bone-crushing machine, which looks like a tumble dryer, a cremated adult weighs around six and a half pounds, which means that many of us weigh at the very end of our existences what we weighed when we were newborn babies. You can get the ashes back the same day in just four hours, 'but they are still hot'. There is no direct contact between crematorium staff and the corpse.

Back for her second visit, Rita – who works in 'men's neckwear' – must be a rarity. 'I so enjoyed it last year that I've brought my two sisters and a friend. I don't think it's morbid. You find out what really goes on. You see that they really do burn the coffins.' Another young woman peers into a cremator. 'How long does it take and how do you know if it's done?' Mr Lee explains: 'There's a viewing window at the back. This part takes about ninety minutes, depending on the size of the person and the time of day. On Mondays it takes longer because there's no heat in the brickwork.' His colleague Michael adds: 'The perfect cremation is a nice bit of oak and the fat of the human body, but you don't often get that because oak is very dear.' Behind the crematorium a mass of recent floral tributes lie on the concrete. Flower heads wired to make a ball of knitting and a bingo card, the letters 'UM' in white chrysanthemums (the first 'M' had blown over) – these are poignant reminders that death as a final parting is very different from death as a day-trip for the curious.

More than any other death rite, cremation characterises the modern way of death, accounting for around 80 per cent of all funerals in the year 2000, compared to 1 per cent in 1900, although there are considerable regional differences – for example, in Scotland cremation accounts for around 50 per cent of funerals. As one would expect there is a rural versus urban divide. Predictably, burial rates remain high in rural Ireland, while cremation is the norm on the south coast of England. Globally, only Japan's cremation rate, at 97 per cent, exceeds that of Britain; conversely, in America the figure is strikingly low, at 21 per cent. As a fast, efficient form of body disposal, cremation signifies a practical approach to the problem of accommodating the dead in places where land for the living is at a premium. As a death-style, it also complements the lifestyle of a society where time is at a premium. Fast food and fast funerals are a twentieth-century sadness, signifying the fact we live at a pace that causes us to experience life and death in convenient, formulaic experiences which ultimately fail to satisfy us. In much the same way that we have lost the art of taking time and trouble over the more mundane ritual of a family meal, the fast funeral that is cremation is an extension of the same mentality, with the added dimension of fear.

The slow spread of cremation to the point at which it has become the dominant form of disposal of the dead in Britain marks the evolution of a sanitised, secular model of death involving an important transfer of responsibility for disposal away from church to local authority. It also represents a system that has tended to subjugate the wishes of the bereaved, who as a matter of course fall in with the tight timetables of busy crematoria. At a different level, the current structure of crematoria and cemetery services means that they are subjugated to the control of other departments: instead of giving them an autonomous department, local councils locate them within community and leisure services! This lack of consistency and absence of strategic planning threatens to have serious consequences in the foreseeable future, particularly in London. Key areas of concern which have the potential to become crises are the lack of space for burial where there is urgent need for a clear policy about grave reuse, the increasing deterioration of cemeteries, and the prospect of ever-more-stringent pollution control regulations for crematoria involving considerable costs. Faced with these problems, local authorities are finding sustainability an increasingly challenging issue. Notwithstanding technological progress, disposal of the dead in the urban environment is in some ways as problematic today as it was in the nineteenth century, when it was first identified as a serious 'sanitary' problem. In the modern idiom this translates as an 'environmental' problem, and concern about pollution remains at the core of the debate about how best to dispose of the dead.

The title of an essay by Lord Sutherland Gower published in 1910, 'Cleanliness Versus Corruption', summarises the dichotomy, and juxtaposes the hygienic qualities of cremation with a repellent vision of earth burial. He strengthens his case by drawing on Jeremy Taylor's gruesome description, dating from the seventeenth century, of the grave as 'a place of rottenness and cold dishonour [where] our beauty is so changed that our acquaintance quickly know us not'. This distinction resonates through the arguments for cremation. The nineteenth-century pioneers made much of the quality of purification by fire, as opposed to putrefaction by burial. Typical is an essay by George Hopps entitled 'The Etherealistion of the Body'. Published in 1900, it is suffused with aesthetic imagery comparing cremation to 'a bath of the fragrance of summer roses'. The concept of cremation as clean is even more explicit in an advertising campaign by the Cremation Society in the 1930s in which the following slogans appeared on promotional posters: 'There are two ways to dispose of the dead. Purification by fire. Pollution by burial. Choose cremation'; and 'Cremation prevents pollution of the earth we live upon, air we breathe, water we drink. Dispose of the dead without danger to the living'.

In an interesting change of direction, however, fear about the emissions resulting from the cremation process means that the original arguments used to promote cremation as a cost-effective, environmentally friendly form of disposal are now being used to promote 'green' burial. There are striking parallels between the progressive spirit of the environmentalists championing the cause of woodland burial and the single-minded 'sanitarians' of the nineteenth century who took on the Establishment to change attitudes to disposal of the dead. The contemporary fear about the dangers of dioxins, recently described as the 'Darth Vader of pollutants', echoes the Victorian fixation with 'fatal miasmas' emitted from unhealthy and overcrowded burial grounds, which caused Sir Edwin Chadwick to conclude in his influential government report of 1843, 'All interments in towns, where bodies decompose, contribute to the mass of atmospheric impurity, which is injurious to the public health.' Just as the word 'organic' describes the cultural zeitgeist today, the word 'sanitary' resonated throughout public life from the mid nineteenth century onwards, as the population boom in cities made pollution a pressing concern. As discussed already, pollution has played an integral role in shaping the landscape of death. The advent of woodland burial sites in the 1990s is the latest in a series of backlashes and trends in disposal motivated by environmental concern. These developments have contributed both to the distancing of death from everyday life, and to the deritualisation of death as it starts to be seen from the perspective of public health.

The breeze blocks and bureaucracy of modern cremation suit the mentality of a society that wants to downplay death. This clinical style of cremation could not be further from the burning rituals of Norse mythology, which Matthew Arnold evokes so powerfully in his epic poem *Balder Dead* (1855).

> But through the dark they watched the burning ship
> still carried o'er the distant waters on,
> Farther and father like an eye of fire.
> And long, in the far dark, blazed Balder's pile;
> But fainter, as the stars rose high, it flared,
> The bodies were consumed, ash choked the pile.
> And as in a decaying winter fire,
> A charr'd log falling, makes a shower of sparks –

> So with a shower of sparks fell in,
> Reddening the sea around and all was dark.

Stripped of the poetry of pyre, the modern method of burning the dead is impoverished and impersonal. The hidden process of committal to the cremator deprives mourners of the imagery of closure that is such an integral part of the ritual of burial. This concealment is anathema to Hindu practice, where great importance is attached to the family witnessing the burning. In India male relatives push the *ghee*-covered body on to the *ghat* and the burning body is smelt and heard; the skull cracking signifies the release of the soul. In Britain, apart from rare instances such as the erection of pyres on the downs near Brighton during the First World War to burn Hindu soldiers who died in the Kitchener Hospital, cremation does not happen outdoors. Generally, Hindus go behind the scenes and touch the coffin before the operatives consign it to the furnaces, but in spite of the cultural diversity of contemporary Britain, as yet there are no dedicated Hindu crematoria. British Hindus either send ashes back to India or mix them with water sent from the Ganges and then scatter them over free-flowing rivers. In London, several funeral directors use Cherry Garden Pier in Bermondsey, taking families there to scatter ashes on the Thames.

It is hard for us to imagine, but those pioneering cremation had an aesthetic vision of its future in this country. In a Cremation Society lecture in 1914, George Noble had grand plans for urn gardens and graceful columbaria in keeping with classical tradition:

> Like the funerary urns of some ancient Greek hero, they might depict in sculptured relief events in the life or symbols of the attainments of those whose ashes they contained. Other folk of more simple requirement could have their innocuous dust mingled with the earth or flower beds, then in a far truer sense might the epitaph of Laertes be applied: 'Lay her in earth and from her fair and unpolluted flesh may violets spring.'

This ambitious fantasy bears no resemblance to the banality of crematoria design in England, where the average crematorium fails miserably in those aspects of architecture which help a building to express humanity. The standard-issue green plastic canisters for ashes are also a far cry from the aesthetic of the cinerary urn, and sadly the practice at some crematoria of pouring unclaimed ashes down gratings is more ignominious than poetic.

Modern crematoria are not conducive to ceremony. Backstage, the health and safety regulations and fire extinguishers, the stainless steel surfaces and computerised control panels give the impression of an industrial unit. The production line feel is reinforced by the rows of plastic twist-top containers lined with polythene where cremated remains are stored. This sterile environment reveals the funeral as a form of high-tech waste disposal. Front of house it is the same, for no one touches the coffin, the curtains open by remote control and the rollers of the conveyor belt move the coffin out of view. With the bright lights and sound systems, the furniture arranged, as if for presentation, the atmosphere is overtly functional. In these uninspiring surroundings a cremation service can feel like an under-rehearsed amateur dramatic production, especially when the officiants don't know the deceased and sound as if they don't know their lines. The lay-out of chairs at a distance from an elevated coffin and the curtains confer the sense of the mourners as spectators in an auditorium, rather than participants in a ceremony. In one London crematorium, a retired sound assistant who had worked for years in a local cinema enhanced this impression when he requested that the Pearl and Dean 'pah-pah pah-pah pah-pah pah-pah PAH' music was played as the curtains swung together at his cremation service.

The fact that the most important part of the proceedings happens out of sight has led to many misconceptions. One of the most enduring is that when the coffin disappears it goes straight into the cremator. George Bernard Shaw dispels this false impression in his account of his mother's cremation at Golders Green crematorium in 1913:

> A door opened in the wall and the violet coffin mysteriously passed out through it and vanished as it closed. People think that door the door of the furnace; but it isn't. I went behind the scenes at the end of the service and saw the real thing. People are afraid to see it; but it is wonderful. I found there the violet coffin opposite another door, a real unmistakable furnace door. When it lifted there was a plain little chamber of cement and fire-brick. No heat. No noise. No roaring draught. No flame. No feel. It looked cool, clean, sunny, though no sun could get there.

Shaw goes on to give a vivid eyewitness account of the committal.

> The feet burst miraculously into streaming ribbons of garnet-coloured lovely flame, smokeless and eager like pentecostal tongues, and as the whole coffin passed in it sprang into flame all over; and my mother became that beautiful fire.

Evidently he was so impressed by the process that later that day he made a note to himself to invest money in the cremation business.

The central tenets of cremation are utilitarian rather than religious. By reorienting the disposal of the dead according to factors of economy, hygiene and public health, and away from the more esoteric realms of ritual and religion, the history of cremation is a fascinating aspect of the secularisation of death. It is an interesting coincidence that the first cremation to be carried out in England – that of Mrs Pickersgill at Woking, Surrey – happened in 1885, the same year in which Nietzsche questioned the usefulness of religion.

> We seem to have arrived at a time when among the arguments for and against religion, those which relate to its usefulness assume an important place. We are in an age of weak beliefs. (*Three Essays on Religion*, 1885)

The crisis of religious confidence in the nineteenth century is relevant to the rise of cremation – indeed, at one level it is an expression of it – and it happens in tandem with mounting concern about the dead as hazardous to the health of the living. Stripped of religious symbolism and beyond the emotional trauma of bereavement, death in the raw is about a dead body and what to do with it. Dilemmas concerning the best methods of disposal, burial or cremation date from the 1870s. This was when Sir Henry Thompson, the chief exponent of cremation, locked horns with Sir Francis Seymour Haden, chief opponent of cremation, in a spirited intellectual tussle which lasted for around thirty years and which has been inherited by the Natural Death Centre and the Federation of British Cremation Authorities.

The line of progress from Sir Henry Thompson's enthusiasm for the concept of cremation after seeing a furnace designed by the Italian engineer Brunetti at the Great Exhibition in Vienna in 1873, to cremation as the principal form of disposal in Britain with over 200 crematoria modified to EU requirements under the Environmental Protection Act of 1990, is an interesting index of a changing set of relationships: our relationship with God, our relationship with Nature, our relationship with the dead body. Where once these relationships constituted a stable social framework within which death was codified, gradually – from the second half of the nineteenth century, as urbanisation transformed how people lived and secularisation changed what they believed – there was strain in each of these spheres. As death became more ideologically challenging, a more material attitude to the disposal of bodies emerged, of which cremation and the scattering of ashes are the most radical expressions. The accelerated progress of cremation in the twentieth century correlates to the deepening level of death denial in the post-war period and a readiness to adopt a more abbreviated form of funeral. Simply put, the less faith binds industrial societies, and in the absence of satisfactory alternatives to religious ritual, the more deodorised their death rites become.

Concern about the redirection of death ritual starts to be expressed by the Ecclesiologists in 1851. They objected to the atheistical character of funerals and the intrusion of secular iconography. They also feared that public health concerns were eclipsing religious beliefs.

> Sanitary considerations then are the first and greatest; let this be allowed by all means; we only wish to have it remembered that they are not all. But also religious concerns. (*Funerals and Funeral Arrangements*, published by the Ecclesiological Society, late Cambridge Camden Society, 1851)

They were worried about the increasingly un-Christian element creeping into attitudes to disposal of the dead.

> The funeral itself is not to be hastened over as a mere burying our dead out of our sight, a mere hurrying a nuisance out of the way, but it is to be treated as the performance of an act of faith, that we believe in the resurrection, an act of hope that we trust again to see the form which the coffin now conceals from us ...

They also observed a growing sensitivity about the facts of death that feels like a distant murmur of contemporary attitudes.

> Our forefathers did not banish from their thoughts and eyes everything connected with death. The bier and grave ropes and perhaps the spades still stand in the aisle of many a country church – a most wholesome warning. But now such plain things are too often banished to closets under stairs, or blocked-off towers.

The clear impression from Chadwick and the Ecclesiologists is of a society with an increasingly secular attitude to the disposal of the dead, a preoccupation with public health – and of an accelerated pace of life, an industrial society getting out of step with death. On top of this, the publication of Darwin's *On the Origin of Species by Means of Natural Selection* in 1859 further destabilised society's relationship with God. Where there had been rumblings of religious doubt, now there was suddenly a massive fissure in the foundations of faith.

It was in this climate of ideological instability that Sir Henry Thompson introduced the concept of cremation to the British public. The impassioned debate it inspired shows a society in transition with regard to attitudes to death. From the contemporary perspective where cremation is the norm, it is hard to appreciate just how revolutionary a concept it was. With pagan associations, cremation challenged the central Christian doctrine of bodily resurrection. Closely associated with scientists and sanitarians who promoted it primarily as a public health benefit, the priorities of the cremation campaign were a source of great consternation to the Church. In 1874 the Bishop of Lincoln preached a stirring anti-cremation sermon in Westminster Abbey in which he was unequivocal in his view of cremation as a subversive practice. He feared that by undermining the doctrine of the resurrection of the body, cremation would bring about 'a most disastrous social revolution' to the extent of 'confirming and increasing the widespread licentiousness and immorality which prevail in all the great capitals of the world'. This anti-religious association proved detrimental to the development of cremation. It was something on which opponents could capitalise all too easily, particularly the Earth to Earth Society with its explicit allusion to the Christian burial service. Notwithstanding the climate of religious doubt in Victorian England, a utilitarian vision of progress was insufficient to overturn the weight of tradition, particularly in such a sensitive area as disposal of the dead, where societies tend to be resistant to change. This resistance meant that cremation was not adopted by the British public in the nineteenth century and remained a minority interest until after the First World War.

Another factor relevant to the context in which Sir Henry Thompson launched his campaign concerns changing attitudes to the dead body. If burial reform was just one part of a phalanx of public health improvements including sanitation and improved water supply, the toxicity of the dead body caused the greatest consternation. The sense of the body as a source of repugnance and negative associations, which is so forcefully expressed in Chadwick's reports, represents an important side-effect of the urban environment. The conditions in the dirty, densely populated, disease-ridden cities were a significant factor in corroding the customs and community experience of death that happened in rural areas. In rural parts the dead body was seen much less as an object of possible contagion and a health risk; rather, it was the subject of a wealth of customs involving much more positive interaction. There are accounts dating from the seventeenth century of a bawdy game called Hot Cockles, which was played around the corpse in Yorkshire. According to historian Claire Gittings, it was 'a sexual variation of blind man's buff'. In Wales 'trouncing on trippets' was a popular game at wakes in the eighteenth and nineteenth centuries. It involved stepping up and down on benches while carrying the corpse. In Scotland there were 'lyke wakes' that involved friends assembling around the dead body and sitting up with it all night.

A plate or cellar of salt was placed on the breast of the corpse and lighted candles set at the head and feet; but as the occasion partook more of festivity than sorrow all the materials of feasting, drinking and smoking were plentifully provided for the watchers. The practice was at last so much abused that a person's lyke wake was often as expensive as his wedding. (*Notices Historical and Miscellaneous Concerning Mourning Apparel in England*, 1850)

Another rural custom centring on the dead body involved employing the services of a 'sin-eater', usually a poor parishioner who, in a parody of Holy Communion and the concept of redemption, would accept payment to eat food placed over the body.

A loaf of bread, a mazard bowl full of beer and a piece of money were delivered over the coffin to the sin-eater who in consideration of these gifts took upon himself *ipso facto* all the sins of the defunct and freed him or her from waking after death. (Lady Colin Campbell, 1893)

Irrespective of regional differences in how long these customs survived, the presence of the dead body in the domestic context was more positive than in the urban environment, when it became antisocial. The rich framework of superstition, religion and custom that was so strong in rural areas gave way to a more material attitude dominated by fear about funding a funeral and avoiding the horror of lime and a pauper's grave. In this way, cremation polarised urban and rural societies. It corroded centuries-long traditions of rural folklore and greatly impoverished the symbolism and poetry that had connected the dead to the living. Such practices included dropping a loaf of bread with quicksilver into water in which someone had drowned three days before as a way of locating the body in the belief that the loaf would above the spot. The country was permeated with beliefs about death that centred on the natural environment.

Portents of death – such as the idea that a fruit tree blooming out of season signifies impending death – were powerfully cohesive in small communities. In Lincolnshire, ordinary pigeons were feared as 'death doves', and when they came and perched near people it was seen as an omen. In 1895 an article in *The Antiquary* related a story about the author's own grandfather, Thomas Peacock. Although he was believed to be in good health, some doves from the cote at the Old Hall at Northorpe settled round his feet as he sat in the garden. 'The pigeons had clearer insight than his own people', and he was soon dead. The telling of death was a two-way need, for 'not telling the bees' of an impending death in the family was feared to cause them to leave the hive, or to die. It is lucky that bees understand dialects, for in a village near Grimsby there is a story of how a woman told the bees of her husband's death and 'asked them "to be trig and work for her". On being required to explain what 'trig' meant she said 'wist', wist being understood to mean quiet and orderly.'

This psychological shift whereby the body is perceived both as an object of moral and physical danger and as a source of 'dreadful demoralisation' to the bereaved is strongly expressed by Chadwick. He was especially concerned about the squalid circumstances which compelled the poor to live in the same room as a corpse for as long as it took them to arrange the necessary funds for the funeral. He includes the evidence of a vicar who describes the irreverence resulting from enforced proximity to the dead:

> From familiarity it is a short step to desecration, the body stretched out on two chairs is pulled about by the children, made to serve as a resting place for any article that is in the way and is not seldom the hiding place for the beer bottle or the gin if any visitor arrives inopportunely.

Another witness, a doctor, describes the problem of seepage from coffins which sometimes rendered them unfit to be taken into church for the funeral service, with the sleeves of the bearers 'quite dripping with the sanies that leaked from the coffin'. He gives a graphic account of the disgusting consequences of this common problem as

> the putrid discharge from the coffin dripping down along the clothes of the undertakers men who carried it, so that the whole line of the funeral procession from the gate to the grave might be traced by the drippings on the ground.

Most importantly, Chadwick – anticipating contemporary practice – introduces the notion of the desirability of taking the dead body away from the domestic context. A section on the 'effects of appropriate establishments for the reception and care of the dead previously to interment' contains the first references to the earliest version of what we understand as a funeral home, in the form of 'the reception house'. This was a German concept which enjoyed considerable, if short-lived, success in Frankfurt, Munich and a number of other German cities. A German resident in London describes the popularity of these 'innovative institutions' which were designed to encourage the separation of the dead from the bereaved with their speedy removal from the domestic environment. The effect was

> to allay all feelings of reluctance to part with the remains and to create on

the contrary a general desire for their removal from the private house early after death, that they may be placed under the care of skilful and responsible officers. (Edwin Chadwick, 1843)

So begins the delegation of death, as well as the pattern of Germany pioneering efficient methods of dealing with the dead which went on to be expressed in their attitude to cremation.

The British ambassador provides an appraisal of the reception house in Munich for Chadwick's report.

The arrangements made for the speedy removal of the body after death are considered highly beneficial in a sanitive point of view, as tending to check the spread of contagious and unclean disorders, more particularly in the crowded parts of the towns.

Sanitary concerns, however, were secondary motives in the establishment of the German reception houses. Their primary function is much more intriguing. It is revealed by the Frankfurt reception house's declaration of objectives as follows:

A. To give perfect security against the danger of premature interment.
B. To offer a respectable place for the reception of the dead in order to remove the corpse from the confined dwellings of the survivors.

The fact that fear of premature burial was a major reason for deferring burial gives a fascinating perspective on the nineteenth-century attitude to the dead body, and specifically to putrefaction. Chadwick asserts that, even when funeral costs could be met, people elected to delay burial because putrefaction comforted them with proof that someone was really dead.

The delay of interment is greatly increased by the expense of the funerals; but in a considerable number of cases where the expense is provided for the delay still occurs chiefly from feelings which require to be consulted – the fear of premature interment before life is extinct.

The argument for introducing the reception house concept to England was enthusiastically taken up by one of the leading lights of the funerary reform movement, the Ecclesiological Society, which stated:

We must introduce the use of dead houses. They have worked admirably in foreign parts; they have in many cases prevented the horror of burial alive nor is there anything objectionable in them, except perhaps the name; and that is easily altered.

The Ecclesiologists objected to the term 'reception house': 'It is a vague un-satisfactory phrase applicable to twenty other different subjects besides that really intended.' They engaged in a spirited semantic assessment of a range of alternatives in the conviction that the right name was crucial to deter-mine public repugnance or acceptance of such a radical innovation.

> Now it is all very well to say that the word 'Dead House' simply means a house for the dead. Of course it does, and nothing more. But we cannot deny that it has an awful sound. The compound 'Dead' has come to be used with ideas and scenes of more terror than the mere fact of death. We need only instance the 'dead cart' and the 'dead thraw'. We want a term which shall be as clear, but not so dreadful.
>
> It is plain the vague terms, as 'Burial House', or 'Rest House', or 'Funeral House', will never come into vogue, as not practical enough for the practi-cal English mind. Long words like 'Mortuary House' will either not be used, or will be grotesquely abbreviated. 'Corpse House' is as bad as, or worse than a dead house. We therefore propose, – and we do it with some degree of confidence – Lich house.

How wrong they were, for 'funeral home' is closer to 'funeral house' than 'lich house', which clearly did not catch on. And how intriguing the differ-ent functions of the contemporary funeral home and the German recep-tion house. The nineteenth-century dormitories for the dead – supervised by nuns or nurses, where German corpses lay rigged up to ringing mecha-nisms and positioned over zinc troughs of antiseptic hidden by flowers – were designed to affirm the facts of death, to ensure that death could not be denied. They comforted the living by proving that the dead were dead. By contrast, the culture of the twentieth-century funeral home, of which embalming is an integral part, is entirely about denial of death and com-forting the living by creating a cosmetic illusion of continuity by pumping the body with preservative to banish any outwards sign of putrefaction.

In fact, the German concept was elitist and expensive, and the funeral home did not become part of the nineteenth-century culture of death; it was not introduced to England until the 1930s. Yet, within a hundred years the way the living related to the dead changed from fear for the corpse to fear of the corpse. The psychological stance changed from projecting the horror of being immured alive on to the corpse – people even requested that their hearts were driven through by daggers to prevent this occurrence – to a more basic fear of seeing one's own death reflected back by the corpse. The horror of post-mortem revival or 'reanimation' in the nine-teenth century contrasts to the horror of putrefaction in the twentieth.

The different focus of fears also relates to the impact of medical progress on our relationship with the dead body, for the Victorians lacked the confirmation of death afforded by the ECG and the EEG and the injections of formaldehyde to prevent putrefaction. Their familiarity with the outward appearance of the dead body and the natural facts of death was far greater than their understanding of the complex internal functioning of the vital organs and the less obvious medical facts which help to establish that death has occurred. For us, it is the opposite.

As the dead are seen more and more through the lens of public health, one can chart a transition in which disposal of dead bodies moves away from religion, custom and community and the framework of rural tradition to becoming a matter of bureaucracy, hygiene and economics dictated by the urban environment. In tandem with waning religious belief, a better understanding of preventative medicine and, especially, the link between sanitation and mortality rates in urban areas further undermined the traditional view of death as God's will and supplanted it with a more rational perspective. An extension of the idea of the dead body as a health hazard can be seen in concern about the funeral ceremony itself as a potential risk to the health of the mourners. The notion that 'in burying the dead we kill the living' is a recurring theme from the mid-nineteenth century onwards in publications advocating funerary reform, which draw attention to the dangers posed by inclement weather at the graveside and the risk of contagion from the burial ground and the body. This sense of the hazards of the traditional outdoors funeral is pertinent to the gradual acceptance of cremation. Similarly relevant to the context of cremation is the concept of convenience as applied to attending a funeral that dates from this time. An article in the *Lancet*, 24 January 1874, entitled 'Doctors At Funerals' conveys this concern for practicality. The gist of the piece is the inconvenience to doctors of attending the funerals of former patients, specifically 'the many valuable hours' involved going to and from suburban cemeteries,

[f]or whilst in country places the churchyard of the neighbouring village is still God's Acre, in London and other large cities the distance to the suburban cemeteries is often great and many valuable hours are taken up going to and returning from the ceremony.

The *Lancet* article continued:

The feeling of modern times is we are happy to know in favour of diminishing rather than increasing the pomp and cost of funerals. Dickens never did a better public service than when he satirised the folly of modern funerals by the mouth of the Raven in *Household Words* and he set a good example by the directions he left for his own funeral. We believe that all doctors of the present day hold attendance at a funeral to be an unmitigated bore, and it would be as well therefore that the public generally should understand that the absence of an invitation to take part in the last obsequies of a patient would not be regarded as a slight.

This indicates a significant shift of attitude away from the funeral as a demonstration of social cohesion toward a more pragmatic approach. It highlights concerns about pomp, and cost in both terms of time and money, which were precisely the targets of the cremation campaigners. The article appeared in the *Lancet* in January 1874, the same month that Sir Henry Thompson published his ground-breaking article on cremation in the *Contemporary Review*.

Thompson's controversial article 'On the Treatment of the Body After Death' made a terrific impact. It was reprinted several times, translated and published abroad, issued as a book and sparked a long correspondence in *The Times*. It was the first time the subject of cremation had been put to the British people since the famous scholarly treatise *Hydriotaphia: Urn Burial*, written by Sir Thomas Browne in the seventeenth century. Sir Thomas demolished the idea of the dignity of the grave with exuberant and eloquent prose:

> [T]o be gnawed out of our graves, to have our skulls made drinking bowls and our bones turned into pipes, to delight and sport our enemies are tragical abominations escaped in burning burials.

By contrast, Sir Henry Thompson is less literary than literal. He opens with a graphic account of the processes of putrefaction.

> Here then begins the eternal rest, the Rest! No, not for an instant. Never was there greater activity than at this moment exists in that still corpse. Activity, but of a different kind to that which was before. Already 1,000 changes have commenced. Forces innumerable have attacked the dead. The rapidity of the vulture, with its keen scent of animal decay, is nothing to that of nature's ceaseless agent now at full work before us ...

Thompson's arguments for cremation centred on health and economics. He took practicality too far for many of his audience, however, when he suggested that the use of cremated remains as fertiliser would save the British people an estimated £500,000 on importing bonemeal. Even more bizarrely, he proposed that the by-products of the process could also be harnessed to manufacture 'illuminating gas for general purposes'. Resonating through his essay is repugnance at the process of putrefaction, which burial prolongs, and unease about 'the unhealthy character of cadaveric emanations'. Shortly after publication he formed the Cremation Society, with a clearly defined utiliarian philosophy.

> We disapprove of the present custom of burying the dead and desire to substitute some mode which shall rapidly resolve the body into its component elements by a process which cannot offend the living and shall render the remains absolutely innocuous. Until some better method is devised we desire to adapt that usually known as cremation.

The Cremation Society promoted cremation as a 'safe, sanitary and inexpensive method of disposal of the dead without danger to the living'. Cremation became a major topic of discussion for the nineteenth-century chattering classes, and an almost constant presence in medical periodicals and letters pages. An editorial in the *Dublin Review* noted that, at the height of interest in the subject, 'All the talk of clubs and drawing room was tinged with funeral pyres and noxious exhalations'. The *Lancet* injected some levity into the debate in August 1874 when it ran a piece called 'The Comic Aspect of Cremation':

> The question of burning the dead is exciting much discussion in California. One paper suggests some readings on plates of funeral urns in the future. 'Charles Pupker, three and a quarter lbs, cremated July 9th 1874. For wife of above see first pickle bottle on next shelf.'

Thompson's lifespan (1820–1904) coincides almost exactly with that of Queen Victoria (1819–1901). As her surgeon, his professional eminence lent credence to his campaign. The movement quickly became associated with the intellectual and literary elite, as well as with scientists, so that membership of the Cremation Society enjoyed impressive representation from the upper echelons of society. Cremation could not have had a more committed activist. From the moment in 1873 when he saw Brunetti's designs in Vienna, Thompson was completely dedicated to furthering the cause of cremation. He was president of the Cremation Society for twenty-five years. He spent the last years of his life painstakingly collating data about the progress of cremation around the world by sending forms to the managers of all crematoria. Before he published his famous article he carried out in private a series of practical experiments on animals. In one such exercise, which took place in Birmingham using a special furnace designed by Siemens, he incinerated a 227lb hog in 55 minutes. Satisfied with these feasibility studies, he published his article and ignited a blaze of publicity.

The *Lancet* seemed particularly captivated by the subject. Its initial response was unequivocally positive.

> In a sanitary point of view no question can be entertained on which side the advantage lies. In cremation the ultimate chemical compounds are formed at once without prejudice to the living, whilst in burial the intermediate products are extremely harmful and, to say the least, are capable of inducing disease and death in the living. Even in cheapness the advantage is altogether on the side of cremation, for a body may be burnt at a cost little exceeding half a crown in fuel. (3 January 1874)

Although it paid lip service to religious concerns – 'the burial service requirement for bodies to rise again in an incorruptible state must not be lightly disregarded" – in the early days its enthusiasm for cremation tended to obscure the religious aspects. The *Lancet* followed the course of Thompson's campaign with careful interest and considered the subject from many angles. For instance, the magazine compared cremation to sea burial:

> It is enough to remind our readers that bodies so exposed are speedily devoured by the inhabitants of the deep and that as these creatures come to us in the form of food the result although superlatively economic may not be always satisfactory. (9 May 1874)

The same article concludes:

> We are constrained to believe that the arguments in favour of cremation are almost irresistible, and that those who work at preventative medicine should add it to their code of subjects and urge it continuously on the attention of the public.

The *Lancet* compared cremation to an even more radical innovation in body disposal. This was the brainchild of a German, Dr Steinbeis, the president of the Board of Trade and Industry for Wurtenberg. Steinbeis had come up with a concept to rival the apparatus for cremation that was drawing international recognition for his fellow countryman Herr Siemens and gaining for Germany a reputation for excellence in the technology of body disposal. According to the *Lancet*, Steinbeis proposed that the corpse should be placed in a trough made of cement which would then be filled up with liquid cement, so as to cover completely the dead body:

> The cement soon hardens and absorbs all the moisture from the body – converts it, in fact, into a preservable mummy at small expense and trouble. As soon as the cement hardens, the square coffins may be piled one upon the other like blocks of stone. The furnace, however, seems to pos-

sess the superior recommendations of reducing the body to much smaller bulk.

Thankfully, this Carl Andre approach to dealing with the dead did not catch on.

As innovators and pioneers, the Italians and Germans were considerably more advanced than the British. To highlight the lag in British acceptance of cremation, eleven years passed – interspersed with Home Office objections, tortuous legal wrangling and intense debate – from the publication of Thompson's article in 1874 to the first legal cremation in Britain in 1885. In Germany, by contrast, the concept was first mooted as early as 1855 and, after experiments in Dresden, the first official cremation took place in Gotha in 1879. In *Fire Burial Amongst Our Teutonic Forefathers*, published in 1875, Karl Blind describes the German interest:

> At Vienna and Berlin, at Leipzig, Dresden, Breslau, Stuttgart and other German towns, agitations in favour of fire burial [*Feuerbestattung*] as the new term is, are in full course. In some cases the communal councils are heading the movement.

But Blind emphasises the point that interest in cremation was

> not of such a recent date in Germany as many seem to suppose. It has been put forth and advocated there for upwards of a quarter of a century; not least ably by Dr Trusen in 1855, and again in 1860 with the motto: *salis publica suprema lex*. But the eagerness with which the proposal of Dr Trusen and Sir Henry Thompson is at present being worked out on German soil, is certainly such as to have almost the appearance to a return to early notions and cherished customs, which centuries of a contemporary practice have not been able to root out from the nation's minds. It is as if a spark of that spirit were again stirring which urged our light and fire worshipping ancestors to consign their dead to the purifying flame.

Whether viewed as Teutonic tradition or as innovation, in Germany the concept of cremation was gaining such acceptance that in 1885 a petition was presented to the Reichstag proposing that cremation should be allowed in all German cities. Prince Bismarck declared that he had no objection to enactment of a general law regulating and permitting cremation throughout the empire although, as it transpired, Prussia took longer to sanction the practice than did the other states. The German avidity for cremation is striking. Periodicals in the 1870s are peppered with references to German progress in this field. In 1874, when England had just one Cremation Society based in London, eighty-two German cities had cremation societies, *Deutsche Feuerbestattungstasse Flamme* as well as a separate industrial division, the *Volks-Feuerbestattungs Verein*. Bremen even offered a cash prize as an incentive to discover 'the most economical and aesthetic mode of performing cremation'. When England did not have a single crematorium, Siemens were often in the news for improving the design of apparatus. A report in the *Lancet* from June 1874 describes how an improved furnace by Professors Reclam and Siemens reduced 200 cwt of animal carcass to ash in merely an hour and a half 'at no more than three shillings outlay. During the process no sound nor smell was appreciable.' Without labouring the point, the fact that the infrastructure for the industrial disposal of the dead was gaining Germany a reputation for excellence and innovation in the nineteenth century cannot be ignored, given the course of events in the twentieth century. After all, the ovens of the 1940s bore the same name as the company of engineers who pioneered the early apparatus. Although with modern cremators you rarely see a plume of black smoke and funeral directors never speak of 'ovens', the associations with the Holocaust remain powerful. Modern cremation is haunted by twentieth-century history. Once, after a conducted tour of Craighton crematorium near Glasgow, an official from the Institute of Cremation Authorities commented '*Schindler's List* was very bad for us'.

When cremation was illegal in this country, the aristocrat Sir Charles Dilke went to inordinate trouble and expense to take his wife's body to Dresden so that it could be cremated in one of 'Herr Siemens' famous furnaces'. Permission was granted for this unusual export on condition that the representatives of various public bodies, including the Church, were present. Lady Dilke's cremation was therefore carried out more as a demonstration than as a private ceremony, and for this reason the furnace was not completely closed as it would have been under normal circumstances. All those present were requested to maintain the strictest secrecy, but – much to the distress of Sir Charles – somebody grassed and supplied a graphic account of the proceedings to the British press. This eyewitness account of poor Lady Dilke's incineration was unfortunate publicity for the cremation campaign and misrepresented 'a last wish carried out at great trouble and sacrifice of private feeling'.

> When the company had complied with Herr Siemens' request to offer up a mental prayer, the coffin was placed on the chamber of the furnace; six minutes later the coffin burst; five minutes more and the flesh began to melt away; ten minutes and the bones began to crumble. Seventy-five minutes after the introduction of the coffin into the furnace, all that remained

of Lady Dilke and the coffin were 6lbs of dust, placed in an urn. (*The Lancet*, 17 October 1874)

A later article in the *Lancet* expressed outrage by the breach of trust involved in this report, which presented 'in the most revolting light possible' and as 'a coarse experiment' the fulfilment of a final request of a woman who had 'extreme horror of the idea of earth burial'.

The most persuasive of the opponents to cremation and a worthy rival to Sir Henry Thompson was another eminent physician, Sir Francis Seymour Haden, who argued that the solution to the problem of sanitary disposal of the dead did not lie with cremation, but rather with improving burial practice. His Earth to Earth Society offered an alternative agenda to that of the Cremation Society. The commitment of Seymour Haden to the cause of 'earth to earth' burial was as whole-hearted – one might say, as obsessive – as Thompson's belief in the benefits of incineration, and the competition between the two men was intense.

In the best tradition of English eccentrics and doughty crusaders, they engaged in energetic practical work in order to prove their theories. Sir Henry's zeal for burning animals was matched by that of Sir Francis for digging up the remains of animals he had buried. Guests visiting Sir Henry's home in Wimpole Street were shown the results of his practical experiments. Edmund Yates describes being ushered into a drawing room by his host:

'Step this way and I will show you a curiosity. Those glass cubes of about 5 inches contain the solid remains of 2 bodies one of which weighed 12 and the other 18 stone, both cremated in Siemens' regenerating gas furnace. One at Birmingham, the other at Maudslay's below bridge. There is nothing offensive in either specimen, nothing but mineral matter remains, and the quantity as you see is not very great.' (Vincent Cope, *Versatile Victorian*, 1951)

Sir Francis Seymour Haden presented equally compelling evidence of innocuous remains achieved by nature in his book entitled *Earth to Earth* (1875).

On Christmas day 1870, I buried in a corner of my garden a favourite dog. On the first November, 1874 – the other day I dug down upon the spot and recovered all that was recoverable of the body of my old companion. The residue lies upon a sheet of white foolscap paper on the table before me. It consists of a few scattered bones with a little friable matter loosely attached to them which has all the physical characteristics of common earth without the slightest odour of anything to indicate that it had once been animal tissue.

Sir Francis Seymour Hayden was, in effect, proposing what we understand as 'green' burial, anticipating both the arguments of the Natural Death Centre that are provoking so much attention today and their interest in biodegradable coffins. He believed the evils of interment were 'of our own creation' and that there was great scope to improve the way in which the dead were buried. The focus of his criticism was the irrational practice of keeping bodies for too long before burial, and then interring them in hermetically sealed imperishable coffins, brick graves and vaults – a practice

> in the highest degree unphilosophical since it engages us in a vain resistance to an inevitable dispensation and has led us to accumulate in our midst a vast store of human remains in every stage and condition of decay.

His arguments centred on the fact that when a body is in a sealed or semi-sealed space which prevents wholesome contact with the earth, it remains in a permanent state of 'advanced but unprogressive putrefaction'. If you imagine what happens to meat in a deep freeze when there is a power cut you can appreciate his reasoning. His solution was to bury the dead

> within a reasonable time of their dissolution in coffins of such a construction as will not prevent their resolution. (The Necropolis Earth to Earth coffin has been invented and patented and is admirably adapted to the purpose.)

His invention of perishable wicker coffins which were used in burials at Brookwood cemetery in Surrey confirms his status as a Victorian version of a Friend of the Earth, an aristocratic ecowarrior and pioneer of green burial.

As a natural process, but moreover a process that did not challenge the format of the traditional Christian funeral, the concept of burial in perishable coffins was a compelling alternative to the revolutionary mechanics of cremation. A *Times* leader in 1875 commented that

> Custom is a great influence and 'earth to earth' are words with which we have been so long familiar that we do not shrink from what they describe as we do from the application of other agencies which science, and as it would appear mistaken science, has been vainly pressing on us to adapt.

By 1876 burial reform was winning the debate, and cremation, after a brief burst of enthusiasm, seemed to have fizzled out of favour. A leading article in *The Times* states

> We have, in fact, been fighting hitherto against nature, and with very imperfect weapons. The Cremationists would improve upon our present species of warfare; but they, too, would be no less certainly beaten in the long run by the power against which they are matching themselves. We have only to yield wisely to the dictates of natural laws, and we shall find our account in a cheaper, a less troublesome, a less pernicious and a more efficacious way of proceeding than we have been able to invent for ourselves. (12 January 1876)

Against nature and against God, cremation was losing the argument. The *Lancet* did a volte face. In 1874 the journal had given its wholehearted support to cremation; in 1879 it averred 'Nothing so imbecile as an adoption of the heathen practice of burning the dead will be tolerated in England'.

Cremation was a complex issue because of its equivocal functions. On the one hand, and more straightforwardly, it was a low-key, low-cost, practical approach to disposal of the dead which fitted into the public health agenda. On a more abstract level, it tapped into a seam of religious doubt running through the final decades of the late nineteenth century. For cremation represented an attempt to impose a material system on an aspect of life that for many people could no longer be processed meaningfully by conventional religious formalities. Leslie Stephen, Virginia Woolf's father, conveys the late nineteenth-century mood of disaffection with religion in a powerful piece entitled 'An Agnostic's Apology' (1876):

> Pain is not an evil, death is not a separation, sickness is but a blessing in disguise. Have the gloomiest speculations of avowed pessimists ever tortured sufferers like these kindly platitudes?

The deficiency of religion as a palliative to the pain of bereavement seems to be an important aspect of the context in which cremation evolved. One thinks of Charles Darwin's emotional agony and his personal struggle for mental survival on the death of his daughter:

> It was impossible for me to experience joy ever again. I was no longer sure of God's existence.

One thinks, too, of Tennyson's eloquent despair on the death of his friend A.H. Hallam as expressed in *In Memoriam* (1850), which conveys the strength of despair more effectively than it does the strength of faith to alleviate that despair. One senses that at this time the emotions of man were starting to become bigger than the religious system within which they were previously contained and codified.

From the Stephen family, one gains a fascinating perspective of attitudes pertinent to the adoption of cremation in England. Where Leslie Stephen's public floundering with his crisis of faith is relevant to the psychological context in which the cremation campaign occurred, a relative, Mr Justice Stephen, was involved in the practical context, playing a crucial role in bringing about the legalisation of cremation in Britain. In 1884 he presided over a landmark court case at the Glamorganshire Assizes in Cardiff, in which he cleared a Welsh eccentric, Dr William Price, of a criminal offence after Price attempted to burn the body of his infant son, Jesu Christ Price, in a ten-gallon cask of petroleum. Price stood charge on two counts: first of failing to register the death of his child and ignoring the coroner's request for a medical certificate, and second for his crude public cremation. The logic behind the acquittal was that, according to English law, nothing can be deemed a crime which is not explicitly forbidden by law. Summing up, Stephen commented

> After full consideration I am of the opinion that a person who burns instead of burying a dead body, does not commit a criminal act unless he does it in such a manner as to amount to a public nuisance at common law.

The key point of his decision was that burning, if carried out decently and inoffensively, was lawful, or at least not criminal.

This ruling gave a green light to the Cremation Society. At last they were able to use the crematorium they had first erected in 1879, and which had provoked such a public outcry when they had cremated a horse that the Home Office had threatened prosecution, causing them to put their plans on hold. At this juncture it is perhaps worth recalling the chronology of cremation as stark evidence of the reticence of the British public to translate its theoretical interest in cremation into practice. In 1874, Sir Henry Thompson's article was published and the Cremation Society was founded; in 1879 the Cremation Society constructed a crematorium at Woking, Surrey; in 1884 Judge Stephen ruled that cremation was not illegal; in 1885 Mrs Pickersgill was cremated in the first officially sanctioned cremation; and in 1902 the Cremation Act was passed regulating the operation of crematoria in Britain.

Legislation, however, was not enough to bring about a major change of attitudes. Cremation remained a minority interest in Britain in the early part of the twentieth century. After the considerable notoriety of Woking crematorium in 1885, the construction of crematoria reflects the slow pace of the movement's progress. Crematoria were opened in Manchester (1892), Glasgow (1895), Liverpool (1896), Hull (1901), Darlington (1901), Leicester (1902), Golders Green (1902), Birmingham (1903) and in 1905 the City of London, Leeds, Bradford and Sheffield. Although cremation was promoted as an aesthetic alternative to burial, the imaginative potential of cinerary urns and classical vocabulary was not expressed in the design of the early crematoria. In fact, the British tended to take a very conservative and functional approach, not least compared to the Europeans who rose to the challenge of crematoria design with considerably more elan. In Britain there is no equivalent to the grand design of the crematorium at Père Lachaise, designed by the famous architect Formige, in which the furnaces are concealed within elegant sarcophagi, or the German crematorium in Hagen, Prussia by the modernist architect Peter Behrens. The Hagen crematorium won critical acclaim as a progressive building and became a major tourist attraction where thousands of people came to witness mock cremations in which empty coffins were fed into the flames of the furnace. Crematoria in Britain are a blot on our architectural landscape, woefully uninspiring since their earliest days. As the architectural historian James Stevens Curl has observed,

> Most crematoria in Britain are distressingly banal and poorly designed, and are composed of disparate elements that are uncomfortably unresolved. Many early crematoria were disguised to look like churches, with the flues installed in the 'bell-towers'. The louvres that should have emitted joyful peals often belched smoke. (*A Celebration of Death*, 1993)

One small consolation – a result of our national affinity for gardens – is the existence of two exceptional columbaria in garden settings: the Hedon Road rock garden built in Hull in 1901, and the Ernest George columbarium in Golders Green, a three-sided building with a central lawn and lily pond which took from 1922 until 1928 to complete, and which was described as 'the most beautiful and expensive building of its kind ever made'.

If cremation today represents egalitarian body disposal, at the start of the twentieth century it retained the elitist associations of its nineteenth-century pioneers. Given the small scale of the Cremation Society, the aristocracy were well represented. The Duke of Westminster opened Manchester crematorium in 1892, and in the early days of the Cremation Society the Duke of Bedford was vice-president. In a Cremation Society lecture in 1914 George Noble said:

It is safe to say that in the early years nearly every body cremated was that of a person of note, as the advantages from the aesthetic point of view as well as the more pressing considerations of public health and decency appealed to thinking men and women of all shades of thought and opinion.

The crème de la crem included Lord Bramwell, Lord Playfair, Sir Spencer Wells, Sir Isaac Pitman, the painters Edward Burne-Jones, William Holman Hunt and John Everett Millais and the philanthropist Dr Barnardo. Lord Ronald Sutherland Gower epitomised the character of the early campaigners. A trustee of the National Portrait Gallery, he wrote in 1910 that

> We are such as nation of snobs that I believe if more dukes were cremated than has been the case up to the present, cremation would be followed by many who love to imitate the aristocracy. Of course, even the cremation of a bishop would be a good example and how happy the cremationists would be if we could reduce to ashes an archbishop.

This association with elitism was such that in the 1930s the magazine *Pharos*, which was launched as a promotional tool for the cremation campaign, included in its objectives that of reassuring the British public that cremation 'was not purely a requisite of the intellectual and monied section of society'.

So how did cremation move from being an elitist minority interest to a widely accepted practice in the twentieth century? Part of the answer lies with the impact of the First World War, which accelerated the disintegration of traditional death rites that had started towards the end of the nineteenth century. Specifically, as we have seen, the cataclysmic separation that was enforced by the policy of non-repatriation of dead soldiers deprived the bereaved of access to the bodies of their loved ones. This paved the way for death rites that were no longer dependent on the presence of the body, but focused on absence and remembrance. Although bodies were not generally repatriated in Wellington's Peninsular campaign or in any of Queen Victoria's 'small wars', individual families could and did choose to do this. It is the enforced First World War policy of non-repatriation, coupled with a ban on private memorials, that is relevant to the rise of cremation, for it introduced into society the concept of uniformity in death and de-emphasised the importance of the body. A vivid expression of the present-day antipathy towards mortal remains can be found in the large number of uncollected containers of ashes abandoned at crematoria throughout the country – a telling stockpile.

Another manifestation of our contemporary non-relationship with the dead body is the growth in popularity of the memorial service. Once the preserve of the great and the good, it is increasingly common for low-key private cremations to be followed by elaborate celebrations of the life of the deceased which are attended by large numbers of friends and associates. These tend to be more uninhibited in style as a result of the absence of physical remains. Cremation, by challenging the necessity of a grave as a fixed reference for grief, contributed to the sense of the dead disappearing, and by extension the sense of death disappearing from public view.

War also shifted attitudes to cremation at a psychological level. Rather as in the mid-nineteenth century, overcrowded burial sites and shallow graves had exerted a powerful hold on the public imagination, increasing support for burial reform, the perception of Flanders as a gigantic, shallow grave created a context which made the cleansing and purifying properties inherent in cremation seem particularly attractive. The macabre backdrop of the war – where men lived in mud with worms, rats and the mortal remains of their peers – even if not widely reported to the public, must have permeated their consciousnesses and served as a catalyst for interest in cremation. Just as the sanitarians had capitalised on the shocking conditions of intra-mural burial grounds, the fact that war violated the concept of the sanctity of the grave gave added resonance to the cremationists' arguments. In a Cremation Society lecture in 1914, George Noble said,

> Surely it must be some satisfaction to know that the dead have passed from us swiftly to the ultimate state and not to feel that somewhere they are subjected to lingering decay and the uncertain tenancy of the grave.

In a similar vein, the musician and clergyman the Revd Haweis enthused about cremation:

> How pure, how beautiful! All that is mere earthly about us to be taken and purified by fire, instead of being left to the mouldering corruption of the grave. No more long terrible months with wind and snow and rain above and the dark prison house of decay beneath; nothing but fair golden fire for half an hour and delicate white ash at once symbol of earth life and heavenly beauty. (Noble, 1914)

Beyond abstract reasons for an increasingly receptive attitude to cremation, however, a more significant consequence of the war concerned the dramatic split between body and memory – a split which was imposed by the absence of bodies for the bereaved to mourn. Such absence is intrinsic to the process of cremation. Cremation is a socially sanctioned form of the obliteration of corporeal identity and the annihilation of individuals in the

First World War was a barbaric but similarly socially sanctioned destruction of corporeal identity. American performance artist Laurie Anderson once said that when her father died it was like a library being burned down. It is an apt description, for seeing the granulated remains of people in plastic containers, indistinguishable from each other, is to be confronted with a brutal obliteration of identity and individuality. It magnifies on a vast scale the feeling of loss experienced when letters are thrown into fires or archives go up in flames, and when the irreplaceable knowledge, information and sentiments of original authorship can only be salvaged by the memory of those left behind. Ludovic Kennedy, a well-known advocate of euthanasia, put it well when he said in 1960 that 'what cremation does is to make the transfer from body to memory that much quicker'. The neat rows of names on war memorials fulfil a similar function to the uniform lines in the book of remembrance at the crematorium. They both relate to bodies that are, in effect, missing.

With interesting symmetry, the wave of memorial building in the 1920s, together with great significance attached to naming the dead, corresponds to the increased construction of new crematoria in the two decades following the war. The foundation in 1924 of the Federation of Cremation Authorities in Great Britain – an organisation with the specific aim of raising the profile of cremation – also furthered its acceptance. In 1914 there were thirteen crematoria in Britain while by 1934 there were fifty-nine. The rhythm of change was such that the increased social acceptability of cremation occurred just as the cult of remembrance gathered momentum. For example, in 1928 the newly completed Menin Gate, widely regarded as the most poignant memorial of the First World War, attracted 20,000 visitors and by 1937 the figure had risen to 60,000.

After the war the attitude to the body in the domestic environment changed dramatically, a change which also played a part in encouraging cremation. The advent of the funeral home in the 1930s and the practice of commercial embalming mark the start of a process of distancing which has increased throughout the course of the twentieth century. An important aspect of this is the concept of 'viewing' the body – an act which takes on the dynamic of object and spectator in an impersonal space, usually a chilled backroom on an undertaker's premises described as a 'chapel of rest'. Squeamishness about the dead body intensified in the twentieth century. In *Funerals and Funeral Arrangements*, written by R. Willoughby in 1936, a negative perception of the dead body as something that contaminates its surroundings is conveyed in the recommendation that the bereaved redecorate completely the room where a person has died.

After the funeral the room should be thoroughly aired, and before it is used again the walls, ceiling and paintwork should be completely redecorated. In the case of walls they need to be stripped of all paper and well washed over.

When someone dies away from home, the author suggests that it is good form

to send a note to the owner expressing the wish that he gives instructions for the room to be redecorated and asking that the bill be sent along when it will be attended to.

This book also gives a vivid impression of the post-war attitude to cremation.

It is clean; there is not contamination of soil, it is sanitary. It does not use up valuable space as every cemetery in a town area does. It does not subject mourners to a graveside ceremony in perhaps inclement weather. It does not or need not offend any religious susceptibility and lastly it is not in any way expensive.

Willoughby observes that a shortage of facilities for cremation had been the principle reason for the continued popularity of earth burial, but that the situation was changing.

Now, however, crematoria are to be found in various parts of the country and with the help of motor vehicles, a funeral may be conducted from almost any address to the nearest crematorium without insuperable difficulty.

The Second World War also had an impact on the development of cremation in Britain, proving a particularly efficient means by which to cope with the grim business of disposing of the civilian war dead. Significantly, three months after the start of the war, Princess Louise, Duchess of Argyll – a daughter of Queen Victoria – was the first member of the Royal Family to be cremated, although her ashes were interred in a coffin for her funeral in St George's Chapel, Windsor. For the wider population cremation seemed the most sensible option, not least because early on in the war the Cremation Society appealed to the Home Office to minimise the red tape surrounding cremation – an appeal which the Home Office accepted. In February 1941 their official magazine *Pharos* reported the amendments:

Under the new regulations, every facility will be given to enable the cremation of an air raid victim to be carried out with the minimum of formality and delay.

This included dispensing with the need for medical certificates in cases where the death was registered as resulting from war operations. As well as bureaucratic simplification, there were financial incentives. In August 1941 Mortlake Crematorium offered reduced rates for deaths due to enemy action – £2.2s per adult, as opposed to £4.4s previously. At Southampton it was announced that

> [t]he city of Southampton considers the idea of cremation to be so well accepted by the public that the corporation have agreed to cremation being substituted for burial without cost to the relatives in the case of funerals carried out by the local authority of persons whose deaths are due to war operations. Here again is proof, if proof is needed, that municipalities understand the value of cremation not only on grounds of hygiene but of economy and public welfare.

To indicate the scale of civilian casualties in the war, there was a month in which 50 per cent of all cremations in one London crematorium were carried out on air-raid victims.

Practical and economical, cremation encapsulated the chief requirements of coping in wartime. It suited a war conducted on the home front as well as overseas, in which 'life must go on' whatever the cost in human suffering and bereavement. In the May 1941 issue of *Pharos*, under a headline 'War Accelerating Interest in Cremation' the editor enthused,

> What we now call the First Great War created an increased interest in cremation and I believe it is safe to prophesy that the Second Great War will take this interest still further. There is already a record number of persons cremated and for the first time in its history cremation is being placed on an equal footing with burial.

In the 1940s those championing the cause were positively evangelical about cremation as a vision of progress, as indicated in 'Crematoria in Postwar Planning' in *Pharos*, November 1941:

> In common with many such groups cremationists have constructive ideas to offer the planners of our New England, ideas which we truly believe could make for the betterment of social life and thought, and we may be encouraged in the advancing of our claims by the sure knowledge that cremation will make a greater appeal to the people of this country in the after

war years than ever before. Progress towards the Cremation Ideal has been slow, but it has been unhesitating, deliberate and sure as the innate conservatism of the race has yielded to its convincing appeals, so that today cremation stands in the minds of hundreds of thousands of people as the most rational means of disposing of human remains, and moreover a means whereby the demands of space limitation, hygiene, aesthetics and sanity are most completely satisfied.

In the climate of austerity and cost-consciousness after the war, cremation rates did indeed soar, and rationality replaced religion as the principal factor in determining how the dead were to be disposed of. By 1967, the number of British crematoria had risen to 199 and cremation had overtaken earth burial as the dominant method of disposal of the dead. It is interesting that this happened in the swinging 1960s, almost as if – in the hedonistic climate of sexual liberation and the empowerment of birth control – death was anathema, to be dealt with as quickly and unobtrusively as possible. A further feature of the period was the vastly increased power of the young in shaping popular culture, as manifested by screaming teenage pop fans, schoolgirl models and the notorious school kids' issue of Oz magazine. This youth orientation combined with the frenetic pace of fashion to create a terrific sense of energy and boundless possibilities for the enjoyment of life, which the abbreviated style of cremation helped to sustain by promoting the powerful illusion of death's disappearance from life. Cremation reflects the values of a society that wants to spend the minimum amount of time addressing death. This is exemplified by the speed with which we despatch the dead body to the funeral home, the speed with which it disappears from our sight at the crematorium within the allocated time slot of 20 to 30 minutes, and the way it spares us the maintenance of a grave.

Above all, contemporary cremation satisfies our mental requirement for distance from the dead body. It is a paradigm of deodorised death which distinguishes twentieth-century attitudes from those of earlier centuries. The romance of Edward Trelawny rescuing Shelley's heart from the beach pyre at Leghorn, Italy, in 1822 is not something with which we can easily identify. Our fear of the dead body is compounded by unfamiliarity, and is expressed by the widespread practice of embalming – one of the twentieth century's most idiosyncratic practices.

Embalming taps into arguably the most potent aspect of the modern death taboo, namely our fear of physical deterioration. The twin terrors of the contemporary psyche are age and flesh, and these concerns inform our behaviour towards the dead. Embalming, for example, is an elaborate psychological defence system designed to prevent the dead body from becoming a mirror of our own mortality. The justification for carrying out the invasive procedure, which involves the body being drained of blood and pumped with preservatives via arterial injection, owes far more to psychology than healthcare. The synthetic illusion of continuity embalming achieves, whereby the dead conform to a certain physical standard, is not dissimilar from the illusions achieved with cosmetic surgery. Our use of silicone as the chemical of sex appeal parallels our use of formaldehyde as the chemical of death appeal – both are symptomatic of the tyranny of lookism. A sad sign of human vanity is the fact that in crematoria in California there is a problem with the gloopy residue from silicon breast implants accumulating on the floors of furnaces.

The history of embalming is a fascinating index of changing attitudes to the body, and an integral part of the development of the sanitised approach to modern death rites exemplified by cremation. Although it has a long history, it was only in the twentieth century that embalming became a fully-fledged commercial practice carried out as a matter of course as part of the funeral director's package. The changing function of embalming – from long-term preservation of the great and the good to short-term presentation of everybody – reflects changing sensibilities. These are conveyed by the different phrases used to describe the process. In the less squeamish past it was referred to as 'ripping out', the modern phrase is 'hygienic treatment'. The semantic span between these phrases is taboo, denial and disgust – the time span, about 500 years. In the early days 'ripping out' was the privilege of royalty and nobility and a procedure designed to ensure that if they died away from home, they could be transported back and still look reasonable. Royal viscera chests were interred separately from the rest of the mortal remains. As has been mentioned, in 1817 graphic accounts of the embalming procedures carried out on Princess Charlotte were published in her funerary commemorative material. Descriptions of her viscera being placed in an urn containing 'coarse sweets' inspired one of her female admirers to write a poem 'On Embalming Princess Charlotte', in which she complained, 'Must England still such customs own as feeling's nicest sense oppress?'

In addition to preservation for purposes of transportation, in eighteenth-century English society the rise of the surgeon in an age with a passion for anatomy, but without refrigeration, fostered an increased interest in techniques through which to preserve corpses. Embalming captured the public imagination when the surgeon William Hunter, one of the pioneers of arterial injection for preservation purposes, achieved particular success with the corpse of the good-looking wife of Martin Van Butchell, an eccentric dentist and truss-maker living in Mount Street, Mayfair. Van Butchell kept his late wife at home with his extant second wife in a macabre *ménage à trois*. As news of this unusual domestic arrangement spread, members of the public turned up on his doorstep in the hope of being granted an audience with the celebrated corpse. The volume of visitors prompted Van Butchell to make an announcement in the *St James's Chronicle* forbidding strangers to visit his wife 'unless by a friend personally introduced to himself, any day between nine and one, Sundays excepted'. Another newspaper published a mischievous piece of misogyny in the form of an epitaph, *To Mrs Van Butchell Whose Remains Preserved by a Curious and Newly Invented Method of Embalment are the Object of Her Fond Husband's Daily Attention*:

> Thrice Happy Mortal! Envied lot,
> What a rare treasure thou hast got!
> Who to a woman canst lay claim
> Whose temper's everyday the same!

She may not have lost her temper, but she lost her looks, and on inspecting her in 1857 after she was relocated to the museum of the Royal College of Surgeons, a visitor was unimpressed by 'the wretched mockery of a once lovely woman'. He noted that she had been preserved along with her pet parrot, 'whether immolated at the death of its mistress is uncertain – but as it still retains its plumage it is a far less repulsive looking object than the larger biped'. Sadly, Mrs Van Butchell and the parrot were both casualties of a German air raid, so we no longer have the chance to judge this post-mortem beauty contest for ourselves.

Hunter's method of embalming was so time-consuming and labour-intensive that he advised others considering it to charge a minimum of one hundred guineas per client. It was not until the American Civil War, when Thomas Holmes devised a more straightforward method of arterial injection, that the way was paved for commercial development. Holmes was obsessed with the art of embalming, and even took his work home with him. Visitors describe corpses in closets, heads on tables and bottles of beer alongside embalming fluids. His skills enabled thousands of American soldiers to be returned to their families for home burial. In particular, Civil War hero Colonel Ellsworthy became a silent ambassador for embalming when he was displayed in three different cities, to considerable public acclaim. An even more famous advertisement for the Holmes method was President Abraham Lincoln, whose embalmed body was viewed by hundreds of thousands of Americans. If Holmes features prominently as a hero of mortuary history, modern embalmers and Damien Hirst owe the greatest debt to the discovery of formaldehyde in 1867, although its preserving capability was not commercially developed until the end of the century. In 1883, in a pamphlet on funerary reform, the vicar of Yaxley sounded a cautionary note about adopting the 'undesirable' practice of embalming, 'increasingly in vogue in America'. By 1910 the Americans were actively campaigning within the British funeral trade. Professor Dodge, president of the Massachusetts College of Embalming, extolled its benefits for the English undertaker:

> The reputation he would gain for keeping bodies in good condition would rapidly spread and give him a vast advantage over his competitors who do absolutely nothing to prevent those most disagreeable conditions. (*Undertakers Journal*, 1910)

By the 1920s most undertakers were doing it.

How we treat the dead, despatching them to be sliced and sluiced and cosmetically enhanced before being displayed in the 'chapel of rest', the brevity and abruptness with which we take our leave of them signifies the degree to which we have become distant from nature. In an era of supermodels and supermarkets, we have become as estranged from the natural appearance of women as we have from that of food. In the same way that the blank-faced teenagers on the catwalk betray no intimations of mortality, the cling-filmed cleaned-up food in our shops betrays nothing of natural processes. Just as chicken nuggets and fishfingers give nothing away about their beginnings, so it is with the dead on display in the funeral home. Wrapped and chilled, filled with additives, colourants, and preservatives, they ward off any uncomfortable associations that might disconcert the living. Ironically, their waxy wrinkle-free faces are not dissimilar to the smooth flawlessness of those fibbing faces achieved by airbrush deception in a million magazines. Supermarkets, supermodels and chapels of rest at one level fulfil a similar function: they distance us from nature and manifest in their different ways our death denial.

Yet at the start of the new millennium, we are reassessing our relationship with nature. The interest in organic food and concern about genetically modified foods indicate a reappraisal of the price of convenience. This is carrying through to a consideration of how we dispose of the dead, where there are increasing signs of a backlash against cremation. Although it seems a distasteful comparison, the environmental issues involved in the debate about burial and cremation replicate those involved in the problem of household waste and the comparative benefits of landfill versus incinerator. In both cases, there is concern about toxic emissions. A Department of Trade and Industry guide to household waste management attributed 12 per cent of UK atmospheric dioxins to emissions from crematoria as a result of glue, paint, embalming fluid, PVC, rubber soles of shoes and other manmade fibres. In addition to this, metal fillings and other medical implants are a new focus of attention. Cedric Mimms, author of *When We Die* (1998), estimates that an average crematorium carrying out 4,000 cremations a year releases about 11kg of mercury from dental fillings, and Ken West of Carlisle cemetery and crematorium has also recorded an intensity of mercury in the vicinity of crematoria. These currents of concern are reflected in the progress being made by the green burial movement which aims to achieve a basic form of human recycling by putting bodies untreated by formaldehyde into biodegradable coffins, to be buried in graves which are marked not with manmade memorials, but with trees. With their emphasis on unmarked graves in sites that are often a considerable geographical distance from the home of the deceased, and with which the deceased has no connection, woodland burial signifies a natural version of the obliteration of identity that cremation achieves with an industrial process. They both express anonymity and fragment the traditional unity of body, grave, memorial – rejecting the site-specific remembrance of the dead.

Since trends in body disposal reflect attitudes to death, the signs are that we are on the cusp of important change. The *fin de siècle* timing and pattern of the woodland burial movement at the end of the twentieth century mirrors that of the cremation movement at the end of the nineteenth century. The cremationists in the 1880s, like the exponents of green burial in the 1980s, represent small satellites of radical cultural activism, developing from a grass roots level with environmental concern at the core of their campaigns. Currently, woodland burial represents only a tiny percentage of all disposals, and yet it is the fastest-growing green movement in this country and has captured the public imagination, having increased from one site in 1993 to ninety in the year 2000, with more in the pipeline. This is not so different from the position of cremation at the start of the twentieth century, which represented a tiny percentage of disposals being conducted at a handful of crematoria, supported by some high-profile people who were seen as enlightened pioneers. Similarly, the concept of green burial is gaining credibility as a result of some high-profile proponents. These include the Princess of Wales who, in public perception at least, had a woodland burial on private land, while Dame Barbara Cartland's choice of burial on her own land in a cardboard coffin under a tree also gained publicity. Other notable burials breaking with the tradition of consecrated ground include those of the playwright Robert Bolt, who opted for garden burial in a cardboard coffin in a grave dug by friend with a tree planted over it, and the politician Alan Clark, who was interred in the grounds of his home at Saltwood Castle, Kent. Wrapped in a winding sheet, Clark had no coffin at all. He was buried near two favourite dogs, in a funeral which he had planned in every detail himself, with only family and a few close friends present. An elaborate and very public memorial service followed several months later, reinforcing the present-day split between low-key disposal rituals for the physical body and elaborate public rituals of remembrance. These unconventional private burials echo the spirit in which some of the more famous cremationists constructed their own crematoria on their estates before the practice was fully accepted. These include Captain Hanham who, in 1882, was burned in his own furnace in Blandford, Dorset, and the Duke of Bedford, who was cremated in 1891.

Over and beyond our ecological interest, we are also in a state of transition about how we relate to the dead. Instead of delineating our relationship with the deceased in public by tending a grave which is a projection of a domestic property – a memorial stone like a house in a small cultivated area like a garden – increasingly we are maintaining private relationships with the dead by bringing cremated remains into the domestic environment. Recently it came to light that the late Paula Yates had arranged for some of the remains of her husband Michael Hutchence to be stitched into a cushion, and another rock star's wife, Patsy Kensit, also went public with the information that she cradled a decorative urn containing her mother's ashes. This trend towards the objectification of cremated remains is becoming manifest in increasingly imaginative ways. Examples of this include a man whose wife could never boil his egg whose ashes have been incorporated into an egg timer; a bird lover's ashes cemented into the base of a bird-feeder; and a man who met his wife at an art class whose ashes have been used in an oil painting. Many of these variants are now available on a commercial basis from companies who hollow out golf clubs or manufacture jewellery designed to contain cremated remains. Above all, these items tend to be portable and personal, affording a particularly comforting form of proximity to the deceased. Importantly, they disguise their purpose. One design that caught my eye recently was a line of leather-effect book ends simulating classical volumes that gave a 'gentlemen's club' feel to the cremated remains. By blending in with the surroundings of domestic life and giving nothing away, these objects give the dead no visible profile.

This trend to making the dead disappear takes on an even more radical aspect in the concept of composting. This is currently the subject of research by some revolutionary thinkers in the field of body disposal whose zest for their work echoes that of Sir Henry Thompson and Sir Francis Seymour Hayden. Andrew Kerr is pioneering the theory of the compost funeral – a bold alternative to burial and cremation.

> The corpse could be taken to the Compostorium and placed in a specially constructed autoclave or pressure cooker. The corpse would already have been disembowelled and that material placed into a methane digester; this would have averted the potential dangers of pathogens. The gas so generated would contribute to the slow and steady heat required to render the remains to a condition ready to be ground up to a kind of slurry to be 'intimately mixed' with straw and other vegetable wastes.
>
> The whole process would be completed in about twelve weeks or so; a decent time for mourning. The finished compost could then be incorporated into the family memorial garden. This would be far better than burial which is too deep for aerobic processes, or wasteful incineration which is damaging to the environment. (*New Natural Death Handbook*, 2000)

Is this the future of disposal of the dead, with environmental concerns determining practice to the exclusion of other concerns? If so, we should be mindful, for disposal of the dead shaped entirely by environmental concerns represents a materialism akin to that of people without belief. Both signify the redundancy of the rituals that sustained our ancestors. Poised between these two material views, we seem to have lost our bearings about how to relate to the dead. With bodies in unmarked graves located either by Ordnance Survey grid-references, or electronically tagged in woodland burial grounds, and cremated remains concealed in ever more mundane places, is the public profile of death going to decrease so that the dead disappear from our sight completely? In a fragmented society of separated families in which individuals lead long-distance lives, and of growing numbers of single households, the question of how the living are to live with the dead is becoming ever more challenging. In *Twelve Theses on the Economy of the Dead* (1997), John Berger asked and answered it well.

> How do the living live with the dead?
>
> Until the dehumanisation of capitalism, all the living awaited the experience of the dead. It was their ultimate future. By themselves, the living were incomplete. Thus living and dead were interdependent. Always. Only a uniquely modern form of egotism has broken this interdependence. With disastrous consequences for the living who think of the dead as the *eliminated*.

ESPRIT
DE
CORPSE

KEEP MY FUNERAL VIDEO ON MY BOOKSHELF. IT WAS NOT made urgently, or sadly. I am in good health. It is neither sentimental nor profound and, concluding as it does with the *Loony Tunes* theme music, it could scarcely be described as morbid. It includes apologies about the state of my study, which has a recently ransacked look that would convince a burglar he'd been beaten to it, as well as requests to return my library books – both pertinent communications, no matter when my time comes. For when I am in my dotage, surrounded by incontinent pugs and the dissident members of the sheltered housing community, I am sure I will remain on the librarians' equivalent of Interpol on account of my pathological disregard for date stamps, whether on library books or pots of yoghurt.

The video was made in the spirit of collaboration rather than personal whimsy when, intrigued by the title, I signed up for a 'Message from the Grave' workshop taking place at the Natural Death Centre, as part of a programme of activities celebrating the English Day of the Dead. The NDC is an educational charity run by writer and 'social inventor' Nicholas Albery, and two psychotherapists, his wife Josephine Speyer and Christianne Heal. The Day of the Dead is their attempt to reinstate on the third Sunday of April what was originally a Christian festival of death that took place in the spring, until the ninth century when Pope Gregory IV moved it to autumn to coincide with a German tradition. Unlike T. S. Eliot, for whom April was 'the cruellest month', Nicholas is of the opinion that 'It is easier to contemplate death when life is burgeoning on every side.' Although each year the event takes in a different format, the objective remains the same – to encourage people to contemplate mortality.

Sunday afternoon in the London suburb of Willesden Green may seem unlikely time and place to look death in the eye, but behind the net-curtain normality, the Natural Death Centre represents an inspiring cell of cultural activism. This organisation is at the vanguard of important social change concerning how we die, dispose of and remember the dead. Its Natural Death salons invert all the rules of social engagement. Instead of death being a no-no in polite conversation, these congenial gatherings offer an unusual context in which to talk about death – not as some abstract, esoteric brain-baffler, but more prosaically and personally, at the level of planning one's own funeral. By coaxing people to give thought to their funerals, the Day of the Dead indirectly encourages them to contemplate their own demise in such a way as to throw their current priorities into sharp relief. As the American Indian saying goes: 'Today is a good day to die, for all of the things in my life are present.' A significant part of the NDC's agenda focuses on improving funerals by making them more personal, more ecologically sound and less expensive than the conventional conveyor-belt version. Since its inception in 1991 the NDC has become a respected funeral watchdog. The fact that its funeral planning salons are always heavily oversubscribed bears testament to a growing disaffection with conventional death rites. There are signs of a backlash against thin, rushed ceremonies, and mounting interest in creating new rituals to provide an alternative source of the sort of communality and coherence that have traditionally been supplied by institutional religion.

When I arrived at the workshop, the first thing that caught my eye was a pamphlet entitled 'Fruit Tree over the Body.'

> Instead of a tombstone a fruit tree is planted over the body. The roots are nourished by the return of that body to the earth and in the years to follow eating the fruit of that tree will be like partaking of the loved one.

The idea that I might metaphysically become apple pie for my family was a mite too material an interpretation of communion with nature for my taste. However, reassured by the cordiality of the hosts, I gave them the benefit of the doubt and joined the pow-wow to start brainstorming ideas for my own funeral.

We were a diverse group. Clive, a funeral director from Dorking, was attending more in the spirit of market research and professional rivalry than enlightenment. He spoke eloquently about the threat to the mainstream trade of the do-it-yourself approach. 'From the undertaker's point of view, the problem with people doing their own thing and just asking us to store a body for a bit, or supply just a coffin, is like booking a chartered flight and then saying don't charge me baggage handling I'll carry my own bags, and don't charge me for the in-flight meal I'll take my own sandwiches.'

His friend Carol, who ran a cemetery at the aptly named Box Hill and also acted as an officiant, had come to pick up tips about secular ceremonies. Jo, a young fashion designer, had spotted a gap in the market for designer shrouds. Paul, a spindly youth in batik trousers many would not be seen dead in, hoped the day would help him to overcome his premature fear of death. Mary, an octogenarian with more reason to be afraid, had been cajoled into attending by her vicar: 'He's always asking us how we want to be buried.' Helen, her friend, sporting the sort of thick black-framed glasses fashionable among philosophy lecturers, had a problem with the doctrine of resurrection and the relationship of body to soul, whereas Susan, a straight-talking American had a problem with the undertakers who had dealt with her father's death: 'Not to get too gruesome or gross anybody out, but the funeral director dealing with my dad was a real jerk and lost the body.'

Introductions over, we were invited to close our eyes and visualise our own funerals exactly as we wished them to be. Josephine prompted us with an impressive list of things to consider. 'Where will it happen? What about invitations? What sort of music do you want? Will you have presents and balloons? What do you want people to wear? Will you have a master or mistress of ceremonies?' As she ran through her checklist, funeral planning started to feel like party planning – the perfect party, in fact, where your guests look after themselves and for once you won't mind if you're not asked back.

Josephine stopped our reverie and invited us to pair up to compare notes. Practical suggestions came thick and fast. Put red dots in your address book beside the people you want to be invited because 'otherwise you'll end up with the window cleaner, your ex-lover and the French reading group'. Consider compiling a written funeral plan and leave it in the safekeeping of a family member. 'Families have enough to think about after a death without spending hours trying to imagine what the dead person would or would not have wanted.' To make this process easier and to steer people in the right direction, the NDC have devised an advance funeral wishes questionnaire in which you indicate personal preferences by ticking boxes. This is *ars moriendi* for the twenty-first century, the formalities of funerary ritual as multiple choice. Among the more interesting considerations are the following:

The kind of numbers I would like at my funeral service are ...

I see it as ideally a very small family affair / family and friends / all comers.

I would like my funeral service to take account of the fact that my religion
/ belief / philosophy is ...

Rituals I would like include single flowers placed in coffin / grave lined
with hay / football scarf or other identifying symbol placed in or on coffin.

I have / have not left a last message / audiotape / video or other text for
my family or friends (if yes, location) and wish this to be played at the
funeral service / some other occasion (specify).

The last question deals with the afterlife, and probably for the first time
in the history of Christianity tackles the doctrine of the Resurrection as a
'tick as applicable' option:

I do / do not believe in an afterlife which I visualise as ...

The NDC suggest that this document should be undersigned by two
witnesses who do not stand to benefit from the will, and then filed with it.
It is available from the centre for the price of four first-class stamps.

Even if what you actually plan is never executed, the act of planning is
salutary. The session continued with a 'life review' exercise where, in pairs,
we took turns to ask and answer the following questions:

'What did you mean to do with your life?'

'What did you actually do?'

'What are your regrets and what do you rejoice in?'

In between putting out the rubbish and the school run, these are not
questions we generally address. Just as my partner was telling me her
proudest life achievements, Christianne clapped her hands for attention:
'That's it! Time up! Stop talking immediately. Death won't allow you to
have your say – think about that.'

One of the more radical issues the NDC addresses is corpse care, because part of its effort to reclaim death is to challenge the practice of hur-
riedly despatching the body to a funeral home. They want to challenge the
'Look, don't touch' viewing syndrome that goes with embalming, by persuading people to keep the body at home. Ideally, this requires rigging up
refrigeration facilities, for in a morgue bodies are kept at exactly the same
temperature as a domestic fridge. They suggest a canopy erected around an
open fridge door, but this conjures up an undignified picture and seems a
rather clumsy form of improvisation that could be avoided if the electric
cold plates that are common in France were introduced over here. A sim-
pler alternative is to turn down the heating and get in some dry ice, which

will enable you to keep the body at home for about seven days – depending on the cause of death, which affects the rate of decomposition. Contrary to popular belief, rigor mortis only lasts for twenty-four hours, after which time the stiff is not stiff. Rubbing it with essential oils like tea tree and lavender can be therapeutic for the bereaved. Indeed, the NDC are positively enthusiastic about post-mortem cohabitation. 'It's a really beautiful thing. You can sleep with the dead body and watch television with it.' Many women may find this a strangely familiar experience when the time comes.

The NDC has captured the zeitgeist of concern about the form of modern funerals in such a way as to capitalise on the baby boomers' interest in death control. As they enter a stage of life where they are closer to death than birth, the boomers want to own death – to transform not only the manner of dying, but also the funeral into opportunities for self-assertion. The NDC encourages people to think about the plethora of options open to them for arranging a personally relevant ceremony. Central to its ethos is the restoration of autonomy to an area of life which has been taken over by undertakers, whose commercialisation of the aftermath of dying it regards as negatively as the anonymity of institutionalised dying which precedes it in the hospice and the hospital. The spirit in which the NDC is seeking to domesticate death is a logical extension of the energy expended in the 1970s on the domestication of birth. The late Nicholas Albery who tragically died in June 2001 cited a comparison between the natural birth of his son and his father's death as the catalyst which turned his attention to the need to establish a 'natural death movement' to parallel the 'natural childbirth movement'. His campaign for home death and family-assisted funerals which minimise the involvement of the professional funeral director replicates the tenets of home delivery as an alternative to the clinical 'stirrups and stitches' system of birth which, for many years, women felt powerless to challenge. Both hinge on self-assertion and the notion of going through a rite of passage in character. The thinking behind the birth plan, where women make it clear if they do not want pain relief, is seeping into attitudes towards death and dying, most dramatically with the advent of the 'Do Not Resuscitate' tattoo, an American concept. (Conversely, in the UK people are demanding access to their medical files to see whether a doctor has added, 'Do Not Resuscitate' without permission.)

The fashion for funeral directives is an important aspect of the new concern for autonomy. It is becoming commonplace for people to go public with their funeral plans, stating everything from their preferences on viewing and embalming to requests for New Orleans jazz bands and flamboyant dress for mourners. Most baby boomers would be hard pressed to match the grand plans of the definitive ageing hippy, the Marquess of Bath. He wants to build a personal temple modelled on Stonehenge which will be called Thynnehenge. A portion of his ashes would be scattered there, in what he hopes would mark the start of a family tradition whereby 'those who are nearest and dearest to me might choose to have their ashes scattered around the same spot the idea of posthumous togetherness might thus be enhanced'.

This concern for asserting one's wishes in death – specifically in funerary detail – represents a renaissance rather than an innovation, for historically there is rich seam of originality in people's plans for their own funerals. Before death became taboo in the twentieth century, there are many examples of British people forming imaginative responses to the idea of their own funerals – not merely thinking about their own demise, but planning the details of the ceremony. In 1905 Blanche Cripps conceived her own funeral on the principles of *Desert Island Deaths*, requesting that she should be buried with her head on a Bible and her feet on Shakespeare. Less orthodox was the funeral directive of Mr Hugh Haimains, who died in 1850 at Kewstoke, near Weston-super-Mare, aged 84 years. A local paper reported his wishes: 'By his own desire he was buried in his first wife's wedding gown, which was an old-fashioned light chintz printed cotton; and by his own request also his wife's lindsey apron was put in the coffin with him.' Evidently Cripps and Hawains were not originals, but conformed to a long English tradition of eccentricity expressed through death style. The *Quarterly Review* of 1819 gives a flavour of this national characteristic:

> There is no country in the world where those half-mad men, who are styled humorists, have indulged themselves so frequently in what might be called funeral freaks. An old smoker who died in a workhouse about ten years ago, at the age of 106, desired that his pipe might be laid in his coffin. An old foxhunter would be buried with a fox pad in each hand; and had the huntsmen and whippers-in of all the packs with which he had hunted for his mourners. A stout electioneer gave directions that his coffin should be painted blue, and the bearers wear blue ribands. A chaise-driver, who had attained great eminence in that profession, desired that he might be interred as near the turnpike road as possible, that he might enjoy the satisfaction, he said, of hearing the carriages pass. An odd fellow, in a higher rank of life, left one penny to every child that should attend his funeral, a guinea to seven old navigators (as canal men are called in the midland counties), for puddling him up in his grave, and half a guinea to the ringers to strike off a peal of grand bobs when they were putting him in.

In this context, the NDC is resurrecting a tradition. As it has grown in stature with an almost constant media profile, so has attendance at the Day of the Dead. From a handful of people sitting in cosy circle exchanging tips for coffin decoration over cups of tea in 1995, the event has developed, and the celebrations in the year 2000 were altogether more sophisticated. The formal programme included an awards ceremony, with categories including Best Cemetery, Best Cardboard Coffin Supplier, Best Funeral Supplier, and so forth. The awards are given to individuals and organisations who, in the opinion of the NDC, are doing most to raise the standard of funerals by providing people with expanded opportunities to achieve their ceremony of choice at a fair price. The Best Crematorium award went to Carlisle, which also won the Best Cemetery award – its double honour reflecting the dynamism of Ken West, the bereavement manager, who is well known for championing the cause of family-assisted funerals: 'We know that funerals arranged without a funeral director are at least as good, and often better, than those that take the conventional path.'

The trend for funerals in which mourners take an active role in the ceremony is gathering momentum. One of the most moving examples I have come across of a personal funeral which involved not a single payment for professional services at any stage, was that devised by Liz Daniels for her daughter Rosie. Rosie died in 1996 at the age of six from meningitis. She was buried on private land that belonged to a close friend. The plot in Kent was the site of a labyrinth which had been used as a venue for solstice parties, and the fact that Rosie herself had played there enhanced the sense of both positive and personal associations. Instinctively, her family shied away from the idea of burying her on church ground, with which they had no connection. Liz approached her friend tentatively, and together they investigated the legality of a private burial. To their relief, they found that it was feasible. At every stage friends were involved. Rosie's body was put in a bright velvet bag so that it was pleasing to the touch and less intimidating for her young friends. She was laid in a room decorated with photographs and pictures drawn by her friends, who had the chance to be with her in this setting before the burial. The grave was dug and decorated with dreamcatchers and ribbons. Cradling her in his arms, Rosie's father carried her to it and gently laid her down. Children and adults helped to fill in the grave, putting small items into it as they did so – a teddy bear, little clay figures and an apple. Rosie's mother describes the ensuing ceremony: 'We held hands, 150 people in a circle, old and young. We sang, we danced, we played drums, we cried, we shared our sorrow and we felt all of us the limitless love that was present. We let twenty-one white balloons fly free symbolising the departure of her soul and then we lit a fire – a big, big fire – and celebrated Rosie's life.'

Instead of cut flowers, people brought rose bushes, trees and plants in pots so that they could start creating a garden.

Another personal ceremony – this time on public land at a woodland burial ground in Essex – took the imaginative step of dividing pallbearers up in accordance with the chronology of their involvement with the deceased. Peter was born with Down's syndrome and died in 1998, aged 59. Friends transported his body to the burial site in a handmade coffin which was strewn with local flowers. For the first leg of the route to the grave, his oldest friends carried the coffin, then those who had known him in the 1970s took over, and finally they swapped again so that those who had known him most recently could take their turn at carrying him to his final resting place. Some of the mourners said a few words, and one or two wrote a final message on his coffin.

But as well as providing words, mourners consigned to the ground symbolic offerings. Roger, Peter's brother, describes these final gestures: 'Sand and earth from Cornwall, shells, silver birch bark and feathers from New England, cigars and an illuminated message, several generous swigs of Guinness poured on to his casket, bulbs from Oxford and chrysanthemums from London.'

Finally Roger laid down his brother's slippers, a *lungi* (loin cloth), a bib given to Peter by his co-carer Ernest, and his baseball cap printed with the words 'Get Real!'

Celebration of personality is not confined to the tiny percentage of alternative and new age funerals. It has pervaded the mainstream. Illustrating this trend was the Teddy Boy ceremony for 'Sunglasses' Ron, a rock 'n' roll fanatic who died of cancer at the age of 53 and was buried in a south London cemetery. A cortège of motorbikes flanked by mourners on foot, many in winklepickers, followed the hearse, which bore a spectacular wreath in the shape of a huge pair of sunglasses made of black-sprayed carnations. Even the funeral director, Albert Torrance, entered into the spirit of the occasion and gave up his usual sober dress for a leather jacket and denims and, instead of a mute's wand, he carried a guitar over his shoulder. The female mourners wore cowgirl outfits and skin-tight leathers. When they arrived at the cemetery, where loudspeakers were relaying 'Rock Around the Clock', they could not restrain themselves and in a moment of spontaneity they started to jive before going into the chapel. Elvis Presley songs were played as the coffin entered the chapel, and 'Three Steps to Heaven' on the way out. As Ron was lowered into the grave, mourners burst into applause and then started casting mementos after him. Some of the men removed their bootlace ties and threw them into the grave; another emptied his hip-flask of whisky, while a woman leaned over and dropped in a copy of the single 'Leader of the Pack'.

The richness of funerals such as these is a burgeoning, but largely undocumented, aspect of contemporary culture. A seam of imagination is being mined by ordinary people, creating a style of ceremony that is outside the conventional dramaturgy of death. Celebrities are also raising the profile of this trend and influencing public perception of funerals. The fact that the Princess of Wales had pop songs and, in effect, a family-organised funeral with a style of burial indicating a rejection of formality and tradition, presented a powerful example of a personal funeral. As mentioned earlier, the funeral of her step-grandmother, Barbara Cartland, also attracted a lot of media interest. Like the words of her romantic novels which were taken down and transcribed by her secretary, the ceremony was executed to the letter of her instructions. The grand dame of romantic fiction had less of a grand finale than a modestly happy ending. Mourners were advised to wear gumboots and to bring shooting sticks. The cardboard coffin was interred in the grounds of Cartland's Hertfordshire estate under an oak tree which was rigged up with a ghettoblaster that played Perry Como's 'I Believe for Every Drop of Rain that Falls a Flower Grows'. Perhaps to their surprise, as with karaoke, the mourners were expected to sing along.

The fertile funereal imaginations of the famous are the basis of a regular feature in a Sunday newspaper. Will Self wants to be picked clean by birds of prey in a relocation of a Tibetan sky burial to the Orkneys with the added ingredient of a Jamaican reggae band. Peter Stringfellow wants to make an exhibition of himself by being mummified in a mausoleum complete with light show. Lionel Blair wants to become a celestial firework let off by his wife after being cremated along with his tap shoes, top hat and cane. Rabbi Lionel Blue wants a lesbian jazz band he once saw in Amsterdam to do a rousing rendition of 'When the Saints Go Marching In'. The celebrity funeral has also been scheduled as a subject of a Channel Five television series, in which famous people describe in minute detail the funeral ceremonies they wish to have. This includes the objects they want buried with them. Lesley Joseph wants a china shoe her grandmother gave her, while fellow thesp Brian Blessed opts for his climbing gear.

Self-expression is challenging the conventional code of Christianity – sometimes flagrantly, as manifested by a cremation service for a man who died of an AIDS-related illness. In the crematorium, feather boas and red rubber accessories were distributed among the guests and besom sticks were shaken in front of a black coffin into which mourners were invited to drive four-inch nails. This type of unorthodox funeral is part of a subculture of creative ceremonies which evolved, in part, as a result of the strained relationship between mainstream Christianity and homosexuals. The impact of the vibrant originality inherent in these funerals appears to have filtered through to the mainstream. In the darkest days of the AIDS crisis, funerals were sometimes brilliantly flamboyant. Crematorium curtains were parted by men in long white gloves to the strains of the *Wizard of Oz* song, 'Ding-Dong, the Witch is Dead'; champagne corks popped over coffins; corpses were buried with bottles of Campari and baseball caps; cremated remains were even scattered on a dance floor in a disco.

After years of being tongue-tied by death denial, we are becoming more literate. A new wave of alternative funeral facilitators and designers is extending the vocabulary of death rites. Unlike traditional funeral directors, where the relationship with the family is defined by delegation and discretion, with the family listening to the funeral director, the funeral arranger listens to the family and helps them to arrange more imaginative ceremonies. In Lancashire, John and Mary Mallatratt run Peace Funerals, a company which encourages family involvement. Like so many alternative funeral arrangers, the Mallatratts started their business as a reaction to their own experience of impersonal, undignified committals. One of the most unusual ceremonies was a railway funeral for an avid trainspotter. After such a hard frost that parts of the train had to be thawed out, Fred Normanton's mortal remains were transported in a cardboard coffin covered with velvet and a fleece in the guard's van of a steam train from Butterley Station in Derbyshire on a seven-mile journey to Swanwick Junction, near the Midland Railway Centre in Ripley. Mourners travelled in the dining car as the train puffed sedately through the wintry landscape. At Swanwick the coffin was carried by bearers, including Fred's sons, from the train to a nineteenth-century tin tabernacle for a non-religious service. A brass band played Gershwin. Maureen, Fred's wife of thirty-two years, recited W. H. Auden's 'Funeral Blues', the poem made so popular by the film *Four Weddings and a Funeral*. John Mallatratt proposed a toast to Fred 'with Tesco's whisky, his favourite tipple.' As Fred's coffin was buried, the train nearby gave three blasts of the whistle and then the mourners repaired to the dining car for 'Fred's party.' This was a celebration of a life full of love and passion, far more fitting than the restraint of small talk and strong tea which often follows more formal funerals.

Thus there is widespread evidence of a collective reclamation of ritual.

The form that this is taking suggests an interesting shift in the perception of the function of a funeral – namely, that it should be a celebration of individuality more than an affirmation of collective faith. Growing dissatisfaction with the irrelevance and expense of the Victorian/Christian hybrid of ceremony means that people are either rejecting it altogether, or adapting it to express individuality. The old is being made new as traditional funerary spectacle, which once symbolised conformity, is being customised to express individual preferences. This ancient/modern mix was evident at gangster Reggie Kray's funeral, where the traditional imagery of hearse and six plumed horses was juxtaposed with the modern imagery of red armbands worn by male mourners printed with the letters 'RKF' for Reggie Kray's Funeral. A similar mix happened at the funeral of murdered schoolgirl Sarah Payne, with a horse-drawn hearse and mourners wearing lapel badges displaying the iconic school photograph of her smiling face. Similarly identified by mourners at his funeral was the biker Maz Harris, who was killed when his motorbike crashed on the A2 motorway. Fellow bikers honoured him by wearing armbands over their leathers bearing his name, 'Maz'. Another good example of the adaptation of traditional elements to express personality was the funeral of the musician Ian Drury. A glass-sided, horse-drawn hearse had on one side flowers which read 'Ian from Durex', and on the other 'Madness Oi Oi'. A humanist service at Golders Green crematorium started with a recording of sleigh bells and yodelling, and ended with 'I'm Just a Gigolo'!

In every detail, traditions are being personalised. If, when the final whistle goes, trainspotters can go by train to their grave, a dramatic and less expensive alternative is for their cremated remains to be fed into the fire-boxes of steam engines. And even train-robbers' funerals reflect their interests; the funeral flowers for Buster Edwards were in the shape of a large train prepared by the south London florist who also did the flowers for the Kray funerals.

Coffins, too, are being customised in variety of ways. People can either buy a generic casket – such as the popular 'Fairway To Heaven' for a golfer – or they can commission one of a growing number of specialists to hand-paint a coffin reflecting the interests of the deceased. These distil poignant details of a person's life. A woman who was terminally ill asked an artist to capture the view of the estuary that she and her husband always saw on their way home together in the evenings. On one side of her coffin this landscape was depicted in full, down to the wader birds and evening light, while on the other side were motifs reflecting her love of badminton and fell-walking. Alternatively, the coffin can be customised in a more ad hoc way, with mourners scribbling messages on it in felt-tip pen, almost as if they were signing a plaster cast. Ken West has seen one funeral where messages included 'Shut that bloody door!', which had been the constant riposte of the deceased to his children and was a family in-joke.

Another trend is for greater significance to be attached to what the deceased wears. Paula Yates, in keeping with her outrageous starlet image, was buried in a white mink bikini by Jasper Conran, while for a sea burial funeral arranger Paula Rainey Crofts was asked to put the dear departed in his swimming trunks. Funeral directors confirm this trend. One enterprising firm, Vic Fearn of Nottingham, went so far as to inspire the general public by organising a funeral fashion show of grave wear. Young designers were invited to show their designs, and forty designer shrouds were displayed on mesh mannequins rather than live (or dead) models. One young paper-maker catering for the green market made a biodegradable daffodil gown – a flimsy, feminine-looking dress made from real daffodils, with pleasing connotations of resurrection and spring. Another gown featured pockets in which to place amulets so that the remains could be annotated and dated by such symbols as CND signs, radiation symbols, printed circuits and gender marks.

Ken West has said that, apart from swear words in the book of remembrance, anything goes. Many of the new wave of alternative funeral directors say that they are happy to execute even fairly outlandish requests, within the parameters of legality and what is deemed respectful and reasonable. This means that in recent years there has been an extraordinary diversity of ceremonies involving ordinary families. For one of their customers, a man who had planned his own funeral in every detail, the firm Undertaken With Love complied with his request to have 'I told you I was sick' written on the outside of his coffin. Testing even further the limits of conventional thinking was the ceremony for the anarchist Albert Meltzer, which was meticulously planned and aptly anarchic. Behind the horse-drawn hearse a reggae band played, and in the crematorium was a stand-up comic who wisecracked in the pulpit until it was time for the coffin to disappear behind the curtains to the strains of a Marlene Dietrich song. Meltzer was typical of many for wanting a celebration:

> Anyone mourning should be denounced as the representative of a credit card company and thrown out on their ear. Snowballs if in season tomatoes if not can be thrown at anyone uttering even worthy clichés.

Fundamental to the modernity of these funerals is the mood of celebration exemplified by the popping of champagne corks at post-ceremony gatherings, bright clothes and the use of balloons and bunting. In Islington, for the funeral of a local shopkeeper bunting was attached to railings with the message 'It's been good to know you'. The growing popularity of balloons at funerals reinforces the association with celebration, but also of mutability, for balloons, like flowers, are bright but short-lived. They feature at contemporary funerals in a number of ways: tied to the back of the hearse, attached to the coffin – where at one funeral arranged by an alternative funeral designer, they bore the words 'Just Deceased' – or distributed to mourners and let fly away as part of the ceremony. This happened at the funeral of a 19-year-old girl, when her family and friends released nineteen red, heart-shaped balloons as her coffin was lowered into a grave in a cemetery in Eltham.

The cult of individualism, which is transforming the funeral ceremony, is filtering through to commemoration. Echoing the rebellion against impersonal funerals, in recent years there has been a trend towards creating memorials which are 'in character'. For example, for a hairdresser, a comb and scissors in stone was recently commissioned from Harriet Frazer of Memorials by Artists, an organisation that offers aesthetic, one-off memorials designed and executed by the country's leading letter-cutters and stone masons. Each commission is a careful collaboration between the artist and the bereaved to ensure the stone reflects the true personality of the person who has died. Frequently the memorial does not take the shape of the traditional headstone. Rather, stone is used in more imaginative forms. These include the memorial as a sundial, as a standing stone, and as a stepping-stone – a powerful metaphor for transition and someone passing from one world to the next. The raw material is similarly diverse – Cornish granite, Welsh slate, Portland stone, Yorkshire sandstone and Derbyshire limestone. Inscriptions are secular as well as devotional. The combination of hand-cut letters and original design inspires contemplation and brings private grief into the public gaze with an aesthetic power that has been woefully lacking in the twentieth-century cemetery. Encapsulating this is a memorial to a small boy killed in a car crash. On one side of the stone, a butterfly is shown alighting on his name, and underneath is a picture of a dinosaur that he himself had drawn. On the other side is the house where he lived and his bicycle in the position in which he left it, leaning against a tree. The memorial is all the more poignant for being so intensely personal.

In America the theme of personal relevance is treated with less reverence. Affluent baby boomers are creating a new market for customised ceremonies. In response to this, the Batesville Casket Company offers a 'Cool

Jazz' option, where the casket is positioned over two loudspeakers, with the music of Miles Davis creating a mellow rather than morbid mood. For the hunter there is the 'Outdoorsman' option, which transforms the funeral home into a lodge decorated with bearskin rugs and assorted paraphernalia of the chase such as trophy antlers and gun-racks. The company has even turned its premises into a boxing ring where mourners stepped between the ropes to deliver their tributes. This trend extends to memorials, too. For example, in Scippio cemetery, near Harlan, Indiana, a plumber who had amassed many unpaid parking tickets had two old parking meters put over his grave; painted black and with the coin-slots welded shut, they read 'EXPIRED'. In Washington, a man whose wife's profligate spending caused him much grief in life commissioned a headstone in the style of a Visa card with the lettering 'CHARGE IT'.

This level of freedom of expression would be censored in most English dioceses. Instead, there are regularly tense negotiations between registrars, vicars and the bereaved about suitable wording. For example, 'Our Dear Mum' was vetoed in one parish where the authorities thought 'Our Dear Mother' more suitable. Perhaps in the near future there will be a popular uprising on behalf of commemorative rights. This is not so far fetched an idea, for another American initiative which takes the dynamics of self-assertion in a new direction is Plan Your Own Epitaph Day. Devised by Lance Hardie, its central tenet is that having an unmemorable headstone is a fate worse than death, as his website explains.

> If you do nothing someone else will put your name and dates on your gravestone, period. If you are terribly unlucky, they'll add something like 'Dearly Missed' or 'Beloved Cousin' or maybe even worse. Don't give up your power over the most important words of your life. Take control: it's your life, it's your death, it's your stone – YOU say something. (www.hardiehouse.org)

The ground swell of interest – even insistence – on personal relevance in funerals and memorials is creating friction between mainstream churches and their congregations. This was evident in Ireland recently. In response to the proliferation of themed funerals and personal eulogies, senior members of Ireland's Roman Catholic church issued a directive reminding people of the function of the funeral mass as a profession of belief in the afterlife, not a do-it-yourself entertainment. The controversy ran and ran in the pages of the *Irish Times*. The target of the Church's opprobrium was exemplified by the funeral of a sedentary racing enthusiast, which was reported by Kieran Cooke. The deceased spent his life watching race meetings on television and placing bets with his bookie using his mobile phone, with a permanently lit cigarette in his free hand. Given his lifestyle, the odds were against him living to a ripe old age and, as the doctor's favourite candidate for a heart attack, it was perhaps no surprise that when he had one it was while watching a race. At a certain point in his funeral, his friends bought some of his most prized personal effects to the altar – a picture of his favourite racehorse and a box of cigarettes – and they put his mobile phone on the coffin. During the eulogy they also played the commentary of the race he had been listening to when he died. The service ended with a friend of his, dressed in a jockey's racing colours, reciting a poem about the joy of the turf. Then, his mobile phone and cigarettes having been placed in his coffin, he was carried out of church. His friends cheered him on the final furlong.

The Roman Catholic church in Britain is similarly concerned about the popularity of themed funerals, where the whole service is designed to reflect the personality of the deceased. They have cause for concern. In response to a survey conducted by Co-operative Funeral Services in March 2000, 50 per cent of respondents said they wanted a themed funeral, with two-thirds saying they would like pop songs, not hymns, and that they would prefer colourful, upbeat ceremonies to formal religious ones. Father Kieran Conry, a representative of the Roman Catholic church in Britain, commented: 'There's a certain inevitability to the development; it is an indication of the severing of people's links with religious traditions.' This severance with tradition is also evident in a growing trend to rejecting the traditional 'white' church wedding in favour of an ever-increasing number of alternative premises licensed for civil ceremonies.

Ireland, as one of the most church-going countries in Europe, has witnessed a dramatic drop in church attendance, with a recent survey showing that where 80 per cent of the population used to attend mass once a week, now the figure is 50 per cent. Falling attendance is even more problematic for the Church of England. The gloomiest forecast is that of the Scripture Union, who estimate that, at current rates, within forty years only one person in 200 will be a churchgoer, and there is very real threat that the Church will be abandoned. More recently, a Mori poll carried out in December 2000 revealed that only 37 per cent of the population intended to go to church at Christmas. The widespread evidence is that the Church's ownership of death rites is being challenged. This is ironic, for if the present day turning away from formal religion is being influenced by organisations such as the Natural Death Centre and the Humanists – secular bodies – at the end of the nineteenth century an important aspect of the movement to reform the excesses of mourning ritual was religious in nature. Where the present-day pamphleteers and activists are seeking to de-Christianise rites of passage and to make people more aware of the possibility of alternative, non-religious rituals, the nineteenth-century campaign was in part an attempt to re-Christianise the funeral by removing some of the more worldly features.

We live at a time of cultural confusion – pop songs in churches for funerals and pop stars with religious names in fashion – Madonna, All Saints, Angel – even a fashion designer called Imitation of Christ. There is a growing sense of distinction between the non-religious and the spiritual. A materialist rejection of ceremony is happening in tandem with ceremonies being designed to express the spiritual. There is also a sense of interesting cross-reference with some individualist funerals borrowing the trappings of Victorian funeral ritual, while similarly, personally relevant funerals may still use the *Book of Common Prayer* as their framework. A society that has bought into existence the chicken tikka sandwich is similarly adapting ideology and religion to its own taste in funeral ceremonies. Fusion cuisine and fusion funerals are contemporary trends. Increasingly, there is a pick-and-mix approach to ceremony – a bit of Buddhist chanting, a Jewish prayer for the dead, secular ceremonies in churches, prayers in social clubs. The boundaries between the secular and the religious are becoming increasingly elastic. There are religious, semi-religious and non-religious rituals often incorporated within the same ceremony. An example of this was the grand woodland burial of Gervase Jackson-Stops at Greenhaven woodland burial ground, where a William Morris-style rustic cart with shire horses carried the coffin to the grave, but where the service was conducted by the Bishop of Peterborough and a Northamptonshire vicar. A similar incongruity was evident in the service for Maz Harris at the parish church of St Paulinus in Crayford, where Hell's Angels dressed in leathers and shades packed into the pews. This particular funeral, in which the priest had never met the deceased, exemplifies a common situation in which non-churchgoers wish to use a church for funerals. The vicar in this instance admitted that it was the largest congregation he had ever had, and generously commented, 'We have all been terribly impressed by the way in which this funeral has been organised and very pleased to be part of it.'

The use of the church as a backdrop for personal informal funerals of non-believers is an interesting anomaly. In an age of declining baptism services and traditional church weddings, the church is still used for funerals. The Revd Roberto Pravisani, an independent minister, is doing fascinating field work in Greater Manchester addressing the issue of providing personalised funerals for non-churchgoers. Underpinning his work is the dichotomy represented by the fact that in this country nine out of ten funerals are conducted with church rites at a time when so few people go to church.

The Church of England is in a challenging position, having to cope with declining congregations, dwindling numbers of new ordinands and an increasingly materialistic flock who regard the individual as sacred. For the first time there is some urgency for the Church to address consumer demand. The pressure to comply with demands for personal funerals is presenting almost comic situations. For example, for a West Ham supporter, Canon Oates of St Brides, Fleet Street, went so far as to base an address on the club's anthem 'I'm Forever Blowing Bubbles'. 'If you listen to the words it has a universal message; we sometimes blow ourselves up to be more than we are. Most importantly it spoke to those present.' More seriously, following the success of the woodland burial movement, the Church has taken the innovative step of opening the first Church of England woodland burial site in Cambridgeshire, complete with a marketing slogan: 'Go Wild When You Die.' This bold move comes in response to having identified a gap in the market for people who want a link to the environment but also to religion. The title of this Church of England initiative, The Arbory Trust, gives nothing away about its religious affiliation. It is described as a Christian foundation chaired by a bishop, and yet the words 'God' and 'consecrated ground' appear nowhere on their brochure, which features a leaf rather than traditional religious iconography. It also states that 'whilst the Arbory Trust is a Christian foundation it welcomes all regardless of race or religion'. This relaxed approach is symptomatic of a dramatic willingness to accommodate an increasingly secular community, and of a level of tolerance which is indicative of crisis management.

The over-arching Christian narrative is no longer relevant to the majority of people. The question arises: What replaces the *Book of Common Prayer* to codify the rite of passage that is a funeral, and to confer meaning on death? In a climate where popular culture has replaced formal religion as the primary element of social cohesion and pop songs have replaced hymns at funerals, we have lost the moorings of tradition and find ourselves cut adrift. Our cultural confusion is compounded by the fact that self-expression has replaced transcendence as the function of much art, and self-cultivation in general is detaching us even further from the stability that comes with shared belief and the continuity of traditional ceremonies.

The picture, however, is not relentlessly bleak, for if we are no longer constrained by tradition, our imagination can be freed. There is no dearth of new ceremonies. Anja Saunders of 'Rituals for Remarkable Times', rites of passage specialists, gives a vivid insight into the creative energy being put into death. 'We've had ceremonies where people painted the coffin, set wishing balloons off in the air, communally dug an egg-shaped grave, blown thousands of bubbles to lift the spirit and constructed an amphitheatre in the middle of a field. We've had bell ringing, chanting, story telling and massage for afterwards.' Such behaviour is not the preserve of a wacky minority. Ordinary people are doing extraordinary things. I've encountered the following imaginative gestures: the cremated remains of a much-loved mother and grandmother being placed in her handbag with her trademark lipstick and compact, her reading glasses and the partially completed crossword that she was doing when she died, and the bag being buried under a weeping pear tree after which her grandchildren, three sons and their wives helped to fill in the hole; the grave of a youngster who was tragically electrocuted being ceremonially scattered with 13-amp fuses by his friends; a widow in her seventies with a withered hand which was smooth compared to her overworked other hand who made a memorial to her husband that was rough stone on one side and smooth on the other; a young mother who lost twin boys making two dolls out of cloth and laying them on their graves like voodoo fetish dolls, a poignantly primitive representation of her two lost children.

The Brit Art phenomenon has been one factor in making art more accessible and culturally conspicuous. Given this new profile of art in popular culture, and the fact that attendance at art galleries is soaring, it seems logical that at the grass-roots level similar originality is being expressed at funerals. In a fascinating transferral of influence, the rites of passage specialists are coming into their own, and have inherited the role once fulfilled by priests. When the clergy are expected to play masters of ceremonies at themed funerals which pay lipservice to the Prayer Book and which dispense with the hymnal and which treat the church more as an aesthetic stage set than as a temple, their authority is being seriously undermined. As a counterpoint, the authority of those without a religious agenda – those who help people to devise individual meaningful ceremonies with an artistic toolbox – is gaining credence.

A theatre company, Welfare State International, is at the forefront of the movement to reclaim ritual. After building its reputation on devising large-scale, ephemeral events involving thousands of people such as lantern festivals and site-specific fire shows, in recent years it has turned its creative flair to rites of passage. It is part of a burgeoning interest in creating meaningful rites of passage in secular settings. Director John Fox states that 'the question for a fragmented society is not whether we need rite of passage ceremonies, but rather what form should they take and who should provide them'. These questions are fundamental to knitting together the social fabric, and artists and theatre companies seem to have the capacity to help address them, if not completely answer them. WSI's mission statement offers 'to show what can be done when people are given a chance to discover their own imaginative potential'. To inspire people further, it has published *The Dead Good Funerals Guide,* a practical self-help book on improving funeral ceremonies. It is packed with practical information, from blueprints for cardboard coffins to tips on customising urns, for example, suggesting putting studs on the base of an urn for a football supporter. WSI also runs weekend workshops on personalising funerals. I have attended two, one in Cardiff and one in London. They are inspiring. Funeral directing takes on a new meaning when you start thinking about tree dressing, live music, sound, sculpture and designing your own shroud. Practical work on the courses includes making paper cuts to decorate a coffin or to cheer up a crematorium, and learning how to create family banners with masking tape and cloth. The most valuable service WSI provides – besides inspiration – is dispelling widely believed notions of what a funeral should be like. For example, there is no legal requirement to go to a church or crematorium at all. John's wife Sue Gill points out that 'it's perfectly possible to invite people to a community centre, cricket club or your living room'. Her simplest tip for improving any funeral is simply to take flowers out of the cellophane wrapping.

Discussing funerals with Sue and John Fox reminded me that a funeral is a performance – one for which the skills involved in producing good theatre are highly relevant. This is reinforced by the increasing acceptance of applause at funerals. The distinctly modern phenomenon of spontaneous applause – occurring when the cortège passes, or the coffin disappears behind the curtains at the crematorium, or is lowered into the grave – is symbolic. Hands clasped in clapping, not in prayer, it is a good vignette of modern death. Welfare State International stresses the need for mental rehearsals of arrangements to ensure that the ceremony takes shape as the family wishes. This may include making an appointment at a crematorium to discuss technicalities such as seating, lighting and music. WSI also suggest thinking about 'casting' mourners in roles ahead of time – for example, arranging shovels for communal grave-filling or single flowers for each person to put on the coffin.

One Welfare State International associate, Gilly Adams, arranged a celebration to mark the life of a friend's mother in an arts centre in Cardiff. It was co-ordinated like a theatre production with a full-colour programme, a compilation of photos, extracts from condolence letters, poems and readings. Entitled *A Celebration of the Life and Travels of Dorothy Russell*, the cover carried Dorothy's instructions to mourners: 'Don't wear black unless you think you look sensational.' Children were considered with the hiring of the South Glamorgan mobile crèche, but also honoured as mourners in their own right. Presents they had given their dying grandmother were displayed on a table. The audience sat in four rows in a large arc and was welcomed with an informal introduction letting them know exactly what was going to happen. The event was fully scripted with music and poems. A family friend who was a professional continuity announcer read a speech about Dorothy. An intermission allowed people time to reflect and cry. Spring flowers in aqua-packs were given to people when they left. This mixture of performance and participatory event, celebration and contemplation, sharing food and feelings, exemplifies a backlash against the downplayed ceremonies that dominated death rites for most of the last century. It almost signifies a return to the traditional behaviour at funerals some four hundred years ago, when rural customs and religion made funerals an important expression of community.

One of the most striking expressions of the reclamation of ritual is in the area of pet funerals. There are currently sixty licensed pet cemeteries in Britain, and although eight out of ten domestic animals are mass-incinerated, the market for giving a pet a more dignified send-off is burgeoning. Co-operative Funeral Services have recently launched an online funeral service for pets, where there is a standard fee of £295 regardless of the size of the animal. A more personal approach is available at Pet Funeral Services in Wales, run by Terri and John Ward, who take pride in providing pets with the same dignified despatch as their human owners might expect. From burial or cremation with secular or religious ceremonies, to the chance to view the loved one in a pink satin-lined casket, the procedures replicate their human equivalents – although most funeral directors draw the line at presenting relatives with a keepsake keyring containing a lock of the loved one's hair after the funeral. 'It goes down very well – you can see their faces light up, they love the idea that they've always got a bit of their pet with them.' Instead of a chapel of rest there is a kennel of repose; instead of 'Henry Holland', the equivalent canine graveside favourite is 'Doggy Paradise', a sentimental piece of doggerel which reduces many clients to tears:

Do doggies go to heaven? Yes, I really think they do.

It may sound quite fantastic, all the same it may be true,
that human love gives them release and sets their dear souls free,
as love divine gives us our hope of immortality.

For those who prefer a religious ceremony, the pet padre – the Revd James Thompson, a retired Anglican priest – conducts short services of cremation and burial: 'Rather than a fixed liturgy, I pray extempore and adapt the service. Occasionally, we sing a hymn from my book *Hymns for Creatures Great and Small*. Where the Church has failed is in a limited view of God's love and compassion as it only refers to humans. After all, Christ chose a stable not a palace, news of his birth was brought to animal carers, and Jesus had a close affinity to animals. I usually read Isaiah 11:6, about the lion and the lamb lying down together, in which Isaiah tells of his vision of a golden age where man and animals live in total harmony.' The market for this service is booming. From pioneering the idea in 1990 the business has expanded through word of mouth. In the last three years it has incorporated tea rooms and a range of facilities for visitors which most human cemeteries lack.

We are on the cusp of important change. The commercial exploitation of death denial is being undercut by the cult of individualism. But is self-expression in a climate of secularism the answer to how a funeral should be? We need to clarify who the funeral is for, as much as the form it should take. Arguably, the dead should have nothing to do with the ceremonies that honour them, and the funeral should be carried out by those they leave behind as a final expression of love, and as a way to pick up the stitch dropped in a community when one of its members dies. Part of the problem is that, in rejecting the traditional religious paradigm, we are unsure of what to put in its place. We are in a time of indeterminate ideological commitment to anything other than self-expression. We have lost the art of transcendence. How to forget the self is the concept we need to reclaim. In evolving new rites of passage, we could learn much from other cultures. In *Reflections on East and West* Hari Dam writes:

> Self-assertiveness is the key to your success; self-abnegation is the secret of our survival. You're urged everyday to want more and more; we're taught from the cradle to want less and less. *Joie de vivre* is your ideal; conquest of desires is our goal. In the sweet years of life, you retire to enjoy the fruits of your labour; we renounce the world and prepare ourselves for the hereafter.

THE NEW
PORNOGRAPHY
OF DEATH

Read this.
Welcome.
A deadly virus is circulating in the form of a palm-sized blood cell.
You will become infected if someone passes it to your hand.
If the blood cell is passed to you, you must do the following.
Show the disc in your hand to the man on the sound system. He will give you a
flower, pin it to your clothing. Then choose your moment, introduce yourself to
someone without a flower and pass the virus on to them.

 HESE WRITTEN INSTRUCTIONS WERE PRESSED INTO MY palm when I arrived at a 'death party' staged at Battersea Arts Centre to launch 'Matters of Life and Death', a month-long season on the theme of death and dying. The virus 'gag' was a good icebreaker and people played along, scrutinising buttonholes before shaking hands. But it was largely the conversation that distinguished it from most drinks parties. As guests stood around in the pall-black darkness, picking at Twiglets from a (s)morgasbord selection, they chatted about mortality. Small talk was made bigger by the presence at the pay bar of an open coffin complete with 'corpse'. The 'deceased' probably never guessed that work experience would entail a near-death experience, but she was dead good.

The BAC season evolved over a period of four years, when the director, Tom Morris, observed that regular creative brainstorming sessions for artists and performers were becoming dominated by discussions of death. Simultaneously, he found himself witnessing many of his baby boomer friends experiencing as a terrible trauma the deaths of their parents – something which brought home to him the inadequacy of the way in which we deal with death. This is the central paradox that distinguishes the modern way of death: the gulf between death as entertainment and a preoccupation of contemporary artists, and death as crisis management, with bereavement a potent taboo. The resulting season of performance art, plays, exhibitions and workshops – including many events aimed at children – was an attempt to redress the balance, and to provide a stimulus for conversation by creating a forum in which audiences had the chance both to listen to and talk to artists.

An installation in the form of a 'den of death' by actor Nabil Shaban afforded a particularly intimate forum for discussion. Nabil gave me a conducted tour of the Necrospace and told me about his experiences of death. He has never been able to walk as a result of osteoporosis, other health problems and two near-fatal car crashes; his multiple-bereavements of many friends means that he has a more intimate acquaintance with death than many of us. Draped in boulder-brown material, his cave contained a computer displaying a range of internet death sites and a video where the viewer could record personal musings on mortality. Instead of woolly mammoths, the cave paintings were more esoteric expressions of near-death experiences in frames. In a niche, a human skull – 'I picked that up in Turkey from a battlefield and it has played Yorrick!' – lay alongside a grizzly special effects skull with grotesque luminous worms in the eye-sockets. This was a neat metaphor for the real-life split between fantasy death and death as existential crisis. 'Not to be' has become the unspeakable half of that famous dichotomy. Our constant diet of pretend death is at odds with our tendency to act in real life as if death does not exist.

On stage, Japanese performance artist Kazuko Hohki conveyed the sense of being caught out by death, and the mixed emotions you feel when you witness death creeping up on someone you love. In a multimedia elegy, at once stomach-turning and heart-rending, she described her mother's slow death from mouth cancer. She used a macabre Muppet-like puppet to depict her mother in the final stages of life when she was attached to 'a spectacular mucus-sucking machine'. Searing details were tempered by a narrative which was above all gentle, affectionate and humorous. But, interestingly, the audience was cautious about laughing until Hohki looked at us squarely and admonished us, 'Don't be so solemn! You can laugh.' This theatrical moment mimicked real life, where we no longer have a protocol with which to face death. We do not know how we should act, what to say, whether we're allowed to laugh.

Hohki, by making public such an intensely personal narrative of dying, is in step with many contemporary artists and writers who are turning personal bereavement into creative material. *Dead Dad*, a sculpture displayed at the Royal Academy's Sensation exhibition in 1997, exemplified this. A latex model of artist Ron Mueck's father, it was unflinching in its presentation of a naked dead body and remarkably true to death. Yet the much-reduced scale of the work, which gave the viewer a feeling of being Gulliver in Lilliput, added great poignancy, for it captured the sense of people being diminished in death – the way in which death reduces the dead. Like Hohki using a poignant puppet of her mother, Mueck was looking at death dispassionately, almost clinically.

This directness is everywhere, not only in accounts of bereavement, but also of terminal illness, where there is a new trend for writers and artists to treat their conditions as material. In the mid 1990s Harold Brodkey in the US and Oscar Moore in England were both explicit in their accounts of AIDS. In 1996–7 Ruth Picardie provided a female perspective on dying with her extraordinary narrative about a 'full house' of secondary cancers. More recently, John Diamond documented his experience of a particularly savage form of throat cancer, from diagnosis in 1996, to his death, 2 March 2001, when even his last words were widely reported in the press. To look back at newspapers and magazines in the 1990s is to see a preoccupation with pathology, a trend that has continued so that morphine pumps, Hickman lines and accounts of celebrity 'chemo' are now commonplace at the British breakfast table.

Across the board, the boundaries between the personal and the public are being blurred as writers, artists and performers are using personal narratives more directly. This was vividly expressed by the hippie guru Timothy Leary, who was as enthusiastic about checking out as he was about dropping out: 'Dying is a team sport; me and my friends are planning the happiest joyable [sic] organically sensitive dying celebrations in human history.' His public waning on the internet typified the trend for dying in public. On television, Melvyn Bragg's interview with the playwright Dennis Potter conferred a sense of attendance in the sick room. Swigging morphine and champagne, and clearly in pain, it was spell-binding television. Potter spoke lyrically about the way in which knowing he was going to die had heightened his perception of the beauty of the cherry blossom outside his window. It was as if Bragg were performing the last rites of the media age, giving the renegade genius of British broadcasting the chance to make his peace.

Mortality has, of course, always been a mainstay of artistic and creative expression, but whereas historically there is a rich artistic tradition linking mortality with morality, the current wave of work addressing death does not fit within this framework. In both the theatre and the art gallery, the tradition of transcendence and catharsis is being challenged by visceral realism – death shown stripped of any coherent moral or religious reference. The noble tradition of the artist exalting his audience by holding up a lamp to illuminate life, has become more mundane. Frequently the artist is a shock-jock, almost mocking the audience, ripping them from their cocoon of complacency – like Sarah Kane with her savage death dance, *Blasted*, or Damien Hirst, who presents death as an arresting image, as accessible and superficial as an advertisement.

Bereft of symbolism, much of the contemporary artistic representation of death has no meaning beyond itself. What you see is what you get, whether a dead shark or a theatrical gore show. Another crucial difference is the much-altered contemporary context in which the work is shown – the fools' paradise of death denial which characterised the twentieth century. The fact that death is no longer woven into our social fabric, no longer integrated into everyday life, affects our stance as readers, viewers and spectators. Indeed, the silence surrounding death in everyday life and the lack of representation of everyday death in the public realm echoes the climate of sexual ignorance which existed even two generations ago, where it was possible to reach adulthood without seeing visual representations of either simulated sex or real sex. Pre-*Playboy* and Page Three, the naked body was not part of everyday life; for us it is the dead body that is unfamiliar. Similarly, the cancers and heart disease, the car crashes and coronaries, the mundane causes from which many of us will die, or through which we will experience bereavement – these have little public profile, and no dialogue. The overdoses and bedroom hangings that are suburban suicide, the slow fade to an unexceptional finale, the Alzheimer's of the old-timers whom we kill off socially long before actual death – these, too, have been strictly private, endured in fear and isolation. In this regard, John Bayley did something very positive in going public with the details of his wife Iris Murdoch's decline.

In his seminal essay 'The Pornography of Death', published in 1955, anthropologist Geoffrey Gorer explored the dichotomy between the taboo of natural death and the 'pornography' of fantasised death in post-war society. Describing this period, he wrote that 'while natural death became more and more smothered in prudery, violent death has played an ever growing part in the fantasies offered to mass audiences'. Given the greatly altered cultural terrain since Gorer wrote, it seems timely to review his argument and update the picture, for while his theories about the schism between squeamishness about natural death and curiosity about pretend death remain pertinent, his frame of reference is out of date and out of time. Popular culture has undergone nothing short of a major revolution since 1955, with the rise of the mass media, movies, videos and the internet. Most importantly, we have witnessed the rise of the popularity of television. This and the sexual revolution are crucial to our building up an up-to-date picture of the current cultural context in which to consider contemporary representation of death. The sexual revolution pushed back the boundaries of taste and decency, creating a climate of liberalism in terms of what is deemed acceptable entertainment. The fantasy death that informed Gorer's definition of pornography and shaped his argument is like the 'glimpse of stocking' once considered shocking: outmoded and anachronistic in the context of contemporary popular culture. Crucially, the 1955 canon of pornography as described by Gorer referred to the written word. He defined his area of concern as 'detective stories, thrillers, Westerns, war stories, spy stories, science fiction and horror comics'. The modern pornography of death owes much more to the visual culture of photography, film and television. In a visually led culture, the lens, the camera, the screen are integral to our exposure to representations of death.

The rise of the mass media and the technological progress of communications mean that we have more opportunity than ever before to experience death vicariously. We witness it daily, but at a safe remove, on the news and in the newspapers, where anything too challenging is excised in the editing suite. The bloodless wars with no dead Englishmen, the school photograph of the murdered child, the mangled metal of the crash with none of the carnage – these homogenised accounts of violent death, like fictional death in films and books, reinforce distance from 'natural death'. The famous Hindenberg broadcast in 1937 stands out in the annals of media history as a rare glimpse of authentic humanity, spontaneous and profound, in a profession that pedals a particularly sanitised version of death to the public as 'human interest'. The way the presenter wept at witnessing the air ship burst into flames has accrued rarity value, for more commonly grief is expressed in the sound bites of strangers asked 'how they feel' when they have just witnessed death. This daily death parade, with its pseudo-compassionate inflection – a voice lowered for an instant before moving up again for the weather – is as un-real as fiction. The public profile of death is thus split between the formulaic style of current affairs and the similarly stylised representation of death in films. The absence of dead flesh in the former inversely relates to the special effects orgy of carnage in the latter.

In between death as news and death as escapist entertainment there has been silence – silence, at any rate, until the tidal wave of creative interest in death in recent years, which is expanding the scope of representation and giving aspects of death which have been strictly private a public profile. For example, the fashion for frank diaries of terminal illness correlates to a similar candour in the visual medium where there is a sense that the crisis of AIDS kickstarted a contemporary version of *ars moriendi*. The infamous 1992 deathbed photograph of a man dying from AIDS used in a Benetton campaign, and Gary Sollars' intense 1999 memorial portrait entitled *My Partner Philip Monroe died 13.1.89 Aged 34*, which depicts his partner at the moment of death from AIDS, are but two examples. The rise of photography as an art medium is playing an important role in our exposure to the facts of death. Increasingly, the art gallery is a morbid peep-show offering the viewer a rare chance to get up close to death. But whether a dead shark or a photograph of a dead person in a morgue, the opportunities to look at explicit, illicit death are proliferating. The sense of peeking at something normally within the private realm is reinforced by the trend for warnings at the entrance to death exhibitions, which resonate with those posted on the doors of strip shows and sex shops saying 'No Under 18s'. Recently, such notices have been displayed at the Royal Academy and the Anne Faggionato gallery in London, and the National Museum of Film, Photography and Television in Bradford.

The British public's appreciation of contemporary art has been gaining force throughout the 1990s. The art gallery, once seen as an elitist enclave, is now a cool place to go. It is a much more accessible branch of mainstream culture than it was twenty years ago. While an increasingly recalcitrant flock is deserting the fold of the established Church in droves, attendance at art galleries is soaring. For the first time, the Tate Gallery found itself having to turn people away because it had reached full capacity. In a culture more committed to individualism than conventional religion, frequent pilgrimages to cathedrals of self-expression seem logical. The contemporary art market is also bound up with the culture of consumerism and this increases public interest. When the *Sun* ran a headline '*Sun* Readers Love Modern Art', one sensed that the winds of change were blowing. 'Tabloid' has become a byword for sensational, and recently art has gone tabloid. In a climate of cheque-book aesthetics, millions are paid for pieces with a high visual impact but little substance – not unlike paparazzi pictures, with their cash-per-splash pricing policy.

Damien Hirst's famous shark in formaldehyde typifies this trend, and has become a logo for this brand of art. Just as an ad campaign rests on the relationship of caption to image, so it is with *The Physical Impossibility of Death in the Mind of Someone Living* – the title Hirst gave to this work. With an ad man's dexterity he used the pickled predator to present an image of mortality that persuaded us to think of death by being real, yet by not being human it lacked the mirroring power of the traditional skull in *memento mori* and therefore was more palatable. It is unsurprising that the modern answer to the grand patrons of the past is Charles Saatchi, a highly successful ad man who quickly recognised the commercial appeal of this type of accessible aesthetic. It uses shock like a fake gun – the viewer may be taken aback seeing it, but remains unscathed.

In terms of self-propaganda, Hirst presents himself as Damien Death. The Grim Reaper could not have had a more media-friendly publicist. Hirst is a bloke's bloke, with pop star friends and a sense of humour expressed by such wheezes as designing a restaurant called Pharmacy that looks so much like one from the outside that people have been known to mistake it for a late-night chemist and pop in, hoping to pick up pills. Hirst is also partially responsible for the fact that in another fashionable central London restaurant, the skeleton is at the feast – hanging by the bar, with a medical cabinet. Stories abound of his passion for pathology books; the catalogue for his recent show at Gagosian in New York could easily be mistaken for one, with its *faux*-textbook title and grisly photographic illustrations. In interviews he talks animatedly about the most untalked-about subject. As journalist Lynn Barber noted:

> But it is really striking how often he mentions death in conversation – he's always saying 'if I'm still alive' or 'if I don't get hit by a truck', and he talks familiarly about the Reaper as if this were an expression in everyday use.

This obsession with death is vividly conveyed by his friend the writer Gordon Burn in a description of Hirst's studio in the Cotswolds: 'There were (real) skeletons and blood; (prosthetic) human body parts arranged on shelves and bagged in binliners; surgical instruments and corpses.' But this death wish, for which he was granted the Turner Prize and enduring notoriety, threatened to become subject to the law of diminishing returns. For with art that reveals everything in an instant, repetition of imagery – as with pornography – deadens impact. In order for Hirst to continue to crank up the interest he almost needs to drain the tanks or break the glass so we can smell death.

In assessing the modern pornography of death, Damien Hirst is soft-core. His medical cabinets and animal carcasses – his shabby shark, a poor

Jaws – manage to be blatant but also bland. The fact they were shown at the Royal Academy at all also deadened their impact, and in the words of American critic Adam Gopnik, made them part of a 'formal aestheticism' of shock-for-shock's-sake, and therefore anything but shocking. Amidst so many pieces that were like visual gags with very obvious punchlines, such as Sarah Lucas's portrayal of the female body as a table laid with two fried eggs and a kebab, the only sensational thing at Sensation was the vandalised portrait of Myra Hindley – the energy of the assault a surge of raw emotion, genuine feeling in the face of actual loss. Meanwhile Hirst's main legacy is his contribution to making death a fashionable subject, and putting his finger on the pulse of popular culture by turning the stuff of medicine into art. In a society where death has moved so completely to the sphere of medicine, to the extent that dying is seen more as medical failure than biological fate, and where death is a big cover-up, Hirst has grassed on death. By giving us a rare glimpse of rot and death in the raw, he betrays the secret of mutability that modern medicine normally keeps so discreetly. Authenticity – the fact it is real dead flesh and real instruments – matters. Similarly, Hirst's recent work *Hymn* taps into the contemporary fixation with corporeality. His artist's statement claims that it explores 'the curiosity of man'. This giant model of a man – an exact replica of a mass-produced metal model in a child's medical science kit – is a dumbing-down of the artistic tradition of anatomical representation – like the copulating dead cows, a bit of a joke. Where *Hymn* is clinical, the nineteenth-century *ecorchés* had dignity. The flayed men in gladiatorial poses displaying their own innards – sometimes holding up their skins like discarded clothes – were elegant and masterfully drawn. The facts of death were shown in stylised, neoclassical terms that simultaneously expressed the grandeur of man with intimations of nobility and heroism. By contrast with his megamodel, Hirst makes man look very small.

In the modern pornography of death, it is in the realm of photography and film that representation of death becomes hardcore. It has become increasingly fashionable for photographers to expose us to things which have previously been for the privileged private view of professionals in the field of medicine – the forensic pathologist, the mortician, the surgeon, the doctor. In the 1970s the American filmmaker Stan Braccage produced an unflinching documentary recording autopsies carried out by the Pittsburgh police authorities. Called *The Act of Seeing With One's Own Eyes* – the literal meaning of 'autopsy' – this film became an underground art-house classic. It is an uncut film of human bodies being cut up, showing the full, bloody beauty of human biology. A face is peeled off a head like a tight swimming-hat, a skull sawn into a flip-top casket containing brains that echo the perfect symmetry of walnuts. It is an awesome spectacle, a three-dimensional interpretation of 'Know Thyself', the invisible seen. Of this unfamiliar interior, crime writer Michael Dibdin has written a description which perfectly conveys the wonder within us: 'Everything seems so lovingly packaged and arranged like a cabin trunk stowed against breakage with just those things necessary for the voyage.' (*The Pathology Lesson*, 1992.)

Braccage's film has come of age, for the autopsy, the mortuary and the morgue are featuring more and more in contemporary culture, allowing ordinary people the chance to see death with their very own eyes. An arresting photograph of an autopsy – a naked female torso laced with sutures – features on the cover of a CD by the pop group Pro Pain. There has even been a prime-time fly-on-the-wall television programme called *Autopsy*, featuring in graphic detail the work of American forensic specialists, from the time they retrieve the body from the scene of the crime through to the final results of forensic analysis. Innards are in. At a fashionable London art gallery, a selling exhibition included a large blown-up, glossy, full-colour photograph of what at first glance I took to be a vast pile of sun-dried tomatoes – a glistening wet mush. The caption beneath read 'Total destruction of the Skull and Brain in a Pilot Who Crashed to the Ground When His Experimental Aircraft Inverted for No Apparent Reason and Descended Rapidly'. Beside it was more full-colour carnage that only made sense after reading the caption. In one case, the caption explained that what the viewer was seeing was the eye and orbit, which had become detached from the severely damaged head in the other photograph.

> It proved important to collect this evidence and examine it because the cornea showed evidence of early disease which might have been responsible for the crash in this case.

These were the words of Patricia Cornwell made flesh, a real glimpse into the world of forensic pathology, a full-colour full-frontal image of a pulverised person.

Whereas in the early days of photography, pictures of the dead were for family consolation and to send to friends for remembrance, these contemporary photographs are for public consumption. They objectify the dead. They are impersonal. Through the lens of Sue Fox humans are giant hams, flanks of flesh; the post-mortem photographs for which she is famous show humans as if through a butcher's eye. Andres Serrano's grim but glossy cibachromes dissect the dead even further. For example, a child who died from meningitis is presented in a triptych of images: identity-tagged feet, a partially covered face and finally identity-tagged hands. This is a disquieting, intellectual, aesthetic version of hanging, drawing and quartering, for both processes involve both breaking up the whole body and the public display of the dead.

The morality of the way in which death is mediated by the artist is even more fraught in the work of Joel Peter Witkin, whose tableaux of body parts culled from Mexican morgues are grotesque parodies of the still life tradition. Witkin's montages of mortal remains resonate with Gericault's drawings in the early nineteenth century which were inspired by the French Revolution – macabre compositions of severed human limbs and heads – although the breadth of difference between charcoal and flesh affects how the image comes across. If the guillotine was a technological advancement for the mechanics of killing, the camera was an instantaneous death machine, confronting the spectator with shocking new images of human mortality. In this sense it has revolutionised the way we see ourselves. This is the basis of Roland Barthes's famous observations about the particular affinity of photography for death, whereby a photograph can only ever produce death by recording what has been permanently lost: 'It produces death while trying to preserve life.' What the camera is producing in contemporary culture by way of representing death is both profound and shocking, and raises complex questions about how death is displayed. Where the guillotine was concerned, the shock resided almost as much in the images of baskets of full heads, as in the political significance of its victims. As the twentieth century progressed, the shock of images produced by the camera became less political than psychological.

In recent years I have seen many photographic images of death made legitimate by the fine art context in which they are displayed – images which outside such an environment – in, say, a newspaper, or on television– would be unacceptable. The fashion for explicit images of death – the appearance of broken bodies in Bond Street galleries – is intriguing. The work of photographers like Serrano and Witkin is not only acceptable, it is highly collectible and now adorns the walls of many wealthy collectors. This has overtones of the elitism of nineteenth-century pornography, for in the early days of photography erotic daguerreotypes were bought and sold in select circles for large amounts of money. This prompted one contemporary observer to complain that 'there is something positively sacrilegious in the idea of prostituting the light of heaven to such debasing purposes'. While so much has passed muster in the contemporary market for the macabre – photographs of dead babies in preservative from medical museums, Witkin's montages of mutilation, Bill Viola's video of a dying woman in the *Nantes Triptych*, the searing photographic record made by Krass Clement of his mother's death, entitled *About Death,* from last gasp to inside the crematorium – there has been little outrage.

In Britain, the greatest furore has been caused by one artist, Anthony Noel Kelly, who trampled on a taboo by using real body parts in producing sculpture. The controversy over his work was based more on the source of his material than on aesthetic grounds. The press cast him as a twentieth-century body-snatcher, when in fact his aim was to beautify death by casting the images of dead humans in precious metals. But in legal terms, his work transgressed the 1992 Anatomy Act, which proscribes the use of body parts for anything other than medical science. In fact, at a time when the medical is so comprehensively shifting into the realm of the arts, and artists are commonly trespassing on that territory, his offence says more about our residual squeamishness about close contact with cadavers than it does about his alleged depravity and perversion.

Noel Kelly was simply living in the wrong age. There is a strong historical tradition of human remains being harvested as artistic material. In the eighteenth century Dutch anatomist/artist Frederick Ruysch (1664–1750) crafted exquisitely intricate landscapes from real human tissue, which so impressed Peter the Great of Russia that he acquired the artist's entire output, installing it in the Hermitage where examples still remain. A little later than Ruysch, the French anatomist Honoré Fragonard (cousin of the much more famous Fragonard) became renowned for his bizarre montages of flayed cadavers which he had found a unique method of preserving. Some eighteen samples of his work have survived and are in the École Nationale Veterinaire d'Alfort in Paris. The most famous and extraordinary piece is a tableau of *The Winged Horseman of the Apocalypse*, in which a flayed man with hideous popping eyeballs rides a flayed horse. His back muscles have been splayed out behind his head in the manner of surreal, sprouting wings, and around the horse's feet are dancing foetuses. In the context of this canon of art where the human body is the artist's actual material, not merely his inspiration, Anthony Noel Kelly's work – casting likeness, not preserving and displaying actual parts – seems positively conservative. Noel Kelly was more in step with eighteenth-century culture than with our own times. In the eighteenth century the artistic establishment sanctioned the use of cadavers for artistic purposes. A notable example is still to be seen in the Royal Academy collections in the form of *Smuglerius*. This is the body of a hanged smuggler whose corpse was admired by Dr William Hunter, the Royal Academy's professor of anatomy, and was cast in plaster by the sculptor Carlini in a classical pose. The Royal Academy's collection also includes the elaborate plaster cast of another criminal, James Legge, who in order to settle debate about the position of Christ in the Crucifixion was flayed, suspended from a cross and cast by Thomas Banks – all in the name of art.

Presenting a more comprehensive challenge to the ethics of art and medicine is the work of the German contemporary 'artist' and anatomist Günther von Hagens, who in the manner of a modern Fragonard has perfected a process he refers to as 'plastination'. By this method he preserves, dissects and displays cadavers and body parts as authentic anatomical specimens. He has created an exhibition called *Körperwelten die Faszination des Echten*, which includes two hundred of these perverse, puppet people. When it was shown in Japan it attracted an audience of 2.5 million people, and drew over 125,000 in a single month when it went to Mannheim. To date, however, it has not come to Britain or America, where it might be seen as overstretching the meaning of artistic licence, for although the exhibits are voluntary 'donors', their authenticity is deeply disquieting. A physician and professor of anatomy at Heidelberg University, von Hagens has the credentials necessary for cutting up cadavers. Yet the issue of the public display of the dead has catapulted him into controversy. In Vienna, where I saw the exhibition, I felt that I was not in a cabinet of curiosities but a cathedral of curiosities. There were ordinary people, spellbound and queuing to look at each case with almost religious awe, for as a work of art man – freeze-dried, cross-sectioned and rearranged in a thousand different poses – is both compelling and repellent. This is the body as a surreal montage, mortal remains rearranged in startling configurations – for example, dismembered into lots of small pieces suspended from nylon strings like an exploded mannequin, or sawn in half like a true-life version of the magician's trick where suddenly the horror of what you imagine is happening in the box is actually before your very eyes, and you are looking at and walking around and able to touch a man cut into two perfect halves. Disquieting though it is, it is also compelling. The urge to look wrestles with the urge to look away. Going round this exhibition invites a salutary confrontation with our raw, ignoble fascination with the forbidden – a mind-popping conflict of revulsion and compulsion.

To stroll around Soho is to be reminded that we live in the age of the live sex show where, by contrast, until 1868 our ancestors had the opportunity to go to live death shows. We should not underestimate the popularity of the state-sanctioned spectacle of death that was public execution. As public events they attracted thousands of people of every age, sex and class, and were the source of songs and chap-book drawings. They were an important aspect of popular culture and exemplified death as entertainment for the whole family. Accounts of executions were pored over in much the same way that we pore over the details of courtroom drama supplied by murder trials. Above all, the public scaffold afforded an obscene display of death, as described by V. A. C. Gatrell in his account of public execution in England, *The Hanging Tree*: 'People did not die on it neatly. Watched by thousands they urinated, defecated, screamed, kicked, fainted and choked as they died.' The abolition of public execution in favour of a more enlightened, discreet form of state killing was an important step in the disappearance of death from the public realm. It was a marker in the development of squeamishness and unfamiliarity with the dead body, which – wrapped in taboo – has become a focus of great fear. Yet the compulsion to witness death as spectacle has not diminished, and has become the basis of the fantasy death that is so fundamental to our concepts of popular entertainment.

A society which has for so long averted its gaze from death cannot stop staring at it. Just as the public presence of the unclothed body was represented by the nude in art long before it was naked in film and print and porn, at the moment we are at an interesting point concerning the public profile of the dead body in art. From high to popular culture we are manifesting increased interest in the body as a site of morbid rather than erotic interest. We have a new fixation with our corporeality, the body itself as *memento mori*. This raises challenges which replicate those we have had to address as a result of the sexual revolution and the rise of pornography, such as what is acceptable in the public domain and where to draw the line between education and entertainment. For example, raising this problem and echoing the association of video with living-room sleaze, was the commercial video *Everyday Operations* that came out some years ago. It was made up of authentic footage of surgical procedures including brain surgery, thus highlighting our fascination with our physiology, our vulnerability and, by extension, our mortality. This is not a new theme, but one which has been affected by technological advancement. Indeed, *Everyday Operations* was catering for the same market as the notorious film of an operation to separate Siamese twins performed by a French surgeon, Dr Doyen, in 1902. This surgical film was one of the earliest moving pictures ever made, and became the subject of a lawsuit when it was discovered that it had been reproduced for the commercial market and was being shown at fairgrounds.

The surgical content of these cultural representations of death is no accident. The medical and the artistic are moving closer together, as medical and scientific advancements afford us increasingly complex images of ourselves – images which are then, in turn, appropriated by artists. Where once the scalpel dissected the dead to show the living the secrets of life, now increasingly it is the lens. From X-rays to endoscopy and magnetic resonance imaging, the camera is enabling us to penetrate the carapace that is the living human body, and to see ourselves dissected alive. The boundaries that had previously defined our aesthetic sense of ourselves have been much extended. Increased intimacy with our own physiology has radically changed our perception of who and what we are, and – in so far as images of our physicality map our mortality – where we are going. In *Corps Etranger*, artist Mona Hatoum even took us on an internal tour through the glistening corridors of her own insides by means of endoscopy, an art gallery *Deep Throat de nos jours*.

In the increasingly medicalised context of contemporary death, where we count on doctors to postpone the inevitable end, they have assumed an almost God-like status. This is partly reflected by their presence in popular entertainment, where they are the most represented profession on television. The genre of the televisual medical drama is an interesting index of changing attitudes to death. For example, comparing the goings-on in two emergency wards thirty years apart is a poignant illustration of the journey from denial of death to realism. In the very English *Emergency Ward 10*, which ran for ten years from 1957, doctors were presented as Olympian beings – clearly with supernatural powers, for in spite of their working on an emergency ward, the first death only took place after two and a half years! When the episode was broadcast in which a patient died from a pulmonary embolism after appendicitis, the public outcry was so great that it was agreed from then on that death should only be shown as resulting from an accident. Fast forward to the 1990s. The American medical drama *ER* presents death very differently. Death is a regular event, and sometimes even the doctors' fault. Doctors are shown as human beings under stress, misunderstood like ordinary mortals, irreverent and sometimes irresponsible, a far cry from their 1950s counterparts – the debonair Dr Kildare, for example – who were invincible. Safe death has left the medical drama, and unprotected death has arrived. Our fixation with drama and adrenalin affords us, as an audience, a particularly compelling form of near-death experience. In a society which has hospitalised death, the hospital drama reinforces our perception of doctors as potential saviours, for in spite of their greater realism these dramas are still more about survival than loss. They are glamorous, there's always a frisson of 'doctors and nurses', female

viewers swoon over heartthrob George Clooney. In short, these programmes function as a way to go to the brink and survive, a cathartic form
of death fantasy, and a popular one. Since it was first screened in 1996, *ER*
has been watched by 35 million viewers in the United States alone.

This obsession with the frailty of human flesh carries through to the
cinema. If every decade has a zeitgeist movie, then *Emmanuelle* is to the cinematic history of sex what *Crash* is to the cinematic history of death. Each
is controversial, polarising popular opinion, a turn-on or a turn-off, with no
room for indifference. Each captures the particular psychosocial concerns
of a generation, expressed in a different axis of interest in human flesh.
Where *Emmanuelle* signified the cinema falling heels-over-head in sex, *Crash*
– a cinematic adaptation of J. G. Ballard's 1973 novel of the same name –
was a head-on collision between Thanatos and Eros, a movie of twisted
metal and twisted minds, which won the Cannes Film Festival jury special
prize in 1996. It seemed all the more audacious at a time when in real life,
AIDS had accelerated the risk-to-thrills ratio of sex. In one scene, two characters discuss staging a re-enactment of the car crash that killed actress
Jayne Mansfield:

> VAUGHAN: I'd really like to work out the details of the Jayne Mansfield crash
> with you. We could do the decapitation – her head embedded in the wind-
> shield – and the little dead dog thing. You know the chiahuhua in the back
> seat. I've got it figured out.
> SEAGRAVE: You know I'll be ready.
> VAUGHAN: But I'll want to wear really big tits out to here so the crowd can
> see them get cut up and crushed on the dashboard.

Crash was about the broken body as a source of sexual gratification –
scars and cars, blood and semen. With its representation of the body as
wounded, debased and degraded, objectified in a morbid sense, it presented an extreme version of the voyeuristic attitude to death that informs
much popular culture. Its framework of cars – those powerful emblems of
twentieth-century consumerism – also confer on it relevance beyond itself.
The film is a joyless ride through human depravity, but its twin themes –
consumerism and voyeurism – are central to the contemporary culture of
death.

In fact, however, despite all the controversy, *Crash* was simply a hardcore raw version of something which is happening in more seemingly innocuous ways, disguised as entertainment in the form of 'real-life tragedy'.
For example, a prime-time television programme called *Crimefighters*, packaged as a documentary about the work of the Kent police force, shows the

graphic reality of road accidents. 'A fatal road accident in Taplow' was how one episode was enticingly billed in newspaper television listings. Less fly-on-the-wall than blood-on-the-road, the programme featured the mangled wreckage of a motorbike with a blow-by-blow account of the rider's final movements: 'The motorcyclist shredded himself on that road sign', we are told, while his helmet is shown near the wreckage and we see the police putting into plastic bags the personal effects and loose money that have been catapulted from his body on impact. We also see the dead man's distraught friend crumple in grief as he arrives at the scene, his identity is obscured with those blocks of blur, but his gut-wrenching cries are all too clear. At some level this living-room voyeurism is even more disturbing than Ballard's fiction. It is one of a growing genre of programmes dealing with real-life scenarios in which people are shown either in mortal danger or dead. These programmes masquerade under the catch-all phrase 'human interest', which is becoming a euphemism for mawkish interest in death.

Flesh and blood are exerting a renewed fascination for us. They define what we are, our mutability and mortality. They have become materials for a generation of artists, writers and performers, both mainstream and marginal, to confront us with a bleak material view of ourselves, which highlights mortality more than sexuality – a view in which the body is more about death than desire. The bloodshed of mass killing that is such a grim legacy of inhumanity in the twentieth century is analogous to a smaller-scale cultural blood bath. For since the 1960s blood has stained and seeped progressively through every layer of contemporary culture. Jackie O's blood-spattered shift and Gianni Versace's designer shoe on the blood-stained doorstep of his Malibu mansion are but two iconic references that featured on news stands and news bulletins around the world. In the mid-1990s, blood became bigger in the box office than nudity with such films as *Natural Born Killers* and *La Reine Margot*, which brought the St Bartholomew's Day Massacre to the big screen. At the same time, Quentin Tarantino conferred on bloodshed a fashionable flippancy. Widely regarded as one of the best comic moments in contemporary cinema is the scene in *Pulp Fiction*, when, in the course of driving over a bump, a gunman accidentally shoots his backseat passenger, splashing his brains all over the car's interior. But whether a stylish shoot-out in *Reservoir Dogs*, the sleek white shirts under sharp suits showing up crimson to great advantage, or a shooting-up scene in *Trainspotting* where the image of blood blossoming in a syringe fills the whole screen to an hypnotically pulsating soundtrack – the best advertisement heroin ever had – contemporary culture is clotted with blood. It can be experienced by the pint in the art gallery in the form of Mark Quinn's bust *Self*, a plasma sorbet made from freezing nine pints of his own blood which was displayed in a chilled case in Sensation, or by the glass in the film thriller *Interview with a Vampire* where Tom Cruise, as the vampire Lestat, orally decants a rat by opening its throat, or drop by painful drop from the performance artist Franko B, who bleeds beautifully in public on a stage swirling with dry ice.

Our morbid interest in the body is also evident in crime fiction. Just as film is a measure of fears and fashion at any one time, the crime fiction genre fulfils a similarly reflective function. This genre caters for a similar market as medical drama, but it addresses death within a different narrative sequence. Medical cases create drama by moving in the direction of death as only one of a number of possible endings, whereas crime stories start with the drama of death. Both tease us with life-threatening situations: the danger that the doctor may not save the patient, the danger that the forensic pathologist may not save future victims by failing to track down the killer. Psychopaths strike both fear and fascination into our psyches, and there is a literary tradition of skilful sleuths outwitting evildoers by using their thought processes. But in our death-obsessed culture, detectives are not what they were. In the course of a century we have gone from Sherlock Holmes's supremely rational approach of using logic to work out whodunit, and Lord Peter Wimsey's rarefied country house Cluedo, all the way to Kay Scarpetta's buckets-of-guts approach where the dead themselves tell us what was done with their DNA, their hair and bodily fluids.

The increasing prominence of the forensic pathologist in popular culture is an interesting modern phenomenon. It involves intimate physical relationships with the dead in a social framework of segregation and unfamiliarity with them. Female forensic pathologists are the new *femmes fatales*. After a long tradition of damsels in distress – Fay Wray flailing in the grip of King Kong, silent heroines tied to the railway tracks, endless starlets as comely corpses discovered by dapper detectives – the reversal, in which the women are the brains outwitting male murderers, scooping out the insides of bodies as opposed to being bodies, is significant. In 1997 a television advertisement for a glossy men's magazine tapped into this popularisation of pathology and the death appeal of the *femme* forensic. In the advert, the camera pans into the path lab and on to a series of body parts – feet in a steel basin, an ear, a tummy, ominous sounds of crunch and slice – and then we get glimpses of a female in surgical gloves and gown as she talks us through the post-mortem she is doing on the 'White, Male'. She then takes off her mask and as her hair falls loosely around her face she tells us, 'He could have eaten a bit less, drunk a bit less – but you could say he died of boredom.' The ad then launches into a sexy action sequence of testosterone and sport, conveying the message that this new magazine is a way to get a life before you lose one. The male/female reversal in death is taken even further in a curious Canadian art-house film called *Kissed*, which again fuses sex and death. In it, an attractive female necrophile has a series of affairs with the dead gorgeous men she meets at work – a funeral home where she is an embalmer. The film extends the reversal of the conventional power base in relationships with a memorable inversion of the lipstick-on-the-collar cliché, in which the heroine's (living) boyfriend gets suspicious when she turns up for a date smelling of formaldehyde! Remarkably, given the subject matter, this low-budget, high-impact production was a restrained and relatively tasteful treatment of the subject. One suspects, however, that less sensitivity would have meant better returns at the box office, given the general currents of voyeurism.

As the market for death entertainment expands in a climate of recreational voyeurism, there is pressure on those catering to our interest to be innovative in order to sustain it. At the heart of the problem is negotiating the precarious line between reality and representation, the apex of all pornography. When desire to look at death is the primary motivation for the burgeoning market in morbid material – not necessarily linked with the desire to learn – then we are on dubious moral ground. As with our curiosity about sex in the climate of repression two generations ago, we need to acknowledge the difference between entertainment and education. Can we really claim that our fascination with forensic pathology and serial killers stems from being a nation of detectives? We are in danger of losing our capacity for self-honesty; the markets which cater for our self-deception are booming. In recent years there has been a trend for explicit sex videos and cd-roms marketed as education, giving new application to the term self-help. But death education is fraught with difficulty. The Jack the Ripper Experience at the London Dungeon, one of the capital's most popular attractions, encapsulates the problem.

In the twenty-first century, family days out have turned into 'experiences', and the Jack the Ripper Experience is the jewel in the crown of this phenomenon – a multi-million-pound exhibition which, on a busy day, draws over 4,000 punters, a good deal more than the number who turn up for the Buckingham Palace experience which opened in the same year. At the entrance a sign reads 'Due to the popularity of the Jack the Ripper Experience visitors may have to queue at peak times'. The London Dungeon does not carry a PG warning, nor is there an age limit, so mothers and fa-

thers happily queue to take Junior along to see a display of the machinery
of death and its victims, all depicted by life-size models, authentic torture
instruments and a soundtrack of screams. At 'Hanging, Drawing and Quartering' a young girl calls to her mother, 'This one had his bowls taken out
when he was still alive.' 'BOWELS' her mother corrects her, and the man
in front flinches.

In much the same way that a nightclub exploits our sex drive, the London Dungeon profits from our attraction to brutality and death. Just as you
wouldn't want to go to a disco with the lights on, you certainly would not
want to see the London Dungeon under a high-wattage bulb. To do so
would be to acknowledge how easy it is to make a monkey out of most of
us by the simple expedient of turning out the lights and granting our death
wish with a selection of macabre models.

In the long queue for Jack the Ripper there are assorted family groups –
mothers with buggies, teenagers linking arms, inquisitive 7-year-olds firing
questions at their fathers. By 'Burning Alive': 'What's a stake?' 'It's like the
thing we use with the tent'. In a subdued crocodile we shuffle past 'Boiling
To Death', 'Hand Torture', 'Pressing' and assorted tableaux showing de-
capitated corpses, decomposing corpses, and everywhere butcher-red
blood and guts. As we edge nearer a young female guide in Victorian dress
does her best to conjure up some atmosphere. 'You'll git yer bloody throats
cut if you stay around 'ere!' An audio-visual display invites us to step back
through time 'to retrace the bloody footsteps of Jack the Ripper, whose
crimes were so gross, so bloody, horrible and evil that he's the most infamous serial killer of all time'. After this, we file through a narrow alley, past
models of two female corpses with slit throats, into a simulated Mitre
Square. Here we assemble around another dead woman as a second audio-
visual display supplies a blow-by-blow account of her murder and mutilation. This is accompanied by large reproductions of the original
photographs of the victim's gaping abdomen. Then a window lights up,
and we see in silhouette another woman being murdered and blood being
spattered all over the window panes. Again, authentic photographs of her
mutilated body are flashed in front of us as we are told how her heart and
kidney had been removed and left on the bedside table. The experience
concludes with a visit to the 'Mortuary', complete with jars of organs,
where we see a tableau of two surgeons cutting through the chest of our
fifth dead body in twenty minutes.

On the way out I pass Ripper's Rapid Snacks, where a 'Hot on the Slab'
board offers pizza, and then the Shock Shop which markets a Ripper Mania
range of souvenirs including drinks, coasters and glasses. I buy a glossy

guide, which in fact gives me the most stomach-turning experience of the day, for beside a picture of a dove are the following words:

> We must remember that even today there are many parts of the world where atrocities still occur, from natural disasters to wars, torture and brutality. That's why we hope that through education and public awareness the mistakes of the past will never be repeated in the future.

To accept the idea that the London Dungeon is the worthy face of death education and that the queues are there because people want to broaden their minds, is to believe that those who go to the scenes of plane crashes do so because they are interested in aerodynamics.

The ongoing battle between representation and reality that determines the difference between soft and hard porn is starting to infiltrate the representation of death in popular culture. For example, the recent natural history programme *Predator* took the wildlife concept and turned it into wild death. This extraordinary series was like a natural history snuff video made with all the gadgetry of pornography. The emphasis was the moment of killing, 'the vital nanoseconds where death hangs in the balance'. It was 'nature red in tooth and claw' as it has never been seen before, with mini-cams attached to the throat of a cheetah, X-ray imagery to bump up the thrill of the chase, adrenalin-pumping techno music, and slow-motion replays. 'Here it is again and again and again', the voice-over told us as the eagle landed on the hare's throat: 'dinner for one, death for the other, and all decided in an instant'. This was an animal skin flick; never has death looked so sexy on television. Where on the small screen *Predator* showed real death via the cruelty of the natural world, on the big screen there was *Gladiator*, which showed dramatic death via the cruelty of mortal combat for sport in the Roman Empire. With astonishing special effects, the point of *Gladiator* – like *Predator* – was the moment of killing, heads spinning off torsos, blood in torrents. The programme *Big Brother* played to the same audience, showed the extent of our voyeuristic appetite for a mental *Gladiator* – a psychological battle for survival in a public arena, lasting until one person is hailed as the winner before a crowd of millions. The point is that recreational voyeurism is progressing at an alarming pace. This has implications for our interest in death.

From the fashion for death in the art gallery to the contemporary version of *ars moriendi* in the bookshop, morbidity is *à la mode*. In 1994 at The Learning Annex in New York, the largest adult education centre in America and a barometer of social trends, a director told me, 'Death and dying are very popular. When we had more people for Elizabeth Kubler Ross than "How To Flirt" we realised death was bigger than sex.'

Death does, indeed, seem to be challenging the cultural supremacy of sex. There's a good reason for this. If sex began in 1963, then arguably death began in 1982 with AIDS. Two comparative snapshots in different decades spring to mind. In the 1960s, John and Yoko hit the headlines when they staged a lie-in as performance art with intimations of sexuality, holding court in public on a bed with crumpled sheets; in the 1990s, people queued for hours to see the porcelain-skinned actress Tilda Swinton lie in state in the Serpentine Gallery, awash with intimations of mortality, in a piece called *The Maybe*. When sex became deadly, death became sexy and assumed a new profile in popular culture. Of course, AIDS is not the only explanation for the fact that the skeleton has come out of the closet. In the same way that war, medicine, fashion and the mass media affected the changing dynamics of sex in popular culture at different stages of the twentieth century, these things have influenced changing attitudes to death. The fact that AIDS decimated such a vocal and creative sector of society – the roll of honour including a disproportionate number of casualties from the worlds of fashion, dance, art and film – accelerated the process whereby death gained a new presence in these arenas. Two dances of death stand out in particular. In 1994, the American choreographer Bill T. Jones caused a storm of controversy with a ballet, *Still Here*, in which the company performed around vast video screens on which people dying from AIDS spoke about their plight; in 1996 the Royal Ballet's prima ballerina Darcy Bussell wore vivid red to dance the part of the AIDS virus, with the *corps de ballet* portraying the white cells, in Matthew Hart's ballet *Dances With Death*.

Death is the focus of a new permissiveness. The way that this has been developing since the mid-1990s – the distinctive currents of mood – replicates with striking symmetry the dynamics of change that heralded the birth of the permissive society in the 1960s. Those who lived through the swinging 1960s, when sex was the motor of major cultural change from film to fashion, are now experiencing a similar revolution around death. All this is happening at a time when, in terms of sex, culturally and socially, we're running out of fuel. Nakedness has become ubiquitous, copulation commonplace, the F-word an adjective in everyday speech, 'shag' a verb. The pill – a pill that for a generation represented sexual liberation, zipless sex, one-night stands, promiscuity, experimentation – is now little more than contraceptive history. It was a prescription that went with a lifestyle. Now Viagra bespeaks of a collective cultural loss of libido. Birth control and abortion, once the subjects animating angry young men and women, have been replaced by death control and euthanasia as topics of concern to the middle-aged men and women they have now become. For the first generation with the privilege and power to experience the beginnings of life as an autonomous decision, and to bring self-assertiveness to the maternity ward, it is a logical progression to wish to control the manner of their demise. We are entering an era where we desperately need the moral philosopher at the hospital, for she is better equipped than the doctor to make the decisions about terminating life.

AIDS crept up behind us and reminded us of our mortality. When sex became dangerous, death became a safer subject – more talked about, explored creatively in the art gallery as a form of mourning, and even used on a bill board by Benetton in the form of a photograph of a man dying of AIDS. Sex has long been the hidden persuader in a consumer culture, but now death sells. From Death cigarettes – a brand smoked by the hip, flip fashion crowd in the late 1990s – to mainstream advertising campaigns including high-fashion store Harvey Nichols and high-street fashion chain Wallis, death has a assumed a new and hitherto unimaginable presence in consumer culture.

The trend towards featuring the imagery of death for commercial ends can be traced back to 1996. This was the year when in the fashion world it was *de rigeur mortis*. Fashion reflects mood, and the mood was black. At the cinema the must-see movie was *Trainspotting*, in which the nihilistic narrator asked 'Choose life – now why should I do a thing like that?' In *The Face* magazine, Hamlet inspired a fashion shoot in which model Emma Balfour posed with a real human skull and a bunch of bones. In London's art world, Hirst was hot. Tapping into this, fashion designer Alistair McQueen staged a show in the eerie atmosphere of a cavernous candle-lit church where the flickering glow illuminated a skeleton he had placed in the front row. One fashion commentator enthused, 'Everywhere there were references to death; masks set with crucifixes; earrings of dangling bird claws; arms caught in silver crowns of thorns; Victorian jet beading and a mourning colour palette of black, bone beige mauves and greys.' In America, Richard Avedon marked his return to fashion photography with a 26-page fashion story for the *New Yorker* featuring a supermodel with a skeleton.

The trend continued. In 1997 in London, Paris and New York, death was in. McQueen's Paris show that year was entitled *Eclect Dissect*, and hype had fashion mavens believing the *enfant terrible* had surpassed himself by incorporating real human body parts into the collections; to their relief, however, the skeletal hands adorning some of the models were made of resin. Authenticity was confined to bird skulls, animal pelts and an abundance of feathers featuring prominently both on models and still attached to live birds – churchyard ravens in cages, their blackness complemented perfectly by the blood red drapery that had transformed the Paris medical faculty. The macabre mood was enhanced by the fact that McQueen used fox fur, horse hair, crocodile skin and ostrich feathers. It was in New York that the trend for glamorising death finally showed signs of having over-reached itself. After a season of deathly pale models made up to look as if they were about to die from heroin abuse, skeletal-thin limbs and flat-battery eyes, President Bill Clinton rounded on the fashion industry, taking it to task over heroin chic. 'This is not about art, it's about life and death, and glorifying death is not good for any society.'

Yet glamorising death shows no sign of going out of fashion in mainstream advertising. An industry renown for exploiting nakedness suddenly seemed fixated by the idea of the body in peril. Savile Row, that bastion of sartorial conservatism, caused a row when it branched out and used suicide as a peg on which to hang a cinema advertisement for tailor Richard James. In a luxurious bachelor pad a 1990s, alpha male, dapper dandy selects an outfit from a wardrobe full of sharp clothes. He shaves, dresses, checks himself in the mirror and then takes the lift up to the roof. He walks across the roof and we hear the sound of a thud. The screen fades to black and the tailor's name appears.

Far from signifying a creative director's off day, this type of black humour seemed to be endemic, as if Tarantino's flippancy had filtered into the ether of the commercial world. In Australia, a campaign targeted at 18–30-year-olds advertised sunglasses with the caption 'Don't be seen dead in anything else'. A man in crisp shirt, suit and shades is seen dead in the bath. In England, Jigsaw Menswear featured a man jumping off a roof, a man dead beside a bicycle and a man after an apparently fatal fall down stairs. Wallis, operating under the slogan 'Dressed To Kill' ran a campaign in which men were placed in mortal danger by looking at women. A Porsche is seen crashing through railings, its driver having taken his eyes of the road; more macabre still, a man driving a heavy-duty mowing machine is distracted by a woman walking by, unaware that a man lying in front of him reading a book is perilously close to having his head in the blades; finally, a tube driver sticks his head out of an Underground train to ogle a woman on the platform, unaware that he's about to get his own head knocked off because the train is entering a tunnel at speed.

But it is not just men who have been playing dead. Notably, in an ad for Dolce e Gabbana, a woman is seen lying on the tarmac like road kill. This trend has continued. Recently, a high-profile campaign for Italian shoe designer Caesare Paciotti showed a cemetery. A woman is seen astride a grave

– in provocative pose, legs akimbo, black stockings, flashes of thigh, and killer heels – clearly not mourning whoever is in the nearby coffin. But death is not only being used to sell fashion. The trend has even extended to hi-fi. A recent campaign shows a model in mourning dress, black lace mantilla, single white lily in hand, staring wistfully at a traditional black speaker. The caption goes: 'Music is alive, why put it in a coffin?'

In 1955 Gorer concluded his essay: 'If we dislike the modern pornography of death, then we must give back to death – natural death – its parade and publicity, re-admit grief and mourning.' The challenge, however, is how to civilise death without trivialising it. Part of the problem is that we remain so distant from 'natural' death. Our perception of death is filtered through health and wealth. In the 1980s, AIDS brutally forced us to address death and – like the Emperor's New Clothes – exposed as an illusion the invincibility of modern medicine. The progress of retro-viral drugs since then has conferred a sense of crisis contained. Thankfully – at least for those in the wealthy and privileged First World – the darkest days are behind us. A most uplifting indication of this can be seen at the London Lighthouse, only recently a place of dying – candles on the reception desk signifying the recently departed, waiting lists for death beds, the Ian McKellen room in use weekly for funerals. Nowadays, the Lighthouse is undimmed by death. The palliative care unit has been disbanded; the place hums with life. Yet while more people are living with AIDS and there are far fewer red ribbons on lapels, there is still no cure. The disappearance of the dying does not mean the disappearance of death.

We should never be complacent about death. This is to return to a fool's paradise. It is both a curse and a privilege that we live as if death does not exist. Our nineteenth-century ancestors, by contrast, saw death more nearly and clearly through a lens of ill-health and religious conviction. Unlike them, we find it almost impossible to embrace our biological fate. We have not heeded Mary Shelley's *Frankenstein* (1818) as a cautionary tale: 'supremely frightful would be the effect of any human endeavour to mock the stupendous mechanism of the Creator of the world'. This inability to accept our own mortality subsidises both cosmetic surgery and cryonics. Both industries are kept afloat by clients who pay fortunes because they refuse to accept the natural effects of time on human flesh. Given the dizzy pace of science, where human cloning is but a matter of time, the idea of natural death becomes even harder for us to grasp. Since the 1950s, when Gorer urged us to give back to death a public profile, the power struggle between ourselves and nature has intensified so greatly that working out the right formula for 'the parade' and 'publicity' of death invokes its own set of difficulties.

In the space of one week in June 1998, the taboo of death was treated radically, and differently, in two separate television programmes. Firstly, and momentously for the history of broadcasting, the BBC screened the first-ever televised death in the context of a seven-part series, *The Human Body*, hosted by Sir Robert Winston. Calmly, and in the guise of promoting 'a greater understanding of human biology', we were able to see the moment at which a man with cancer died 'peacefully at home', as a newspaper would say. A few days later, Channel 4 broadcast *The Drop Dead Show*, presented by Davina 'Big Brother' McColl, a game show about death. In the chat show, chat-up style, Davina greeted the viewers with, 'One thing that comes to all of us – death – but when? Which of you fine specimens is likely to die first? By the end of the programme you'll know how long you're likely to live.' The 'Mortality Game' was a running theme, and contestants from the audience received Drop Dead Urns and £10 for their funeral of choice by way of prizes. The programme was not the indulgence of a small, way-out production company, but the creation of Channel 4's own current affairs department, whose credits include *World In Action*. The commissioning editor commented of the show:

> *The Drop Dead Show* is the ultimate hybrid: part game show, part quiz show, part health education show, and part current affairs show. And it is all concerned with the TV-unfriendly subject of death and illness.

Real death and game show death, highlighting the two poles of representation – yet was one more acceptable than the other? Was sitting in our armchair at the deathbed of a stranger more acceptable and educational than contemplating own life expectancy as a source of light entertainment, in scenes which included three men defecating in special on-stage cubicles so a bowel cancer expert could analyse their movements? It was as if the programme makers were taking too literally the Dutch doctor Bert Keizer's assertion that 'death is a great turd'. Theoretically, the demystification of death represents a positive liberation from denial and repression and, as such, carries with it the potential to transform our lives. In practice, however, the difficulty lies in discovering how best to break the taboo.

The commercialisation of sex has turned pornography into wallpaper. We should take note of this in considering how we re-admit death to public life, for similar issues are at stake. Philippe Comar, the French artist and author of *The Human Body: Image and Emotion* writes of the naked body:

> Our perception of the body is constructed according to a set of conven-

tional attitudes, largely mediated through fashion, advertising and film. We use these mass culture filters to identify what degrees of nakedness are acceptable, what sorts of bodies should or should not be seen and in what manner or context they may be seen.

This seems as pertinent to the naked as to the dead, and how we show them. In recent years we have had a long death parade. Death has become a cheap trick turned by artists: 'corpses' in advertisements, body part art, authentic suicide notes as the basis of an art exhibition which also displayed body bags from the LA police department. Arguably, these things signify less of an enlightened re-admission of death to everyday life, than a waning of sensibility. This exposure to death underscores the bleak, black, material view we have come to have of ourselves. The blood and guts, flesh and bone reality they convey seems to omit the soul. Where once society portrait painters captured character, now society artist Alexander de Cadenet takes X-rays of the skulls of the rich and famous.

Nothing means anything beyond itself any more. Like art without symbolism, there's sex without love, and death without belief. Each of these implies the absence of something that has the power to transform and enrich experience – an optional extra, but a significant one, and one which is starting to feel important. We need to appreciate that second-hand experience is not enough. Looking is not the same as learning, seeing is not the same as feeling, and information is not the same as wisdom. When voyeurism is becoming a national obsession, death by proxy is a compelling, but dubious, form of escapism. Johnny Rotten put it well when he snarled about 'a cheap holiday in other people's misery'. This is an all too plausible destination, given the centrefold stories of celebrity cot death tragedies, the close-ups of grief-stricken relatives arriving at the scene of the air crash, the sickening emotional strip show that followed the death of schoolgirl murder victim Sarah Payne.

And yet, despite our voracious appetite for consuming the deaths of strangers, we rarely contemplate our own. In recent years we have been told the facts of death, in both pictures and words. We've heard them from both sides – from those suffering from terminal illness and those treating them. Derek Jarman and Dennis Potter are just two of the many people we have seen dying. Sherwin Nuland gave us the biological and clinical reality of death with his explicit preview *How We Die*, an international bestseller which spared us neither the smells nor the sounds of death. In his bestselling book *Dancing With Mister D*, Dutch doctor Bert Keizer also gave it to us straight. He told us about the stench emitting from the cadaver of his dead mother that has haunted him ever since, and of the inconsequential last words of one of his patients: 'no potatoes at dinner'. If anything, their books reinforce our fear.

In 1895, in a letter to her father W. E. B. Gladstone, Mary Drew mentioned 'the utter grimness of death unbrightened by faith'. This strikes a chord, for the loss of faith, like a permanent power cut, plunged the twentieth century into darkness. In the dark, a culture of creative degradation has thrived. In the absence of the anchorage of faith we find ourselves cut adrift from opportunities for contemplation, mystery and awe – all the things supplied by religion that have helped others to accept death. Art, too, is no longer a source of inspiration or transcendence, and the media neither consoles nor enlightens us.

It would seem the time is right to seek solutions closer to home about how to re-admit death to life. To start with, we should use the D word. We should leave the territory of human interest for a while for the province of humanity, abandon internet sites and seek first-hand exchanges with people we know – exchanges about death, theirs and ours, our thoughts and fears. We should be brave and dare to ask our parents, to whom we speak regularly but rarely communicate, the things we want to know. The dying have been in Coventry for too long – we should let them back and alleviate their loneliness by daring to listen to them.

As for the people we love who die, we should not shun them. We should dare to fraternise with these 'people of pearl', as Emily Dickinson described them – after all, we are not afraid to peek at dead strangers in art galleries, or to read about them in the news. It is time to focus on the third of T. S. Eliot's triad of life experiences, 'birth, copulation and death'. We need to reclaim death, for it belongs to life as much as birth and copulation. 'The walk is in the raising of the foot as in the laying of it down.'

SUGGESTED READING

A rainforest-threatening amount of material has been published about death and over the last six years I have looked at an eyesight threatening, although fractional, amount of what is available. Herewith a personal selection of books which I found illuminating, inspiring and accessible.

Background
The following authors, either in collections of essays, or their own books, are the leaders in the pack in death studies. For academic authority combined with clarity, their works are highly recommended.

Peter Jupp, Glennys Howarth, Douglas Davies, Ralph Houlbrooke, Ruth Richardson, Julie Rugg and Clare Gittings.

The Art of Death: Visual Culture in English Death Ritual (1991) Nigel Llewellyn
The Body Emblazoned: Dissection and the Human Body in Renaissance Culture (1995) Jonathan Sawday
The Changing Face of Death (1997) Peter C. Jupp and Glennys Howarth
Death and Bereavement Across Cultures (1997) Colin Murray Parkes (ed.)
Death, Burial and the Individual in Early Modern England (1988) Clare Gittings
Death, dissection and the destitute (1987) Ruth Richardson
Death, Heaven and the Victorians (1971) John Morley
Death in England: An illustrated history (1999) Peter C. Jupp and Clare Gittings (eds)
Death in the Victorian Family (1996) Pat Jalland
Death, Ritual and Bereavement (1989) Ralph Houlbrooke (ed.)

The English Way of Death: The Common Funeral since 1450 (1992) Julian
  Littern. With his encyclopaedic knowledge, Julian would be the friend
  to phone should the million pound question chance to be on the
  history of funerals. For an experience, which is similarly educational
  and entertaining, it is well worth going on one of the conducted tours
  he leads around Kensal Green cemetery at their open day.
The Fireside Book of Death (1990) Robert Wilkins
*From Dust to Ashes, the replacement of the burial by cremation in England
  1840–1967* (1990) Peter Jupp
Funeral customs, their origin and development (1926) Bertram Puckle.
  (Amusing rather than accurate.)
The Grim Reader (1997) Spiegel and Tristman (eds)
The Hanging Tree: Execution and the English People 1770–1868 (1994)
  V.A.C. Gattrell
Mirrors of Mortality (1981) Whaley (ed.)
The Victorian Celebration of Death (1972) James Stevens Curl

On Cemeteries

An Introduction to Brookwood Cemetery (1992) J. Clarke. (This is charming. I
  recommend all Necropolis publications, especially their magazine,
  Necropolis News.)
London Cemeteries: An illustrated guide and gazetteer (1981) H. Mellor
Mortal Remains (1989) Chris Brooks

For texture, colour and the vividness of authenticity, it is invaluable reading
nineteenth-century material, periodicals, pamphlets, ephemera, fashion
magazines and form guides, which are a rich source of social history. However, be warned, at times this material may cause you to break the silence
rule at the library by laughing!

Anti-Mourning: A Lecture (1876) Mary Hume-Rothery
The Glass of Fashion by The Lounger (1881)
The Lancet (1874) James Wakely (ed.)
The Manners of the Aristocracy by one of themselves (1881)
Mourning Mottos (1846)
The Uncommercial Traveller. For the most complete collection of essays, the
  1890 edition is the best. Dickens's non-fiction prose is superb. In
  'Recollections of Mortality', the description of visiting a morgue in
  Paris distils the strangeness of the experience of looking at a corpse
  quite brilliantly.

War

At the Going Down of the Sun: British First World War Memorials (1988)
    Derek Boorman
Dismembering the Male (1999) Joanna Bourke
The Immoral Heritage (1937) Fabian Ware
J.M. Barrie and the Lost Boys (1979) A. Birkin
The Life of Sir Edwin Lutyens (1950) Christopher Hussey
The Old Lie, the Great War and the Public School Ethos (1987) Peter Parker
The Silence of Memory (1994) A. Gregory
Sites of Memory, Sites of Mourning the Great War in European Cultural History
    (1996) Jay Winter
The Story of the Unknown Warrior, 11 November 1920 (1995)
    Michael Gavaghan
The Victorian Public School (1975) Simon and Bradley (eds)
War Memorials (1991) Allan Borg

Princess Charlotte

Bearing the Dead (1994) Ester Schor
Memoirs of Her Late Royal Highness Charlotte Augusta (1818) Robert Huish
Over Her Dead Body: Death, femininity and the aesthetic (1992)
    Elisabeth Bronfen

Contemporary Death

The Dead Good Funerals Book (1996) Sue Gill and John Fox
The Mourning for Diana (1999) Tony Walter (ed.)
The New Natural Death Handbook (1997) Nicholas Albery, Gill Eliot and
    Joseph Eliot
The Natural Death Centre, 20 Heber Road, London NW2 6AA. The
    centre produces a wide range of publications that are essential reading
    for anyone interested in practical information on inexpensive, green,
    family-focused funerals.
The Revival of Death (1994) Tony Walter

Classic Texts

The American Way of Death (1963) Jessica Mitford
Western Attitudes to Death (1974) Philip Aries
Death, Grief and Mourning (1965) Geoffrey Gorer